Information Asymmetries and Investment Banking in Mergers & Acquisitions

Bibliographic Information published by the Deutsche Nationalbibliothek
The Deutsche Nationalbibliothek lists this publication in the Deutsche Nationalbibliografie; detailed bibliographic data is available in the internet at <http://www.d-nb.de>.

Zugl.: Tübingen, Univ., Diss., 2006

Mit Unterstützung der

Stiftung
Landesbank Baden-Württemberg

LB≡BW

D 21
ISSN 0531-7339
ISBN 978-3-631-56310-6

www.peterlang.de

VORWORT

Die vorliegende Arbeit wurde an der wirtschaftswissenschaftlichen Fakultät der Eberhard-Karls-Universität Tübingen im Juli 2006 als Dissertation angenommen. Sie entstand während meiner Tätigkeit am Lehrstuhl für Bankwirtschaft von Prof. Dr. Werner Neus. Ihm gilt mein besonderer Dank für die fundierte wissenschaftliche Betreuung dieser Arbeit und für vielfache, konstruktive Anregungen. Außerdem möchte ich mich an dieser Stelle für seine außergewöhnliche Loyalität und Fairness gegenüber seinen Mitarbeitern bedanken. Mein Dank gilt ferner Herrn Prof. Dr. Manfred Stadler für die freundliche Übernahme und äußerst zügige Abwicklung der Zweitberichterstattung, sowie Herrn Prof. Dr.-Ing. Rainer Schöbel für die anregende Diskussion während der Disputation.

Für die wertvolle Unterstützung bei mathematischen Programmen bedanke ich mich bei Frau Dipl.-Math. oec. Svenja Hager und Herrn Tobias Enderle. Stets in Erinnerung bleiben wird mir die angenehme Arbeitsatmosphäre am Lehrstuhl, sowie die anregende gemeinsame Bürozeit mit Herrn Dr. Moritz Weber und Frau Dipl.-Kffr. Rosali Gohl. Für die nötige Entspannung und Ablenkung sorgten die gemeinsamen Mittagspausen mit meinen Freunden Frau Dipl.-Kffr. Natalie Höllig, Frau Dr. Kiriakoula Kapousouzi, Herr Dipl.-Kfm. Andreas Pfauth, Frau Dipl.-Kffr. Katja Neugebauer und Frau Dipl.-Kffr. Carola Weise.

Der Stiftung Landesbank Baden-Württemberg danke ich für die großzügige Gewährung eines Druckkostenzuschusses.

Insbesondere möchte ich meinen Eltern Inge und Fritz Häcker danken, die mich nicht nur in akademischen Belangen stets unterstützt und vorangetrieben haben, sondern mir durch ihren liebevollen und starken Rückhalt die Möglichkeit gaben, meine Träume zu verwirklichen. Ihnen ist diese Arbeit gewidmet. Meinem wunderbaren Vater, der leider die erfolgreiche Fertigstellung dieser Arbeit nicht mehr erleben konnte, sowie meiner liebenswerten Mutter, die mich mit ihrer ansteckenden Fröhlichkeit sehr geprägt hat. Mein herzlichster Dank gilt außerdem meinem Bruder Prof. Dr. Dr. Joachim Häcker, der mich unablässig vorangetrieben und mir immerzu neue Wege aufgezeigt hat.

My deepest gratitude and love I express to Prof. Dr. Ted Azarmi, who was so much more than one could ever ask a partner to be. He was there to mentally support and motivate me at all times. He also took the thankless task upon himself to proof-read and edit my work. I thank him for the very valuable suggestions and constructive criticism that he continually provided. And above all, I thank him for his unfaltering trust in my abilities that propelled me to a level that I never thought attainable.

Christine Häcker

TABLE OF CONTENTS

LIST OF ABBREVIATIONS

DCF	Discounted cash flow
Discl.	Disclosure
EBITDA	Earnings before interest, taxes, depreciation and amortization
EVA	Economic value added
FB	Financial buyer
GmbH	Gesellschaft mit beschränkter Haftung
HB	Horizontal strategic buyer
HGB	Handelsgesetzbuch
IB	Investment banker
IPO	Initial public offering
LBO	Leveraged buyout
M&A	Mergers and acquisitions
MASP	Minimum acceptable selling price
MBO	Management buyout
MS	Monopoly surplus
ND	Non-disclosure
NPV	Net present value
Part. Discl.	Partial disclosure
PD	Partial disclosure
PEGs	Private equity groups
PV	Present value
ROIC	Return on invested capital
S	Seller
SWOT	Strengths, weaknesses, opportunities, and threats
VBC	Vertical buyer, a customer
VBS	Vertical buyer, a supplier
WACC	Weighted average cost of capital

LIST OF SYMBOLS

c_m	Competitive damages (increase in unit costs) to the target based on disclosure of unit cost information to supplier "m"
d_i	Synergy (increase in demand) of the customer "i"
$E[k]$	Expected value of unit costs
g_n	Expected gain to the seller from buyer n's offer
h_i	Competitive damages (decrease in demand) to the target and competitor HB based on disclosure of unit cost information to customer "i"
k	Unit costs
K_S	"Old" cost of capital for the selling firm
p_{FB}	Offering price of the financial buyer
p_{HB}	Offering price of the horizontal buyer
p_{VBC}	Offering price of the vertical buyer, a customer
p_{VBS}	Offering price of the vertical buyer, a supplier
s_m	Synergy (reduction in unit costs) of the supplier "m"
x_{HB}	Quantity produced by the horizontal strategic buyer (the competitor)
x_S	Quantity produced by the seller
ΔK	Differential cost of new capital
δ	Demand parameter indicating size of product market
ϕ_n	Probability of a buyer "n" acquiring the target
π_M	Monopoly profit if HB acquires S
π_n	Profit for firm "n" in Cournot duopoly

1 Introduction

Worldwide transaction volume of mergers and acquisitions (M&A) has rapidly increased over the last century. Five merger waves have significantly shaped this development. The first merger wave between 1897 and 1904 was sparked through the industrial revolution and consisted of horizontal mergers.[1] New antitrust laws in the US led to a vertical merger wave between 1916 and 1929, followed by a conglomerate merger wave in the sixties (1965 to 1969) that was based on diversification motives. The fourth merger wave between 1984 and 1989 was marked by a focus on the core business through divestitures and by leveraged buyouts and bustup[2] acquisitions of financial buyers. Since 1993, globalization, the new economy shakeout, and an increased focus on shareholder value driven management led to a surge in strategic mergers.

In 2005, 1016 M&A transactions with German involvement were completed, of which six transactions can be classified as "mega"[3] deals.[4] Total transaction volume amounted to 158 billion euros in 2005, which translates to an estimated average transaction volume of 155 million euros.[5] Based on the ongoing high demand of financial buyers and the recent strong increase in demand of strategic buyers, continuing positive development of the German M&A market is expected. German targets are attractive to foreign firms (35.1% of total 2005 transactions) and German buyers are increasingly interested in foreign markets (23.6% of total 2005 transactions, versus 17.5% in 2004). International acquisitions with German involvement with either a foreign buyer or a foreign target account for 58.7% of total 2005 M&A transactions.

This brief synopsis of the historical development and the current level of M&A activity shows that mergers and acquisitions are an important and highly relevant topic. Accordingly, mergers and acquisitions have been widely researched from many different points of view. Among the most common themes are (1) the motives for acquisitions[6], (2) hostile take-

[1] Jansen and Müller-Stewens (2001), pp. 3-4.
[2] Bustup acquisitions were undertaken by corporate buyers who targeted companies whose entities were worth more separately than the whole and divested segments after the acquisition. Weston, Siu, and Johnson (2001), pp. 193.
[3] Mega deals are transactions with a transaction volume greater than 5 billion euros.
[4] See M&A International (2006), p. 1, for current M&A data.
[5] Actual offer prices were only disclosed for 22% of total transactions. For these 224 acquisitions, the average transaction volume amounts to 527 million euros.
[6] Jansen (2001), pp. 72-107; Scherer (2002), p. 2; Brealey and Myers (2003), pp. 930-937.

overs and defensive tactics, and (3) valuation issues and post-merger performance studies[7]. In that context the investment banker is usually discussed as an intermediary who facilitates the search process, negotiations, and the due diligence process.[8] The role that the investment banker plays in respect to smoothing the progress of the information flow from the target to the buyer during the negotiation process has however only been sketchily discussed in existing literature[9], typically only in respect to the provision of the so-called offering memorandum[10] or the facilitation of information flow during the due diligence process.

Information disclosure itself in similar circumstances has been examined in several papers, yet the analysis is carried out from an accounting point of view.[11] This implies that the focus of those papers is on how much information to disclose and when to do so. My contribution is that I will examine the information asymmetry problem between buyer and seller from a finance point of view. I focus on developing a theoretical model that reflects reality and models the M&A process with all its players and the information disclosure issue. Specifically, the effect of private information disclosure on the valuation of the target firm and the role of the investment banker in the negotiation phase in respect to generating value for the selling client will be scrutinized. Central issues are as follows: 1) does the existence of an investment banker in the mergers & acquisitions process decrease the information asymmetry between seller and buyer; 2) are there additional benefits from using an investment banker as an intermediary; 3) can the investment banker formulate universally valid recommendations for the seller regarding which buyer to choose to maximize seller's expected gain; and 4) can a higher offer price be generated through the existence of an investment banker.

The rest of this dissertation is organized as follows. Chapter 2 lays the foundation for the subsequent discussions by briefly introducing the major mergers & acquisitions principles, the main elements of the M&A process, and important players. The mergers and acquisition process in section 2 with the planning stage, implementation stage, and integration stage is discussed both from the buyer's and the seller's perspective. Thereby, the focus is on the implementation stage to scrutinize the information flow between seller and buyer in detail. Additionally, the discussion concentrates on the seller's perspective of the mergers and acquisition process, because this perspective has rarely been taken in literature. In the third section, the

---

[7] Jensen and Ruback (1983), pp. 5 et sqq; Scherer (2002), pp. 1 et sqq.
[8] Jansen (2001), pp. 17-19; Hooke (1997), pp. 315 et sqq.
[9] Dibelius (2002), pp. 51-57; Hodgkinson (1996), pp. 336 et sqq.
[10] When the investment banker is engaged by the selling company, he prepares a comprehensive information memorandum for potential buyers, which describes the target company and highlights its strengths.
[11] References will be given in detail in Chapter 5.

most important M&A intermediaries are introduced and their main tasks briefly explained. Focusing on the investment banker, different incentive-based compensation structures are discussed.

In Chapter 3, capital market imperfections are discussed in detail. First, it is shown that intermediaries cannot exist if capital markets are perfect. Therefore, imperfect capital markets are studied in the second section. Two characteristics of imperfect capital markets are presented and applied to the case of mergers and acquisitions. In Section 3.2.1, it is derived that investment bankers as intermediaries may exist because they reduce transaction costs. Information asymmetries as the second characteristic of imperfect markets are discussed in Section 3.2.2. In respect to ex ante information asymmetries, the hidden information problem between seller and buyer is explored in detail. Possible solution approaches to this problem and their respective advantages and disadvantages are analyzed. The major problem with investment bankers in this respect is the moral hazard problem that may arise out of the principal agent relationship between buyer or seller (as principal) and investment banker (as agent). This ex post information asymmetry applied to the investment banker is discussed in section 3.2.2.3 and possible solution approaches are derived.

In Chapter 4, the information flow during the M&A process is examined. In the first section, the degree of private company information that a German or US company is legally required to report to the public is determined. The result is that a large degree of information will be publicly available for an interested buyer if the target is a large, public corporation. For private and smaller companies however, a potential buyer will have access to very little or no public information. Since the majority of German and US companies can be categorized as small or medium sized, buyers of most companies are exposed to a large degree of information asymmetry. In section 2, an appropriate distinction among information categories is made that allows the modeling of the effects of information disclosure to the buyer on the valuation of the target company. In section 3, different buyer types and their respective level of industry information are discussed. In section 4, confidentiality agreements as instruments to safeguard the seller from repercussions resulting from the disclosure of private information are introduced and their weaknesses discussed. Finally, the seller's dilemma in respect to information disclosure to achieve maximum price is discussed.

Chapter 5 theoretically models the information disclosure and maximum price dilemma that was developed in the preceding chapters. Different buyers are considered in this chapter. The investment banker is then modeled as an intermediary that facilitates the acquisition process as the seller strives to maximize his expected gain from the buyers' offers. Thereby the seller's perspective is taken to allow an interpretation of results from a finance point of view. Main results are summarized in a conclusion.

2 Mergers and Acquisitions Principles

2.1 Transaction types

2.1.1 Acquisitions, Divestitures, and Buyouts [12]

An *acquisition* occurs when one company acquires a controlling stake in another firm, a legal subsidiary of another firm, or selected assets of another firm such as a manufacturing facility. On the other hand, a *divestiture* is the sale of all or substantially all of a company or subsidiary to another party for cash or securities.[13] A company will often divest an asset that is not performing well, is not vital to the company's core business, or that is worth more to a potential buyer or as a separate entity than as part of the company. A *leveraged buyout (LBO)* is the purchase of a company using a significant amount of debt (usually 70% or more of the total purchase price). Within a going private framework, an LBO is frequently used by a public company to buy back its stocks to convert the company to a private company. If the existing management of a public company uses a LBO to take the company private, the transaction is called a *management buyout (MBO)*. A firm that acquires or merges with another company is called the *acquiring company, acquiror,* or *buyer*. The firm that is solicited by the buyer is called the *target, target company,* or *seller*. A *takeover* refers to a change in the controlling interest of a corporation, either through a friendly takeover or through an unfriendly or *hostile takeover*[14].

2.1.2 Mergers and Consolidations [15]

From a structural perspective, a *merger* is a combination of two corporations, in which only one corporation survives and the merged corporation goes out of existence. Such a merger can be performed as either a statutory merger or a subsidiary merger. In a *statutory merger*, one of the merging companies continues to exist as a legal entity, rather than being replaced by the new entity. The acquiring company assumes the assets and liabilities of the merged company. In a *subsidiary merger*, the target becomes a subsidiary of the parent company.

---

[12] DePamphilis (2001), pp. 5-7; Gaughan (2002), pp. 7-8.

[13] Divestitures differ from Initial Public offerings (IPO's), in that the subsidiary's equity is not offered to the public, as for instance is the case with split-off IPO's, but rather to one buyer.

[14] A hostile takeover is usually attempted through a public tender offer with the aim of replacing the existing management. According to Thomson Financial Securities Data Corporation, only 17% of hostile takeover bids were successful in the United States within the last decade. Nearly 40% of the takeover targets were eventually sold to a different bidder and 6% to a white knight, while the remaining targets stayed independent.

[15] DePamphilis (2001), pp. 5-7; Gaughan (2002), pp. 7-8.

Even though the terms merger and consolidation are often used interchangeably, a consolidation technically differs from a merger. A *consolidation* is the combination of separate companies into a single one. The difference with a merger is that with a consolidation a separate entity is created, while with a merger only the acquiror or the target company survives.

From an operational perspective, mergers may be classified as horizontal, vertical, and conglomerate.[16] A *horizontal merger* occurs between competitors or two firms in the same industry. A *vertical merger* occurs between two companies at different stages of the value chain. Vertical backward integration is the acquisition of a supplier, while vertical forward integration is the acquisition of a customer. A *conglomerate merger* occurs if the acquiror purchases a firm that is engaged in unrelated types of business activities. Depending on the type of merger, the degree of information asymmetry between seller and buyer varies. There will be the least information asymmetry with horizontal mergers, because buyer and seller are competitors. The highest information asymmetry will exist at the outset of conglomerate mergers, because buyer and seller are totally unfamiliar with each other's businesses.

Having defined key terms and transaction types, the mergers and acquisition process and its different stages will be discussed next.

2.2 The Mergers and Acquisitions Process

The mergers and acquisitions process consists of three stages: (1) the planning or pre-merger stage, (2) the implementation or merger stage, and (3) the integration or post-merger stage (Figure 2-1). Because this dissertation focuses on the information transfer during phase two, stage one and three of Figure 2-1 will only be discussed very briefly.[17] Within the implementation stage especially those steps that require information transfer will be discussed extensively. Additionally, the buyer's perspective of the mergers & acquisition process will be discussed rather briefly, since it has been widely covered in literature.[18] The seller's perspective in the M&A process, on the other hand, has been generally neglected. The subsequent discussions will therefore emphasize and elaborate this point, both drawing on the few sources available in literature[19] and on the author's first-hand experience in the field. Next, the plan-

[16] Azarmi and Häcker (2004), p. 887.
[17] For more details on the planning and integration stage see Jansen (2001), pp. 160-239; Weston, Siu, and Johnson (2001), pp. 625-660; DePamphilis (2001), pp. 136-268.
[18] Gaughan (2002); Jansen (2001); Weston, Siu, and Johnson (2001); and DePamphilis (2001).
[19] Hooke (1997), pp. 314 – 324 and Beitel (2004), pp. 58 – 62.

ning stage of Figure 2-1 will first be briefly examined from the buyer's perspective, followed by an in-depth discussion of this stage from the seller's point of view.

2.2.1 Planning Stage

2.2.1.1 Buyer Perspective

In order to remain competitive and at the forefront of the industry, companies have to continually reassess trends and developments in their industry, with their competitors, and with social and political factors.[20] If the environment changes, an acquisition might be appropriate. A business plan is the first step in any acquisition process, because the acquiring company must first consider its strengths, weaknesses, opportunities, and threats (SWOT), before an appropriate target company can be identified.

The main components of a business plan are as follows:

(1) Determine in which industry or market to compete

(2) Determine how to compete in the identified markets most effectively

(3) Carry out an internal analysis of the firm's strengths, weaknesses, and core competencies

(4) Define a mission statement

(5) Set objectives

(6) Select the optimal strategy to accomplish the identified objectives best and in a timely manner.

Once the acquiring company has performed a SWOT analysis and has set its objectives, it may decide that an acquisition, merger, or divestiture is needed to implement the firm's business strategy. Senior management will then draw up an acquisition plan, which defines expectations for the acquisition and outlines tactics concerning identification criteria for potential acquisition targets, about preferred form of payment, desired timetable, restrictions on contacting competitors, etc.[21]

---

[20] This is especially true for young, fast-growing start-ups.

[21] For a detailed discussion of the planning stage, see DePamphilis (2001), pp. 163-177.

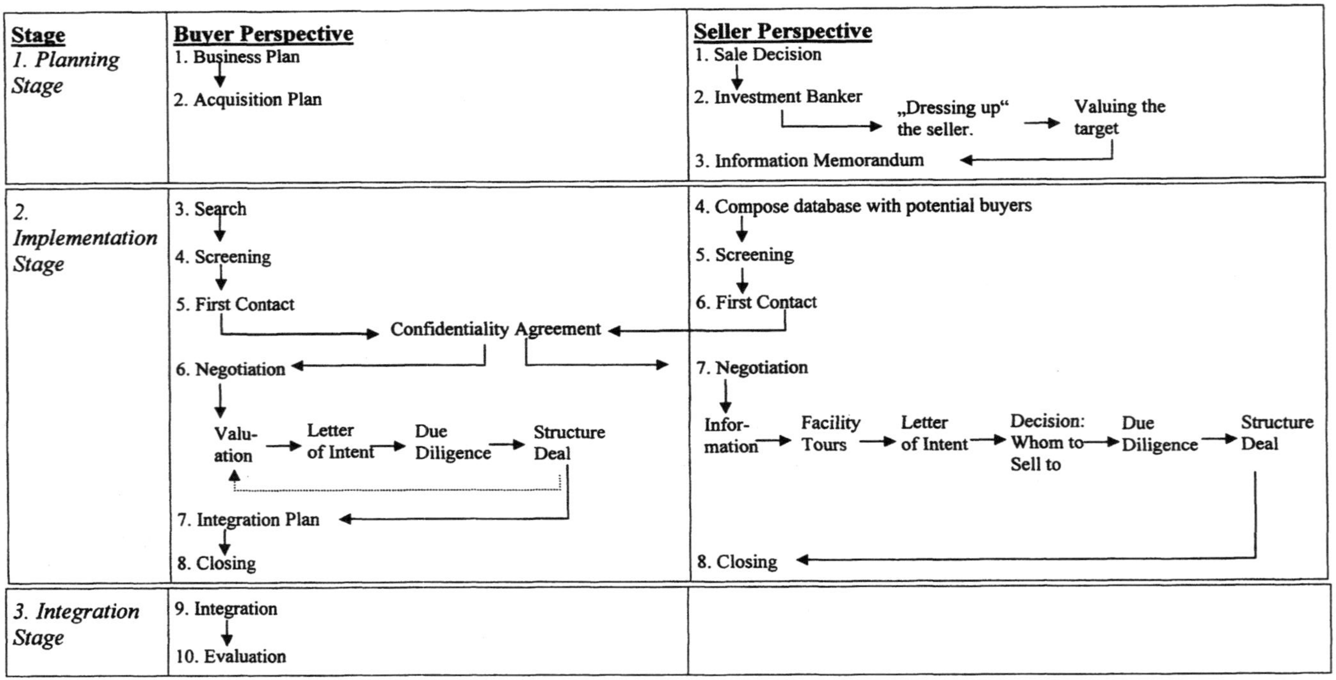

Figure 2-1: Acquisition Process from the Buyer and Seller Perspective (DePamphilis (2001), p. 139; Hooke (1997), pp. 314-324)

2.2.1.2 *Seller Perspective*

The first step in the planning stage from the point of view of the seller is to make the sale decision (Figure 2-1). Hooke (1997) divides sellers into four broad categories: a private, often family-owned business; an entrepreneurial enterprise; a large corporation selling control; and a large corporation divesting a subsidiary or business segment. Reasons for the sale are diverse and differ according to the size and the life cycle of the selling company. Family-owned businesses or entrepreneurial enterprises may sell upon the approaching retirement of the owners or executives. Entrepreneurial firms may decide to sell to a larger company with capital on hand, because the liquidity needs of the rapidly growing business cannot be met otherwise. Larger public companies may divest a subsidiary or business segment and use the proceeds to reinvest in another line of business. They may also divest a subsidiary or business segment because of a shift in strategic focus. In addition to those "strategic" reasons for sale, both small and large companies may also decide to sell based on financial reasons, e.g. at the peak of the market cycle to exit their investment at premium value. Alternatively, if a company is performing poorly and current owners cannot or do not want to turn it around, they may decide to sell.

Once the sale decision is made, most sellers engage an investment banker as intermediary, despite the considerable fees that investment banks charge for their services. The investment banker as an intermediary is in the unique position to create more competition and thus generate a higher price.[22] Specifically, the investment banker has vast experience and devotes more time and effort to the transaction than executives or owners ever could without neglecting their daily duties. Because of his expertise and because he is closer to the market and the buyers, an investment banker can estimate the eventual offer price rather accurately. In his position as an intermediary, an investment banker also provides a unique level of confidentiality to both sides, which is a critical prerequisite for a successful acquisition process. As a negotiating agent, the investment banker serves as a buffer between the seller and the buyer. Even if both sides have opposing opinions, a transaction may be completed because of the investment banker as a mediator. His presence may also lead to unique concessions on either

[22] If there were no investment banker, especially a small selling firm would usually negotiate with one or at most a few buyers. The investment banker with his access to financial buyers and industry databases with information about potential buyers is able to generate a much higher interest level than the seller could on his own.

side. Lastly, as an experienced M&A professional, the investment banker can provide suggestions on how to "improve" the selling firm to make it more marketable.

The investment banker commences his assignment with an initial visit of the selling firm in order to get to know his client's business. Next, the banker undertakes actions that aim at making the target more attractive and generating a higher valuation. This custom of "dressing up" the seller is especially important for those private firms, which do not report company information to the investing public and are often structured to minimize taxes. It is for instance common among privately owned firms to expense private expenditures[23] of the owner that are unrelated to the business through the company in order to reduce taxable income. Such unrelated expenses should be added back to the earnings figure[24], because the buyer will not incur those expenses after the sale.

Additionally, those sellers who do not have audited financial statements must receive this "stamp of verification" prior to sale. Private companies with a large inventory of fixed assets should have their machinery & equipment as well as their real estate officially appraised. If the selling company has a serious issue which may become a major stumbling block to buyers during due diligence, the investment banker will usually focus on the problem right away and find a solution that will be acceptable to buyers. Such a problem could for instance be an ongoing lawsuit or environmental liabilities whose extent cannot be assessed and might be enormous. Another important tool is the "salability analysis", which determines what strategic buyers like to buy in terms of location, product mix, and profitability. If the selling firm does not fit this profile, the investment banker may suggest taking remedial action, which may mean the expansion of a specific product line, complementing the existing product mix with a new product, or entering new markets with a product.

After the selling firm has been "dressed up" to an optimal state, the investment banker will value the target. This initial valuation is both important for the seller and for the investment banker, because the seller will have an initial assessment of fair market value and thus of his expected proceeds after the sale, and the investment banker can assess his expected fee income based on fair market value. Because private companies are not traded on organized exchanges, no public fair market values exist for those firms. Therefore, a private selling company may be especially interested in this valuation, but may not have the valuation skills

[23] This could be travel & entertainment expenses, expenses for a company car or an apartment, etc.

[24] Usually implemented through an adjusted EBITDA (earnings before interest, taxes, depreciations and amortization) figure, on which the buyer will base his valuation.

itself. This is another reason why it is advantageous for the private seller to hire an investment banker.

Four valuation approaches that are most commonly used in mergers and acquisitions are as follows: The earnings-multiple approach is a very rough initial valuation guideline that allows the banker to very quickly derive the private seller's valuation based on historical earnings and a common industry multiple.[25] For instance, an investment banker may assess an industry-wide earnings multiple for private injection molding firms of 5.5.[26] This multiple is based on the banker's industry experience and changes with the cycle of the M&A market. During acquisition booms the future looks brighter, buyers are willing to pay more, and there is more competition. Therefore, multiples will increase during bull markets and decrease during bear markets. If the target company is especially innovative and promising, the investment banker may add a bonus on the industry multiple, because buyers will be willing to pay more than industry-average for such a firm.[27] The advantages of the earnings-multiple approach are that it provides instantaneous results, it does not require many input parameters, and it is easy to use. The weakness of this approach is that it only considers earnings and does not take cyclicality, accounting irregularities, the level of required investment, and timing issues into account.[28]

Additionally, there are two market-based multiple approaches: the comparative company approach and the comparative transaction approach. The comparative company approach values the target company based on the market value of a comparable company within the same industry, with a similar product mix, and with similar profitability. The comparative transaction approach derives a value for the target company based on the value of a recent and comparable M&A transaction. The common problem to both approaches is that is it usually quite difficult to find two companies in the same industry that are readily comparable.

The discounted cash flow (DCF) approach determines the value of a company based on the sum of its expected cash flows, which are discounted at a rate that reflects the risk inherent in these cash flows. Cash flows are projected into the future for a number of years, until such cash flows cannot be estimated with reasonable accuracy. A terminal value for that point in the future is computed, which reflects the discounted value of all subsequent cash flows. Ac-

[25] Listed firms, on the other hand, are valued by the market. An implied earnings-multiple or P/E ratio for a certain firm in a specific industry can be derived by dividing the market price by the company's adjusted earnings.
[26] Azarmi, Eisele, and Häcker (2003), p. 6.
[27] Assuming a multiple of 6 for an innovative injection molding firm and last years adjusted earnings (usually adjusted EBITDA) of 15 million euros, a rough valuation of 90 million euros will result.
[28] Copeland, Koller, and Murrin (2000), p. 67.

cording to Copeland, Koller, and Murrin (2000), terminal value frequently accounts for a large percentage of the total value of the company.[29] Consequently, it is essential to assess the cash flow on which the terminal value is based, the underlying growth rate, and the appropriate discount rate correctly.

Despite the difficulties inherent in the various valuation approaches, a valuation of the selling firm by the investment banker in this stage should be as accurate as possible. The investment banker is experienced with the valuation of similar acquisition targets in the industry. In addition, the investment banker receives full information from the selling client. Because the banker is bound by his fiduciary duty arising from the principal-agent relationship between the selling client and the banker to act in the best interest of his client, the seller can disclose all company information to his agent without having to fear that the information might be misappropriated.

As a last step in the planning stage, the investment banker prepares an information memorandum. The information memorandum usually includes the following items: a narrative and financial overview, audited financial statements for the last 5 years, an overview of the seller's products, information about top customers, an organization chart depicting the structure of the target, information about officers and employee compensation and benefits, and appraisals of machinery & equipment and real estate. Once the investment banker has been provided with the above information, he compiles all information in an information memorandum. This information memorandum is structured so that it provides a potential buyer with the necessary broad information to decide whether to acquire the target firm and what purchase price he should offer.

2.2.2 Implementation Stage

2.2.2.1 Buyer Perspective

The implementation stage (stage 2 of Figure 2-1) from the buyer's perspective begins with the search process (phase 3) for an acquisition target. First, the buyer has to determine his selection criteria[30] as well as a search strategy. In the screening process (phase 4), the long list of feasible targets in the initial M&A database is narrowed down further with the help of secondary and more specific selection criteria. This smaller number of potential targets is contacted

[29] Copeland, Koller, and Murrin (2000), p. 267.
[30] Typical criteria are target size, industry, geographic location, level of profitability, etc.

during phase 5. Thereby, discretion is extremely important, as even mere hints of acquisition negotiations may have considerable negative consequences for the target company.[31] Customers of the target company may be concerned with product warranty or service quality, suppliers about potential disruption to their production schedules, and employees about job security and compensation. Dealing with these disruptions and assuring stakeholders could account for a significant amount of the target's management time and thus negatively affect daily business operations. This is why the buyer has to sign a confidentiality (or non-disclosure) agreement before any information is provided to him.[32]

Phase 6 of the implementation stage can be summarized with "negotiations". After the buyer has signed a confidentiality agreement, he is provided with the information memorandum about the target company. Based on that information and on additional specific information requests that each buyer might have, a valuation of the target firm is determined. Negotiations between buyer and seller and their respective bargaining positions result in an offer price, which is set forth in a letter of intent. A letter of intent is an intermediate document, in which the main areas of agreement between buyer and seller are summarized.

The main components of a letter of intent are as follows:

1. The type of transaction
2. The proposed offer price
3. Main terms and conditions
4. The extent and duration of due diligence
5. The type of data to be exchanged
6. The responsibilities of both parties while the agreement is in effect
7. A date by which the offer expires
8. An exclusivity clause specifying that the seller cannot have sale negotiations with another buyer.[33]

The offer price specified in the letter of intent may not be the maximum price that could be attained, because the seller may determine that it is better for him not to disclose certain sensitive information that could harm his competitive position. This means that the information

---

[31] DePamphilis (2001), pp. 184 et sqq. There could also be negative consequences to the bidder, if the increased awareness about merger negotiations prompts other bidders to submit competing bids.
[32] Confidentiality agreements will be discussed in more detail in section 4.4.
[33] DePamphilis (2001), p. 186.

asymmetry problem will apply in this sixth phase of the acquisition process, in respect to provided information, valuation, and ensuing negotiations.

Due diligence, which is the next step in the acquisition process, is described by DePamphilis (2001) as follows: “Buyer due diligence is the process of validating assumptions underlying valuation. The primary objectives are to identify and confirm sources of value and to mitigate real or potential liability by looking for fatal flaws that reduce value.” After due diligence is completed satisfactorily, the buyer will secure financing for the transaction. A financing plan is prepared and presented to lenders or investors. Depending on the target company’s profitability and buyer’s or seller’s preferences and bargaining position, the transaction is financed with cash, cash and notes, shares of stock, all debt, or a combination thereof. The financing structure of a deal in turn influences the valuation of the target, because the expected cost of financing the transaction is taken into account.[34] A buyer will only undertake the acquisition, if its net present value (NPV) is greater than or equal to zero.[35] This means, that the buyer should at most offer a purchase price (P) that is equal to the present value of the target on a stand-alone basis (PV_{SA}), and restructuring value (PV_{RV})[36], plus synergy value (PV_{SV}) generated by the combination minus integration costs (PV_{IC}) discounted at the buyer’s cost of capital.

$$NPV = PV_{SA} + PV_{RV} + PV_{SV} - PV_{IC} - P \geq 0$$

Upon successful completion of negotiations and due diligence, the buyer develops an integration plan for the target with the buying-entity after the acquisition. Only a smooth integration process will eventually lead to a successful acquisition and help materialize expected synergy benefits. The closing phase as the last step in the implementation stage aims at obtaining all required shareholder, regulatory, and stakeholder[37] approvals to the proposed acquisition. The major component of the closing documents is the definitive agreement of purchase and sale (or purchasing agreement), which specifies the rights and obligations of the seller and buyer before and after closing. All contingencies must be resolved by the closing date, otherwise the purchasing agreement is invalidated. Conditions in the purchase agreement often address issues like the assignment of existing leases, verification of financial statements,

[34] This connection is shown by the dotted line in Figure 2-1.
[35] DePamphilis (2001), p. 197.
[36] Restructuring value in the acquisition context arises if additional value can be created based on the divestiture or spin-off of poorly performing units or through the financial restructuring of the target company.
[37] Stakeholder approvals are for instance required for customer or vendor agreements.

transfer of licenses, or obtaining financing. A financing contingency means that if the buyer fails to obtain financing for the transaction, the purchase agreement will not be binding on him. The closing date and hour is the effective time when the assets of the target company are transferred to the buyer, all liabilities are assumed by the buyer, and the seller receives his purchase price payment.

2.2.2.2 *Seller Perspective*

From the seller's perspective, the implementation stage of Figure 2-1 begins with the composition of a database of potential buyers by the investment banker. Potential buyers may come from many different backgrounds. These buyers may be broadly categorized into strategic buyers and financial buyers. Strategic buyers are horizontal or vertical buyers in the same industry as the target company that can gain synergies from the acquisition. Financial buyers, on the other hand, are private equity groups (PEGs) or individual investors, who provide the financial means to buy the target but have no industry expertise, usually require existing management to stay on, and have no synergy potential. The seller will primarily choose strategic and financial buyers that have geographic proximity to the target company, operate in the same industry, and have an appropriate size. Most importantly, the investment banker will identify the currently most active buyers in the industry.

The screening phase will be rather unrestricted from the seller's perspective. In contrast to the buyer, the seller initially does not like to exclude anyone from the acquisition process. The larger the number of interested buyers, the more seller-friendly the acquisition environment will become and the higher the purchase price. That is, the seller's investment banker will initially contact a large number of potential buyers. However, the seller should be especially careful in dealing with its most important competitors. Because damages are likely to be severe if the seller's willingness to sell and the seller's private information is known among his competitors, the investment banker will have to be extremely careful in contacting such buyers and may want to contact them at a later point during the implementation stage. The investment banker contacts all potential buyers via phone or in writing and provides them with a blind[38], brief overview on the company. With this cursory overview, the investment

[38] The term blind implies that the overview is written in a way so that buyers cannot conclude the selling company's identity from it.

banker is usually able to generate at least 20 interested suitors.[39] Before any specific information on the target is provided, the investment banker asks all interested suitors to sign a confidentiality agreement.

Once confidentiality is ensured, the negotiation phase begins. First, the suitors receive the information memorandum that presents detailed information on the selling company. After studying the information memorandum, serious buyers will be allowed to ask follow-up questions. Additional information requests often focus on cost or pricing details or on additional information about the top customers. Once the investment banker has supplied the buyers with the requested information, he will give facility tours to the top buyers as a next step.[40] In the interest of confidentiality, the investment banker will only allow few buyers to visit the facilities, and will portray them to his workforce as suppliers or customers. Generally, only the seller's top management is aware of the sale negotiations and utmost care is taken that the key employees of the selling firm do not feel unsure about the security of their jobs and look for employment elsewhere. As a next step, the investment banker will set a date by which all letters of intent have to be submitted. The seller decides whom to sell to, based on the offer price and specific terms such as financing or payment structure.[41]

Apart from the obviously important purchase price component, a seller (especially a private seller) may consider the proposed acquisition terms an important factor in their decision-making. Besides purchase price, such sellers may be equally concerned with the management style of the acquiror, his plans for growth and integration, and if the acquiror intends to lay off part of the workforce, etc. This means that a seller may decide to sell to a buyer who has similar goals for the company, even though he may not be the highest bidder. Another important decision criterion is if the financing for the transaction is in place. If such an agreement already consists at the letter of intent stage, it increases the acquisition probability and a seller may prefer such a buyer to a buyer with no existing financing agreement. Another key consideration is the composition of the purchase price and the form of acquisition. The purchase price can be composed of cash, debt, stock, earnouts, or deferred payout vehicles. Generally, the seller prefers immediate compensation and a lower tax burden to a variable

[39] These figures are based on the work experience of the author in a mid-market investment bank over a period of 1.5 years.
[40] The facility tour is especially important for buyers of manufacturing firms, which have expensive machinery and high fixed costs. For a software company with mostly human capital, a facility tour will generally not be necessary before the letter of intent stage.
[41] This assumes that there is more than one buyer. Usually, if an investment banker is involved, there are indeed multiple suitors.

compensation in the future. As the legal acquisition form the seller generally prefers a share deal, because all obligations are transferred to the buyer and tax payments are deferred until the seller actually divests his stocks. The buyer on the other hand usually prefers an asset deal. This is, because the responsibility for undisclosed or contingent liabilities remains with the seller in an asset deal and higher depreciation and amortization expense deduction are possible in these deals.[42]

Most letters of intent include an exclusivity provision, which prevents the seller from conducting sale negotiations with any other prospective acquiror after he accepts the buyer's letter of intent. This condition safeguards the buyer's interest. During the due diligence period, the buyer expends a vast amount of managerial manpower, time, and effort to verify the information that was provided by the seller and to obtain additional information about the selling firm. Attaining and verifying information about the selling firm is costly[43], and expending these information costs is only worthwhile for the buyer if the seller has committed to selling to him. If the seller is reasonably certain that the acquisition will be completed, he will agree to the exclusivity provision because it will enable the buyer to decrease the existing information asymmetry and then offer a higher price. To safeguard his interest, the seller may decide to include a break-up fee provision in the letter of intent that discourages the buyer from breaking off the deal. This provision requires the buyer to pay a specified fee if he breaks up the deal due to reasons other than fraud or material misrepresentation of the seller. A break-up fee is especially important for the seller if the letter of intent contains an exclusivity clause, because it discourages an "exclusive" buyer from breaking off the deal at a late stage. That is, it decreases the probability of the seller having to revisit all potential buyers and to start the negotiation process again.

The seller is especially interested in minimizing the number of contingencies in any preliminary purchasing agreement, because such contingencies enable the buyer to break-off the deal at a late stage in the acquisition process. The seller aims at limiting the probability of advanced negotiations breaking down because of various reasons. Firstly, like the buyer the seller incurs high transaction costs by expending a large degree of effort on acquisition negotiations. A large time commitment of top management is necessary in advanced negotiations, which may be so extensive that management has to neglect ordinary business duties. Secondly, many acquisition negotiations unsettle employees, suppliers, and customers. A break-

[42] DePamphilis (2001), pp. 402 – 404.
[43] Neus (2005), pp. 93, 96.

down in negotiations and an uncertain situation with a new suitor courting the target may result in frustrated stakeholders severing their ties with the target firm, thereby damaging the seller's competitive position. Lastly, the buyer could use the private information he received during the acquisition process to advance his own interest, which may affect the seller's competitive position negatively.

After the seller decides on one specific buyer, both sides sign the letter of intent and the due diligence process commences. For the seller, this mainly means providing the buyer with unrestricted access to his premises, personnel, books and records, and clarifying matters to the buyer. Once the buyer is satisfied that his potential liability is limited and that there was no material misrepresentation in the seller's information, both sides will work together and agree on a definitive agreement of purchase and sale (purchasing agreement). The last step in the implementation stage is the closing of the transaction, as described earlier.

2.2.3 Integration Stage

After the closing, the buyer has to integrate the target into his business as quickly as possible. This integration stage is crucial, since important reasons for the underperformance of many acquisitions are implementation issues. First, the acquiror should prepare a communication plan that addresses every major stakeholder group[44] and aims at creating trust between the stakeholders and the new management. The second step in the integration process is the creation of a new organization that assimilates the corporate organizational structures of the acquiror and the target. Next, staffing plans are developed, with a central focus on the retention of key employees.[45] The integration process concludes with a functional integration and an integration of corporate cultures.[46] Finally, a post-closing evaluation of the acquisition is conducted in phase ten of Figure 2-1. Central issues are if the acquisition fulfills ex ante expectations, what counteractive measures could be employed if needed, and specifying what was done well and what could be improved for subsequent acquisitions.

[44] Major stakeholder groups are employees, suppliers, customers, investors, and communities.
[45] This is especially important for targets with low fixed costs and high intangible value, since a high degree of their valuation is based on their skilled human capital.
[46] For more detailed information see DePamphilis (2001), pp. 223-268.

2.3 Intermediaries

2.3.1 M&A Advisors

2.3.1.1 Accountants and Lawyers

Owing to their extensive contacts in the industry, accountants and lawyers may sporadically take on a "finder role", and bring their client and the seller or buyer together.[47] Primarily however, both accountants and lawyers are active in the due diligence and closing phase. Accountants will be involved in financial due diligence, which includes the valuation of the target firm. Lawyers are responsible for legal due diligence, which includes the scrutinizing of existing contracts, e.g. licensing agreements.[48] Mainly, lawyers are active in the closing phase, i.e. after the seller and buyer have agreed on the basic terms and conditions of the sale. Specifically, lawyers are responsible for drawing up the final contract, or purchase agreement, and seeing the client through the closing phase. Examples for accounting firms active in M&A in Germany are KPMG, PriceWaterhouseCoopers, or Ernst & Young, and examples for legal firms are Shearman & Sterling, Freshfields Bruckhaus Deringer, or Haarmann, Hemmelrath & Partner.[49]

2.3.1.2 Consultants

Consultants primarily get involved in the M&A process, if they have an already existing mandate. Even though consultants may assist in all phases of the M&A process, the most frequent areas include development of strategy, search process, and integration. Consultants may analyze growth and diversification possibilities of the acquiror, may search for suitable acquisition objects, or may develop concepts for the organizational integration of the acquired firm. Some of the major consulting firms in Germany and the US are McKinsey & Company, Boston Consulting Group, Bain & Company, and Booz Allen Hamilton.[50]

2.3.1.3 Business Brokers

Business brokers are small, regional operations that take on small deals in the range of $1 to $10 million.[51] In contrast to investment bankers, business brokers carry a broad inventory of

[47] Hooke (1997), p. 109.
[48] Strasser (2000), p. 106.
[49] Beitel (2004), p. 38.
[50] Vault (2006).
[51] Hooke (1997), p. 107.

firms for sale and spend very little time or effort on being acquainted with their client firms. Business brokers offer much fewer services to the client than investment bankers do. However, brokers do not charge a monthly retainer fee. Usually, business brokers do not offer a valuation analysis, do not compile an information memorandum, and do not lead the negotiations. Their main contribution is that (as so-called "finders") they bring the buying and the selling side together.[52] In the subsequent negotiations, business brokers often do not play a role either. Many times, the same business broker is simultaneously engaged by both the buyer and the seller and receives a fee from both sides.[53] An example for business brokers is the firm George & Company in New England.

2.3.1.4 Investment Banks

The core M&A advisors are called investment banks and can be further categorized as international investment banking firms, the M&A departments of European Universal Banks and German private banks, regional investment banks, as well as M&A boutiques.[54] Some of the most important investment banks involved in M&A are Goldman Sachs, Morgan Stanley Dean Witter, JP Morgan Chase, Merrill Lynch, and Rothschild. Investment banks are mainly active in the implementation stage, and are responsible for the search, contact, valuation, negotiation, and closing phase. U.S. investment banking firms, European universal banks, and German private banks may also take an active role in financing the transaction.[55] Often, there is a mutual exclusivity clause in the contract between the seller (or the buyer) and the investment banker. This clause is a standard agreement, which specifies that for a period after the termination of the agreement, should there be a sale to one of the buyers from the investment banker's list (i.e. a suitor that has been contacted by the investment banker for this transaction) the investment banker will still be entitled to his fee. For example, there may be a two-year period of exclusivity after the termination of the agreement.

Investment banks can be categorized in two groups according to the transactions they mediate, specifically according to the criteria (1) transaction volume, (2) complexity of a transaction, (3) internationality, and (4) public listing.[56] International investment banking firms and European universal banks make up the first group. The firms in this group deal

[52] Strasser (2000), p. 102.
[53] Reed and Reed Lajoux (2000), p. 49.
[54] M&A boutiques are small investment banks generally with a regional focus providing advisory services to smaller companies.
[55] Strasser (2000), pp. 101-102.
[56] Müller-Stewens, Spickers, and Deiss (1999), p. 65; Achleitner (2000), p. 158.

mainly with large[57], complex transactions of publicly listed companies, often with an international perspective. The second group consists of German private banks, regional investment banks, as well as M&A boutiques. Firms in this group are retained for less complex medium-sized[58] transactions that are often privately owned and have a domestic focus. Saunders and Srinivasan (2001) show in their empirical study of 611 U.S. M&A transactions between 1985 and 1998 that larger firms predominantly choose top- and medium-ranked investment banks and smaller firms choose bottom-ranked investment banks.[59] Additionally, transaction volume on average decreases with lower rank of the investment bank.[60]

Once the client has made the selling or buying decision, he will engage an investment banker. The most important characteristics that a client looks for in an investment banker are his record of accomplishment (transaction experience, especially with similar deals), industry experience, and network.[61] Because investment banks have high overhead expenses and the M&A process is lengthy[62], investment bankers often reject sellers or buyers that are not serious as clients. A very effective screening method is a retainer fee, which usually amounts to $50,000 to $100,000, and is payable to the investment banker before he commences his intermediation work. The relationship between the investment banker and the client is characterized by mutual trust, absolute confidentiality, and, largely, matching interests.[63] Because this thesis focuses on the intermediation contribution of the investment banker, the subsequent discussion will center on the investment banker and neglect other intermediaries[64] involved in the M&A process.

2.3.2 Main Advisory Tasks in the M&A Process

An investment banker advises clients on a wide range of financial issues and assists them in negotiating and executing financial transactions (for an overview see Table 2-1). He may provide advice on issues such as how to raise capital through equity or debt instruments, capital

---

[57] Large deals are commonly defined as transactions with a volume of more than $50 million. Hooke (1997), p. 107

[58] Hooke (1997), p. 107 defines medium-sized deals as transactions with a volume between $10 and $50 million.

[59] Thereby, medium-ranked investment banks are defined as ranked 6-20 in M&A market share computation in the calendar year prior to the announcement of the merger. Saunders and Srinivasan (2001), Table 3.

[60] Saunders and Srinivasan (2001), p. 11.

[61] Beitel (2004), p. 42.

[62] Note that the entire M&A process generally takes at least one year.

[63] Beitel (2004), p. 37. The conflicts of interests that may arise between investment banker and buyer or seller are discussed in section 3.2.2.3.

[64] Other intermediaries are accountants and lawyers, consultants, and business brokers.

structure ratio, mergers and acquisitions or the privatization of publicly owned assets. An investment banker also assesses the market environment to ensure that transactions can be executed successfully. Investment banking clients range from government bodies to public and private corporations. Goldman Sachs defines their investment banking services as "identifying, structuring and executing diverse and innovative public and private market transactions for corporations, financial institutions and governments. Transactions include mergers, acquisitions, divestitures, the issuance of equity or debt capital, or a combination of these." [65]

As described in Chapter 2.2, the investment banker is an important intermediary in the mergers and acquisitions process and mainly involved in the implementation stage (see Figure 2-1). During the planning stage, an intermediary may only be involved on the selling side. Specifically, the investment banker provides suggestions on how to "improve" the selling firm to make it more marketable, determine an expected value range, and compose an information memorandum. Because of its expertise and proximity to the market place, investment bankers can value and estimate the closing price rather accurately. In the integration stage, the investment banker typically does not play an active role.[66]

Return-driven activities	**Supporting activities**
Primary market transactions • Structuring, underwriting and marketing of initial and secondary public offerings	*Research*
Secondary market transactions • Sales and trading • Proprietary trading	*Clearing*
Principal investments	*Funding*
Financial advisory • Structured finance, project finance, public finance, financial engineering, etc. • Risk management • Asset management • **Mergers & Acquisitions**	*Information technology*

Table 2-1: Business segments of investment banks (Marshall and Ellis, 1994).

[65] http://www.gs.com/client_services/investment_banking/index.html; retrieved March 01, 2006.
[66] Beitel (2004), p. 58.

During the implementation stage, the investment banker adds value due to his expertise in the area of mergers & acquisitions in general as well as in particular focus industries. The intermediary assists the buyer in composing a clear and workable search profile and then searches its extensive databases and personal network for all the possible targets that fit the search profile. Through the market intelligence gained from involvement in frequent transactions in specific industries, an investment banker accurately gauges a specific target firm's willingness to sell or the expected level of competing bids. Likewise, the investment banker will assist the seller by identifying potential buyers through his databases and personal network. The information memorandum will be passed along to multiple suitors, and bidding will take place in an auction framework. Especially when representing a selling company, an investment banker adds value through the initial anonymity that he provides by functioning as an intermediary. With the sale intent usually carrying a negative connation, it is crucial that an intermediary contacts the large number of potential suitors with a brief blind overview on the selling company. If the seller himself was to initiate the contact, his sale intention could spread to his suppliers, customers and employees, and the competitive position of his business may be negatively influenced. From the buyer's perspective, an anonymous intermediary may also be important. For instance, an anonymous intermediary could add value in a horizontal acquisition process where the buyer initially does not want to show his interest to his main competitor.

During the negotiation phase the investment banker assists the buyer with the valuation of the target company. Especially if a market-based valuation method, such as the comparative transaction method, is used, the investment banker can add value through his industry-specific expertise. Additionally, investment bankers advise the buyer on how to structure his offer and provide an analysis on how the buyer's stock price would be influenced by the offer. As a negotiating agent, investment bankers serve as a buffer between the seller and the buyer, which can lead to unique concessions or may facilitate a deal even if both sides have opposing opinions. If the investment banker was hired by the seller, his main role during the negotiation is to lead and facilitate negotiations resulting in a successful sale. The investment banker devotes more time and effort to the deal than executives do or owners ever could without neglecting their daily duties. Specifically, the investment banker leads the due diligence process and coordinates the information transfer by establishing a data room. Another important task of the investment banker is to analyze all submitted offers, conduct price and deal term negotiations. Because the investment banker is an independent intermediary with vast M&A experience, he is in the unique position to create more competition among buyers by creating an auction environment, which may result in a higher price for the seller. In the closing phase, the investment banker analyzes different price adjustment mechanisms and recommends the optimal one to his selling client.

2.3.3 *Fee Structure*[67]

The agreement about the fee that the investment banker receives for his mediation services is set forth in the engagement letter between the client and the investment banker. The agreed upon fee structure may differ among investment banks or transactions. General fee structure components are (1) retainer fee, (2) flat or fixed fee, (3) break-up fee, and (4) success-based fee or incremental value fee.

Retainer fees are monthly or upfront fees that the investment bank charges to cover its ongoing expenses in connection with the transaction. Such expenses may include traveling expenses, and phone and mail expenses. Retainer fees are frequently chargeable against the success fee, i.e. they decrease the success fee due at closing.[68] The intermediary is often compensated with a success-based fee at the end of the transaction. By charging retainer fees, the investment banker decreases his risk that he receives no income if the transaction fails.

A fixed fee can be structured either as success-based or as a fee payable regardless of the outcome of the negotiations. However, the level of the fee is not related to the volume of the transaction or any other key figure. This fee structure is mainly used for fairness opinions and defense or merger intermediation.[69] The break-up fee is only payable if negotiations break down. In a similar manner to the retainer fee, the break-up fee limits the risk that the investment banker may not to be reimbursed for his expenditures of time and money in the event of the termination of the transaction. The break-up fee can be interpreted as the minimum income that the investment banker receives in a worst-case scenario.

A success-based fee due upon signing of the purchase agreement or upon closing is most frequently used in the industry.[70] The success-based fee may be fixed, based on transaction volume, based on the value of the acquired stake, or based on the book value of assets. The investment banker and the client may agree upon different fee percentages, depending on

---

[67] Investment banker's fee structure, especially in respect to conflicts of interests, will be discussed in more detail in section 3.2.4.
[68] Dufey and Hommel (2000), p. 973.
[69] Beitel (2004), p. 47.
[70] Rau (2000), p. 308.

the level of the purchase price.[71] If the success-based fee is based on transaction volume, the fee percentage generally decreases with an increasing transaction volume.[72] For very large transactions, a so-called fee cap, i.e. a fee limit, is frequently imposed. In Saunders and Srinivasan's (2001) study, the investment banker's fee income varies greatly both on an absolute basis and in percentage terms for all sizes of transactions.[73] Generally, there is a strong negative correlation between the size of the transaction and the percentage level of fees. This implies that investment bankers charge a high percentage fee for small transactions, and vice versa. Over the examined 14 years and 611 transactions, investment-banking fees expressed as a percentage of the transaction value amount to 0.7% on average.[74] Out of the 611 transactions, 64% were infrequent transactors. Their total fees were $2.74 million on average with an average market value of the acquiring firm of $1.48 billion. Frequent transactors[75] exhibit higher total fees with an average figure of $6.04 million, as well as a higher market value with an average of $6.70 billion.

For German firms, information on fee payments is rare. Table 2-2 shows the intermediary fee payments by German firms reported for mergers and acquisitions in the period of 1992-2001 by Thomson Financial SDC. As in Saunders and Srinivasan's (2001) study, the German data show a large variation. Excluding the Fresenius, Siemens, and Henkel deal, this data also exhibit a negative correlation between transaction size and percentage fees, i.e. generally percentage fees are lower with a larger transaction size. On average, over the examined 10 years and 9 transactions, investment banking fees expressed as a percentage of the transaction value amount to 0.77%, which is similar to the 0.7% average fee income that Saunders and Srinivasan (2001) found in the U.S.[76]

Often, an investment banker receives a compensation contract that combines different fee categories. For example, a typical fee structure is composed of (1) a monthly retainer fee

[71] Dufey and Hommel (2000), p. 973.
[72] The compensation formula for investment banking activities initiated by Lehman Brothers was originally structured as follows: 5% for the first million dollars of purchase price, 4% for the second million, 3% for the third million, 2% for the fourth million, and 1% for everything thereafter (i.e. above $4 million). Mastracchio Jr. and Zunitch (2002), p. 41. Because of inflation, investment bankers nowadays often seek some multiple of the original Lehman formula. In addition, the fee structure of Morgan Stanley is used as a benchmark for large transactions. In this compensation formula, there is a 1% fee for a $100 million purchase price, a 0.5% fee for a $500 million deal, and a 0.4% fee for a $1 billion transaction.
[73] Saunders and Srinivasan (2001), p. 9.
[74] Saunders and Srinivasan (2001), Table 4, Panel A.
[75] A frequent transactor is defined as an acquiring firm that had four or more capital market transactions (debt, equity, or mergers) in the four years prior to the announcement of the merger. See Saunders and Srinivasan (2001), Table 3.
[76] Because of the small sample size and imprecise information on one transaction, the results are not representative. However, they provide an indication about the general level of German investment banking fees.

covering the ongoing expenses of the investment bank, (2) a success-based fee due upon closing, and (3) a break-up fee payable in the event of a termination.[77] Rau (2000) determines that fixed and success-based fee components together on average account for 95% of an investment banker's fee income.[78]

Date	Target	Buyer	Transaction Volume	Fee Payment by Buyer	Percentage Fee Paid by the Buyer
07.05.98	Chrysler Corp.	Daimler-Benz AG	40,467	60.0	0.15%
06.02.96	National Medical Care Inc.	Fresenius AG	4,236	1.5 *	0.04%
02.09.99	Lone Star Industries	Dyckerhoff AG	1046	5.2	0.50%
08.06.99	VWR Scientific Products Corp.	Merck KGaA	932	5.8	0.62%
09.01.98	Wyle Electronics Inc.	Raab Karcher AG	751	5.0	0.67%
03.08.94	ElectroCom Automation Inc.	AEG AG	259	2.8	1.08%
13.08.99	Turner Corp.	Hochtief AG	169	2.8	1.66%
09.01.95	Pyramid Technologies Corp.	Siemens Nixdorf Informationssysteme AG	166	1.8	1.08%
14.07.98	DEP Corp.	Henkel KGaA	91	1.0	1.10%
				Mean	0.77%
		Weighted Mean (by transaction volume)			0.18%

Note: All values in $ million, unless otherwise specified.
* It is not certain, if this relatively small fee was merely for a fairness opinion or was charged for full-scale M&A advisory work.
Source: Thomson Financial SDC.

Table 2-2: Fee Payments by German Buyers between 1992 and 2001

[77] Kosnik and Shapiro (1997), p. 16.
[78] Rau (2000), p. 308.

3 Capital Market Imperfections

3.1 Intermediaries and Perfect Capital Markets

A perfect capital market is often assumed in theoretical models in the financial literature. The existence of perfect capital markets implies the following[79]:

- Agents are perfectly rational and pursue utility maximization.
- Agents are perfectly rational and they pursue utility maximization.
- Markets are frictionless. That is, there are no transaction costs (implication: the borrowing rate equals the lending rate), no taxes or constraining regulations, and all assets are perfectly divisible and marketable.
- There is perfect competition in product and securities markets.
- Information efficiency. That is, information is costless and is received simultaneously by all individuals, both corporate insiders and outsiders.

From these assumptions it can be deduced that a financial contract has a well-defined price at all times[80] and an optimal allocation of demand and supply in market equilibrium results. All allocating and coordinating functions are performed optimally by the market participants, and their behavior is not influenced by the existence of an intermediary. Freixas and Rochet (1997)[81] show that in a perfect capital market the financial intermediaries add no value to the equilibrium allocation, because the intermediary cannot improve the allocation resulting from the forces of demand and supply. This implies that the existence of financial intermediaries cannot be explained under the assumption of perfect markets.

3.2 Intermediaries and Imperfect Capital Markets

Because the existence of intermediaries cannot be explained if markets are perfect, imperfect markets are considered. Imperfect markets modify the assumptions of perfect markets, in that transaction costs and information asymmetry are introduced.

---

[79] Franke and Hax (2004), pp. 153 et sqq; Hartmann-Wendels, Pfingsten and Weber (2004), pp. 18-19.
[80] Beitel (2004), p. 11.
[81] Freixas and Rochet (1997), pp. 8-11.

3.2.1 Transaction Costs in Mergers & Acquisitions

Transaction costs were conceptually introduced in Coase's 1937 paper, simply as "the cost of using the price mechanism".[82] Coase reasons that transactions not only incur transaction costs if executed through firms but also if the price mechanism via markets is used. Transaction costs for instance are the costs for discovering what the prices and costs for negotiating and closing a contract are.[83] When prices allocate resources at a cost, then they compete with other allocating mechanisms, such as firms or governments. This implies that market prices are used in directing goods and services, as long as this allocation mechanism incurs the least transaction costs. Transaction costs can be decreased through firms, because contracts are (even though not eliminated), greatly reduced, and simplified within a firm.

According to Williamson (1985), "the principal dimension with respect to which transactions differ are asset specificity, uncertainty, and frequency. The first is the most important and most distinguishes transaction cost economics from other treatments of economic organizations, but the other two play significant roles".[84] Asset specificity implies that highly specific assets intended for use in a particular transaction are of relatively little value in alternative uses. Such highly specific assets represent sunk costs and result in a strong dependence between transaction partners, which, in turn, may cause transaction costs if there is the risk of opportunism and if rationality is bounded. Because of bounded rationality, individuals cannot predict or are uncertain about eventualities that may occur during the course of the transaction in the future.[85] Uncertainty may also arise due to information asymmetry and moral hazard that is based on opportunistic behavior and occurs when the actions of agents cannot be perfectly observed or contracted for directly. Frequency is defined as how often an activity is performed or how often an asset is used. As asset specificity, uncertainty, and frequency increase (thereby making transaction management more difficult), the use of hierarchy for managing transactions also increases.[86]

Accordingly, transaction costs can be defined as "the costs of arranging a contract ex ante and monitoring and enforcing it ex post"[87]; "the costs of running the economic system"[88];

---

[82] Coase (1937), p. 391.
[83] Coase also hints at problems of enforcement, but stops short of a definition of transaction costs.
[84] Williamson (1985), p. 52.
[85] One important criterion influencing the degree of uncertainty is the length of the transaction.
[86] Neus (2005), pp. 127-128.
[87] Matthews (1986), p. 906.
[88] Arrow (1969), p. 48.

and "the economic equivalent of friction in physical systems"[89]. Transaction costs can be further categorized as follows. Firstly, transaction costs can be search costs, which are the costs of locating and processing information relevant to decision-making.[90] Search costs in mergers and acquisitions may for instance be the costs incurred by the buyer while searching for a suitable acquisition target, or due diligence costs that are incurred to assess and confirm the information provided by the seller. A second category of transaction costs are negotiation costs, which are costs incurred while negotiating the terms of the exchange. A third category of transaction costs are enforcement costs. Because individuals are focused on maximizing their utility, they do not necessarily keep promises and adhere to agreements. A contractual obligation will only be fulfilled if the utility of the individual is greater upon adherence than when violating the contract. If one side violates the agreement, the other side will incur costs for enforcing the contract. For instance, the buyer of a company may incur legal fees, if the selling company decides to sell to a different buyer despite an exclusivity clause in the letter of intent.

Generally, intermediaries exist if the transaction with an intermediary incurs less total transaction costs, including the added intermediation costs, than if the transaction is coordinated through the market. An engagement of investment bankers may incur less transaction costs since financial intermediaries "have a comparative advantage in processing documents, in acquiring information about borrower's ability to repay debts, and in monitoring instruments that can be easily converted into generalized purchasing power".[91] Benston and Smith (1976) specify three sources of this comparative advantage as follows:

1. Due to specialization, the intermediary is able to achieve economies of scale; i.e. owing to the frequency of transactions, intermediaries can develop routines and specialized machinery and contracts.
2. Due to the confidential nature of intermediation activity, it is easier and less expensive for financial intermediaries to obtain important information on a market participant.[92]
3. Through the involvement of an intermediary, search transaction costs are reduced for market participants.

---

[89] Williamson (1985), p. 19.
[90] Neus (2005), p. 93.
[91] Benston and Smith (1976), p. 222. Thereby, Benston and Smith examine financial intermediaries as producers of specialized financial commodities (p. 215).
[92] Other market participants (who are likely to make the information available to competitors or others) may be denied access to the information. See Benston and Smith (1976), p. 223.

Similarly, Fama (1985) bases his explanation about the existence of financial intermediaries on their comparative advantage at information collection and processing.[93] He discusses short-term bank loans, where the borrowers' creditworthiness has to be confirmed periodically. Thereby, the collection of information is less costly for an intermediary, because it is better for the borrower to provide an intermediary with confidential information than to circulate confidential information relevant for decision-making to many different lenders. Additionally, it is easier for a financial intermediary to obtain information about the borrowers, because the intermediary usually already possesses information on the borrowers from prior dealings. Ross (1989) explains the existence of investment banks with their special role in the marketing of securities. Because investment bankers are specialized in the search for potential purchasers, they can do so at a lower cost.[94]

Concerning, the principal-agent relationship between managers and stockholders, Campbell (1979) explains that managers are hired to act as the agents of the firm's equity holders in the "collection and processing of information".[95] Because information is costly and there is a return on specialization, the agent may use inside information to maximize the wealth of current owners. Frequently, strategic[96] inside information that has to be kept confidential determines the success of a transaction. The necessary information for the transaction can only be received by trusted individuals, who will not use it to their own advantage. Intermediaries, in their position as agents, are an obvious choice for this role.

The named articles illustrate that the existence of intermediaries may be explained through transaction costs. Financial intermediation therefore possesses two advantages:

1. With the help of an intermediary, the number of transaction relations can be reduced substantially.[97]
2. An intermediary may achieve economies of scale through specialization.

The common weakness of the above papers is twofold. First, the assumption that all information required for a transaction is at all times available at a cost, is flawed. While publicly available information is generally available at a cost, this is not necessarily the case for

[93] Fama (1985), p. 35.
[94] Ross (1989), p. 550.
[95] Campbell (1979), p. 916.
[96] According to Campbell (1979), p. 915, "strategic information refers to marketing and advertising strategies, collusive price agreements ..., organizational techniques, and research and development procedures".
[97] The number of transaction relations can be reduced from (x* y) to (x + y) through an intermediary, whereby x or y stands for the number of buyers or sellers, respectively.

private information.[98] On one hand, the value of the information itself may be variable. For example, a profitable market niche strategy diminishes in value in accordance with the number of people that are aware of it. On the other hand, the information transfer may be impeded, if the reliability of the information cannot be observed by the recipient[99] and because the holder of the private information may have difficulty in appropriating economic returns to that knowledge[100]. Second, in this literature, it is unclear, how one may ensure that the intermediary, as the agent, acts in the interest of the principal instead of enriching himself by opportunistic behavior. Both of those weaknesses are explored in the following discussion about information asymmetry.

3.2.2 Information Asymmetry in Mergers & Acquisitions

3.2.2.1 Overview

This dissertation is founded in the theory of information economics, which "is the study of situations in which different economic agents have access to different information".[101] Heterogeneous information implies that although the parties to a transaction may have differing expectations about specific parameters or variables (e.g. about the durability of a car), no party to the transaction (e.g. producer or customer) systematically has superior information. Information asymmetry (or asymmetrical information), on the other hand, occurs when one party to a transaction has more or better information than the other party. Thereby, the degree of information can be regarded as a range of obtainable information and current information,[102] while both parties are aware of the differing degrees of information.[103] Information asymmetry arises due to information costs in imperfect markets. Since the provision and processing of information is costly, all parties to a transaction will generally have a differing information level.[104] Information asymmetry causes markets to become inefficient, since not all market participants have access to the information they need for their decision-making processes. In addition, assuming rational behavior of individuals, information asymmetry is prob-

---

[98] Leland and Pyle (1977), p. 383; Campbell (1979), pp. 920-923.
[99] Hirshleifer (1971), pp. 561 et sqq.
[100] Grossman and Stiglitz (1980), pp. 393 et sqq.
[101] Milgrom (1981), p. 380.
[102] Wittmann (1959), p. 25.
[103] Schmidt (1993), p. 1045.
[104] Neus (2005), p. 96.

lematic because the better-informed party may try to take advantage of the lesser-informed party. A suitable device has to be put into place that will mitigate this problem.

Information asymmetries are categorized depending on their occurrence before or after the contractual period. Before the contractual period there is the hidden information issue, which leads to adverse selection and is discussed within the signaling framework. After the contractual period, there is the hidden actions issue, which is discussed in principal-agent theory.

3.2.2.2 Ex-ante Information Asymmetries

3.2.2.2.1 Hidden Information and Adverse Selection

Hidden information implies ex ante information asymmetries regarding a contract. Such information asymmetries arise because the seller of a good is best informed about the quality of the good that he is selling, while the buyer cannot observe or know with certainty the quality of the offered goods and services.[105] Since the quality of a product influences its valuation, the hidden information is crucial for the buyer's decision to contract.[106] Better-informed sellers may choose to withhold competitively sensitive information or solely emphasize positive aspects.[107]

Without information transfer, product markets would perform poorly. Because buyers cannot distinguish between products, market value must reflect average product quality.[108] According to Akerlof's Lemons problem[109], good and bad products may sell at the same price, if it is impossible for the buyer to tell the difference in quality ex ante.[110] This could drive sellers with high quality products out of the market, because high prices cannot be enforced.[111] In the extreme case, it is also possible that no market exists at all[112], since "the bad (are) driving out the not-so-bad driving out the medium driving out the not-so-good driving

[105] Hartmann-Wendels (1992), pp. 415-420; Spremann (1990), p. 566; Schumann, Meyer, and Ströbele (1999), p. 416; Dietl (1993), p. 137; Noth (1994), p. 22. Typically, the seller knows more about the product than the buyer does (for instance in the case of used cars), however it is feasible for the buyer to know more than the seller knows (for instance if an individual sells inherited jewels to a jeweler).
[106] Neus (1999), p. 956; Richter and Furubotn (1999), p. 92; Schmidt (1979), p.142.
[107] Balakrishnan and Koza (1993), p. 103.
[108] Leland and Pyle (1977), p. 371.
[109] Akerlof (1970), pp. 488-500.
[110] Elschen (1991), p. 1005; Milde (1988), pp. 1-3; Wohlschieß (1996), p.10; Varian (1999), p. 615.
[111] Neus (2005), pp. 101 et sqq; Schmidt and Terberger (1997), p. 66; Hopf (1983), p. 31.
[112] Milde (1988), p. 5; Spremann (1990), p. 574; Schumann, Meyer, and Ströbele (1999), p. 417.

out the good"[113] in a sequence of events. Such adverse selection may lead to pareto-inefficient transactions, because the "wrong" seller might be chosen[114] and pareto-efficient or advantageous transactions for both parties might not be undertaken.[115]

While the hidden information issue has commonly been applied to the used car[116], insurance[117], labor[118], and capital[119] markets, mergers and acquisitions have rarely been examined from this point of view. Information asymmetries between management and shareholders of corporations have been widely explored, however mostly with emphasis on financing strategies, dividend policy, or accounting practice. The application of information asymmetry to mergers and acquisitions is only common in the special case of management buy-outs.[120] This study helps in closing this gap in literature by specifically exploring the information asymmetry present during the mergers and acquisition process and focusing on the required information transfer.

Hidden information regarding mergers and acquisitions implies that information relevant to valuing the target firm is not equally shared between the buyer and the seller.[121] Because of his outside position, the buyer will not have the same access to relevant valuation information as the seller.[122] The seller knows more about his business than an outside buyer does; particularly, regarding the quality of customer relationships, expected revenue trends, proprietary products and technologies, and the soundness of the business model.[123] That is, the buyer is ex ante uncertain about both the quality of the selling firm and the specific fit or the level of synergy benefits of the target company to the bidder. Therefore, the outside buyer runs the risk of choosing the "wrong" target.

Because information asymmetry adds uncertainty to an acquisition project that is already inherently risky, purchase price is influenced negatively. Buyers are only willing to pay

---

[113] Akerlof (1970), p. 490.
[114] Milgrom and Roberts (1992), p. 129; Neus (1995), p. 148.
[115] Franke and Hax (1999), p. 410.
[116] Akerlof (1970).
[117] Rothschild and Stiglitz (1976) and Wilson (1977).
[118] Spence (1973).
[119] Stiglitz and Weiss (1981).
[120] Possible reasons for the lack of discussion in literature may be the complexity of corporations as a product as well as the wide variety of possible information distribution among market participants. See Ragotzky (2003), p. 13.
[121] Thereby, the degree of information asymmetry varies by buyer type. See section 4.3 for a more detailed discussion.
[122] An exception to this principle would be the case of a management buy-out (MBO). Here, the managers of the firm, i.e. insiders, are the buyers and thus have more relevant information than the owners, if there is separation of control and ownership. See Niemann (1995), p. 2.
[123] Vincenti (2002), p. 55.

for the information that they have and, assuming rational behavior, consider all withheld information to be unfavorable.[124] Therefore, information asymmetry causes the buyer to offer a lower price than he would in the case of efficient markets. This implies that if information asymmetry exists, the seller will require a higher price than the buyer will be willing to pay. A "good" firm will not accept a low price. This causes an adverse selection phenomenon. Inefficiencies arise as some attractive deals break off and buyers aim at gathering more information and conducting more extensive negotiations.[125]

Similarly, a hidden information issue may occur with the involvement of an investment banker as an intermediary in a mergers & acquisition transaction. Before the transaction is initiated, i.e. ex ante, the buyer (or seller) cannot assess the quality of the agent.[126] This hidden information problem may explain why Saunders and Srinivasan (2001) find that, on average, in 70% of new mandates clients hired the same investment-banking firm that they had dealings with within the prior four years.[127] Since the focus of this dissertation is the hidden information between buyer and seller, potential hidden information problems between investment banker and client are neglected. Instead, possible solution approaches for the hidden information problem between buyer and seller are introduced and analyzed in the next section.

3.2.2.2.2 Possible Solutions

Both buyer and seller are interested in reducing information asymmetry prior to the final purchasing agreement.[128] The buyer needs to assess the value components and risks of the target and the seller aims at generating maximum price, which implies the need for symmetrical information. Commonly accepted solution approaches for the adverse selection problem in literature are screening, signaling, and self-selection. These approaches may mitigate information asymmetry or even solve the problem entirely.

With *screening*, the lesser-informed party (the buyer) initiates the process by acquiring additional information to assess the characteristics of the better-informed party. The buyer

[124] Milgrom (1981), p. 382.
[125] Shen and Reuer (2005), p. 396.
[126] Strasser (2000), p. 21.
[127] Saunders and Srinivasan (2001), p. 10. The study includes transactions completed in the period of 1985 to 1998 and results are relatively stable over the study period.
[128] Richter and Furubotn (1999), pp. 144 et sqq.

aims at concluding the unknown information to choose the appropriate target.[129] The lesser-informed party incurs costs for the analysis of the information provided by the better-informed party.

With *signaling*, the better-informed party initiates the process by passing along information to the lesser-informed party indirectly. The lesser-informed party receives the signal and attempts to assess the unknown information. In the labor market, for example, the employer does not know the applicant's quality before he is hired. The applicant can signal his quality with suitable credentials or past job experiences.[130] Naturally, the signal is only credible if it is costly for the applicant to send it. This implies that only "good" types will send the signal, as the signaling costs are not economically justifiable for "bad" types.

With the *self-selection* solution mechanism, the lesser-informed party construes a contract in such a way that the better-informed party reveals its type by accepting or rejecting the offer. That is, in a self-selection solution the better-informed party is induced to reveal its type itself, in a manner similar to the signaling solution. Because of the selection opportunity for the better-informed party, different contracts are designed for different types instead of one pooled contract.[131] If for instance a buyer requests a particularly long guarantee period, "bad" types will not agree to the contract.[132] In literature, this principle has been extensively explored for the insurance market.[133]

In the following section, these three common solution approaches are applied to mergers & acquisitions as a special information asymmetry case. Specific tools to mitigate information asymmetry in this industry are earn-outs, common stock payments, equity stakes, collaborative agreements, and employing investment bankers as intermediaries.

3.2.2.2.2.1 Earnouts

For mergers and acquisitions, the main self-selection tool is called "earnouts". An earnout agreement is a contract between a buyer and a target company that specifies a deferred payment that is contingent upon the target's future performance over a set period and is payable

---

[129] Stiglitz (1975), pp. 283-300.
[130] Spence (1973), p. 358.
[131] Milgrom and Roberts (1992), p. 157-159. Note also that very often all groups might be better off with no signaling, i.e. with one pooled contract, because the cost incurred in generating signals lowers net aggregate product. Spence (1973), p. 367.
[132] Picot, Reichwald, and Wigand (2003), p. 50.
[133] Rothschild and Stiglitz (1976), pp. 629-649.

in addition to a fixed payment at closing.[134] Earnouts are a tool to bridge the valuation gap when buyer and seller cannot agree on price and terms.[135] The advantage of this contingent payout structure is that the final purchase price is not set ex ante but contains a significant deferred payment component that is dependent on the target's performance after closing.[136] This is advantageous under conditions of uncertainty, particularly under asymmetric information, because the buyer reduces his downside risk by transferring it to the better informed target. By accepting the earnout agreement, the target self-selects and signals that it possesses favorable private information, since only "good" seller types are rewarded ex post, while "bad" seller types are penalized.[137] In addition to resolving valuation disputes, earnout agreements are advantageous because they provide the target with significantly higher premiums than stock or cash offers.[138] Furthermore, buyers also show positive excess returns in earnout offers, with excess returns larger than in cash or stock offers.

The advantage of earnout agreements to the buyer is that he is required to pay less money up-front while minimizing his risk of overpaying for the acquisition.[139] Additionally, the buyer receives an experienced manager to guide the target through the transition process. A main problem with earnout agreements is the agency problem that may arise from imperfectly aligned interests. An agency problem from the buyer's perspective may arise, because the seller/manager may be focused on maximizing earnout bonuses rather then maximizing the value of the target company for the buyer. In addition, the limited period of the earnout may induce the seller/manager to maximize short-term profits while neglecting long-term profits.[140] Problems could also arise with revenues as basis for payment assessment, if the seller/manager was to focus entirely on generating revenues, for example with large discounts, while neglecting the effects on profit. Therefore, a key determinant of the success of earnout agreements is the perfect alignment of interests of buyer and seller. An additional

---

[134]Earnout periods usually range between 1 to 3 years. Ernst and Häcker (2002), p. 101. A typical earnout might include payments to the seller every year for three years based on a percentage of operating income that exceeds a specified threshold.

[135] Additonally, earnout agreements can be used as retention bonuses for valuable target human capital. Kohers and Ang (2000), p. 472.

[136] Craig and Smith (2003), p. 45. Mergerstat Review (1994), p. 112, explicitly states that "contingent provisions serve as [..] protection of the buyer against overvaluation by the seller".

[137] Reuer, Shenkar, and Ragozzino (2004), p. 22.

[138] According to Kohers and Ang (2000), p. 473, "the median premium in earnout transactions involving private targets is more than two-and-a-half times the median premium in cash or stock offers [...]. For subsidiary takeovers, the median premium is 1.7-1.9 times larger in earnout offers than that in cash and stock offers, respectively".

[139] Craig and Smith (2003), p. 46.

[140] For example, this may be accomplished by the reduction of research & development expenditures. Datar, Frankel, and Wolfson, (2001), p. 201; Reuer, Shenkar, and Ragozzino (2004), p. 3.

issue in earnout agreements is that these agreements may conflict with the integration of the target.[141] To achieve economies of scale or synergies, the buyer aims at integrating the target's operations into his own. Yet, earnout agreements are most successful when the operating entity continues to be independent after the acquisition. Once operations are integrated, it becomes difficult to determine the appropriate basis for earnout payments.

The main advantage of earnout agreements to the seller is that the business is sold at a higher expected price.[142] The downside inherent in the earnout agreement is that the seller is now required to bear risk. This risk consists of the original business risk arising from the future economic performance of the target company as well as of the uncertainty about the capability of the buyer managing the target's operations.[143] Interests of the seller and the buyer in respect to managing the target's operations may diverge and the management capability of the buyer will become an especially important factor if the buyer (and not the seller) operates the target company. Then the seller has little influence on performance, yet he is compensated based on that performance. Potential agency conflicts from the seller's perspective induce the seller to monitor the buyer's way of computing the performance measures underlying the earnout.[144] Such calculations become even more difficult if the target's business is integrated in the buyer's existing business, requiring especially careful monitoring. The main problem with earnouts for both buyer and seller is the considerable litigation risk, which is exacerbated through the above-mentioned difficulty in measuring the earnout provisions and the increased transaction complexity due to incentive incompatibility issues.[145]

Because designing and negotiating contracts and monitoring compliance is costly, earnouts will primarily be used in situations with greater information asymmetry, or a higher level of private information. Earnout usage is generally more likely for smaller, private companies with buyer and target operating in different industries.[146] Younger target businesses with no record of accomplishment, targets in the high-tech or service industry with few tangi-

---

[141] Craig and Smith (2003), p. 46.
[142] Craig and Smith (2003), p. 46. For private seller/managers, another advantage is that they can ease into retirement through this offer structure.
[143] Datar, Frankel, and Wolfson (2001), p. 203; Craig and Smith (2003), pp. 44, 47.
[144] Datar, Frankel, and Wolfson (2001),p. 203.
[145] Craig and Smith (2003), p. 47.
[146] Datar, Frankel, and Wolfson (2001), p. 204; Shen and Reuer (2005), p. 394; Kohers and Ang (2000), p. 472. Adverse selection may be especially pronounced in acquisitions of non-core targets, because buyers will be less familiar with available target firms and less able to assess the value of the target. Note that Reuer, Shenkar, and Ragozzino (2004), p. 27, find no evidence for this industry criterion.

ble assets, and subsidiary targets frequently utilize earnout agreements.[147] On the other hand, earnouts are used less in industries that experience a high degree of mergers & acquisitions activity.[148] Active mergers & acquisitions markets may exhibit earnout agreements less frequently, because transaction costs are lower due to reduced adverse selection problems. Datar, Frankel, and Wolfson (2001) find that for 7% of private targets earnouts are utilized, whereas for less than 1% of public targets an earnout agreement is included in the payment structure.[149] The authors also suggest that the percentage of earnout usage is likely to be considerably higher, because of limited disclosure on deal terms. According to active M&A professionals, about 20% of mid-sized mergers (acquisitions of less than $100 million) feature earnouts.[150] However, Datar, Frankel, and Wolfson also acknowledge that the use of earnouts may be hampered by monitoring difficulties and contracting costs, which "tend to outweigh the information and incentive alignment benefits of earnouts". [151]

3.2.2.2.2.2 Common Stock Payments

Another tool to overcome information asymmetry in mergers & acquisitions is the use of stock payments. In contrast to cash offers, stock offers have a contingent pricing effect. That is, the adverse selection problem faced by the selling firm is mitigated, because the value of the stock payment that the seller receives is affected by the future performance of the target firm.[152] However, use of common stock creates an additional adverse selection problem that affects the uninformed seller. Hansen (1987) describes this adverse selection problem in a scenario in which both the buyer and the seller have private information on their own value. That is, there is a "double lemon" problem.[153] The composition of the cash and stock mix signals the true post-acquisition value of the acquiring firm, because acquirors tend to offer stock

[147] Datar, Frankel, and Wolfson (2001), p. 231; Reuer, Shenkar, and Ragozzino (2004), p. 28; Kohers and Ang (2000), p. 472.
[148] Datar, Frankel, and Wolfson (2001), p. 232; Reuer, Shenkar, and Ragozzino (2004), p. 27.
[149] Datar, Frankel, and Wolfson (2001), p. 217. These results are based on a total number of 39,706 acquisitions between 1990 and 1997, including target firms in 157 countries.
[150] Datar, Frankel, and Wolfson (2001), p. 216. See also Reuer, Shenkar, and Ragozzino (2004), p. 24, who find that contingent payouts are used in 24.3% of acquisitions in high-tech industries and in 25.9% in the service sector.
[151] Datar, Frankel, and Wolfson (2001), p. 223.
[152] Fishman (1989), p. 41; Datar, Frankel, and Wolfson (2001), p. 219; Hansen (1987), p. 76.
[153] Hansen (1987), p. 76. Note that information asymmetry on the acquiring side may be less pronounced, because acquirors are generally larger and more widely known than target firms.

when their firm is overvalued and offer cash when their firm is undervalued.[154] Note that this problem is reduced and the negative market reaction to the use of common stock diminishes, if active M&A players consistently use stock as acquisition payment.[155]

Datar, Frankel, and Wolfson (2001) show empirically that the use of stock payments is more likely in industries with high expenditures for research and development, high revenue growth, high market-to-book ratios, in employee-intensive industries, in the service industry, and for large target companies.[156] If the use of common stock as means of payment had a mitigating effect on the information asymmetry problem, then common stock payments should be used less frequently in situations with low or no information asymmetry. In line with this argument, the use of stock payments is less likely if the industry that the target operates in is active in mergers & acquisitions, or if the acquisition is a management buyout. Contradictory to the above adverse selection argument, however, Datar, Frankel, and Wolfson (2001) find that the use of stock payments is less likely if the target is in a non-core industry or if the target is a private firm. Therefore, factors besides information asymmetry must trigger the use of stock payments. One important criterion for the use of common stock in acquisitions is financing considerations, which includes the issuance of stock to finance the acquisition if insufficient cash is available.[157] In line with this liquidity explanation, Datar, Frankel, and Wolfson (2001) find that the percentage of mergers and acquisitions involving common stock rises with increasing target size. Another important factor influencing the payment structure of an offer is tax considerations. This means that the use of common stock in the payment structure can mitigate information asymmetry, yet its use is limited by other factors influencing the payment structure of an offer.

3.2.2.2.2.3 Equity Stake

Another method for mitigating information asymmetry is for the buyer not to acquire the entire target firm, but to take an equity stake in it. This way, some of the buyer's acquisition risk is borne by the seller. The acquiror thus decreases his downside risk while allowing for upside

---

[154] Eckbo, Giammarino, and Heinkel (1990), p. 673; Hansen (1987), pp. 76-77. Fishman (1989), p. 42, reasons that cash offers for the target firm signal a high valuation, whereas equity offers are believed to have a low value.
[155] Reuer, Shenkar, and Ragozzino (2004), p. 29.
[156] Datar, Frankel, and Wolfson (2001), p. 228. See Table 8 for a probit estimation of the relation between common stock use and acquisition characteristics.
[157] Datar, Frankel, and Wolfson (2001), p. 219.

potential in case that in the future, conditions prove favorable.[158] The seller's readiness to retain an equity stake in the firm after the sale sends a strong positive signal about his private information to the acquiror.[159] Similarly, Leland and Pyle (1977)[160] show that the willingness of an insider entrepreneur to invest in his own project or his own firm signals the true quality of the firm to the lenders.

However, several problems limit the use of equity stakes as a tool to mitigate information asymmetry. First, even though "bad" types will not agree to sell an equity stake instead of a complete sale, the reverse is not necessarily true. Not all good types would agree to sell just an equity stake. Many private manager/owners sell shortly before retirement, and may not be willing to stay several more years and bear the business risk of the target as well as the uncertainty about the capability of the buyer managing the target's operations. Second, the control of the target firm is an issue. If the acquiror has a majority stake, the seller will be concerned about his influence on the firm, and if the buyer has a minority stake, he may not have the necessary power and control over the target. Third, if the acquiror does not acquire the entire target, he cannot achieve any synergies or economies of scale, because the acquiror and the target remain separate entities. In summary, acquiring only an equity stake in the target firm reduces the risk inherent in a situation of information asymmetry, but has other disadvantages that may outweigh the informational benefits.

3.2.2.2.2.4 Collaborative Agreements

Another approach to reducing information asymmetry is the use of joint ventures[161] or strategic alliances. Balakrishnan and Koza (1993) find that joint ventures are superior to acquisitions if "the costs of valuing complementary assets are non-trivial".[162] Especially for private targets in dissimilar businesses with a high degree of intangible assets, collaborative agree-

---

[158] Note that by only acquiring an equity stake versus the entire target, the buyer not only limits his downside risk but also limits his upside potential.
[159] Reuer, Shenkar, and Ragozzino (2004), p. 23.
[160] Leland and Pyle (1977), p. 371.
[161] Balakrishnan and Koza (1993), p. 99, define joint ventures as "special mechanisms for pooling complementary assets owned by separate firms.
[162] Note that Hennart and Reddy's (1997) results do not support Balakrishnan and Koza's (1993) view that joint ventures lower the information costs of acquisitions. Instead, Hennart and Reddy's results indicate that joint ventures mainly are tools to gain access to the resources of other organizations. However, Balakrishnan and Koza's (1993) view is reinforced by additional research, resulting in evidence that joint ventures are especially valued under information asymmetry conditions. See Reuer and Koza (2000) and to some extent Hennart and Reddy (2000) themselves.

ments reduce information asymmetry for the collaborators.[163] Additionally, such agreements mitigate the information asymmetry for other potential buyers because of signaling effects. Potential suitors may now be able to differentiate between "good" and "bad" quality target types, assuming that the formation of an alliance with a reputable firm is harder to signal for lower quality firms.[164] Because the creation of alliances may be comparatively inexpensive, a weaker signaling value than with other alternatives is implied.

Advantages of joint ventures include the possibility of using the market-specific abilities of the joint venture partners, creating important skills and expertise for future business operations, and collecting information on the value of the partner's assets. Because joint ventures do not constitute a terminal sale or the transfer of property rights, the partners are able to to withdraw from the partnership relatively cheaply.[165] Joint ventures may be an alternative to acquisitions, if legal or institutional barriers complicate the acquisition process. Additionally, joint ventures may be the medium of choice if the assets desired by the acquiror are difficult to extricate from the unwanted assets of the target firm.[166] However, joint ventures incur increased administrative costs of managing and controlling the joint venture inherent in the joint ownership of assets and the lack of unity of command.[167] Joint ventures are also hampered by the inherent free-rider problem, resulting in moral hazard.[168] Renegotiations of the joint venture agreement as well as disputes over the allocation of gains are potentially costly. Three reasons for the increasing coordination costs of shared ownership are that (1) international tax-efficient structuring is hampered by diverging interests of joint venture partners, (2) intellectual property may not be transferred within the joint venture due to fear of appropriation by the partner[169], and (3) the rising degree of intrafirm trade.[170]

Desai, Foley, and Hines (2004) show that between 1982 and 1997 U.S. multinational firms have decreased their joint venture activity, while increasingly internalizing transactions through acquisitions of wholly owned operations. In addition to the increasing coordination

[163] Balakrishnan and Koza (1993), p. 111.
[164] Stuart, Ha, and Hybels (1999), p. 319, show that the mere existence of a reputable affiliate serves to enhance the perception of a new venture's quality.
[165] Balakrishnan and Koza (1993), p. 103. The collaborators possess a real option on the venture, which they can exercise if the joint venture is successful.
[166] See Hennart (1988) for the "digestibility" hypothesis.
[167] Desai, Foley, and Hines (2004), p. 371.
[168] Grossman and Hart (1986) and Hart and Moore (1990) find joint ownership to generally be suboptimal because residual control rights are shared.
[169] See also Oxley (1997) and Anand and Khanna (2000) on the risk of asset appropriation in alliances.
[170] Desai, Foley, and Hines (2004), p. 371. "Specifically, international production coordination, tax planning, and the use of intangible property appear to be much more easily executed with majority- or wholly owned foreign affiliates".

costs of shared ownership, this trend has been fueled by changes in US tax policies and legal requirements of foreign countries. This implies that the positive information asymmetric benefits seem to be outweighed by the inherent disadvantages of collaborative agreements.

3.2.2.2.2.5 Investment Bankers

Leland and Pyle (1977) advocate that information asymmetries are the main reason for the existence of intermediaries.[171] An empirical study by Servaes and Zenner (1996) provides evidence that investment bankers may reduce the information asymmetry between buyers and the target firm.[172] Servaes and Zenner find that investment banks are hired if transactions are more complex, if the buyer has little prior M&A experience, if the target is diversified, and if the acquisition constitutes a takeover[173]. Beitel, Boerner, and Schiereck (2005) show that German bidders more frequently engage investment banks when bidding for diversified target companies and if the target is a new economy company.[174]

With information transfer, the problem of appropriation and credibility of information arises. An intermediary whose business is the collecting and processing of information may overcome this problem. Specifically, intermediaries may reduce transaction costs and validate quality. Transaction costs are lowered due to economies of specialization, scale economies in information acquisition[175], and a decrease in search costs[176]. Since investment bankers standardize their analysis and valuation procedure and learn from previous transactions, they may analyze acquisitions at a lower cost, including the identification of targets, their valuation, and the structuring of a bid.

Biglaiser and Friedman (1999) show that in markets with heterogeneous buyers and sellers where sellers have private information about their goods' quality, efficient trading cannot occur without intermediaries. That is, the intermediaries perform a certification service by

[171] Leland and Pyle (1977), p. 383.
[172] Servaes and Zenner (1996) examine 99 acquisitions between 1981 and 1992 in which the buyer did not use the services of an investment bank and compare them to a sample of acquisitions (n = 198) with investment banking advice.
[173] Servaes and Zenner categorize into (1) takeovers, defined as acquisitions of 50% or more of the shares of another firm, (2) acquisitions of assets or units, which implies the acquisition of a portion of the assets of a firm, and (3) acquisitions of a partial ownership interest, defined as the acquisition of less than 50% of the target's shares. Note that acquisitions (or here takeovers) only account for about half of the total number of assets traded. Maksimovic and Phillips (2001), p. 2019.
[174] Beitel, Boerner, and Schiereck (2005), p. 304.
[175] Servaes and Zenner (1996), p. 790, Hunter and Walker (1990), p. 1117.
[176] See for instance the discussion of Rubinstein and Wolinsky (1987) on the housing market and Benston and Clifford (1976) on financial commodities. For a more detailed discussion about the transaction cost approach see section 3.2.1.

inspecting the goods of a seller with private information about his product's quality and establishing a disclosure rule on how much information will be revealed to the lesser-informed party.[177] Investment bankers as intermediaries in mergers & acquisitions can reduce inefficiencies in a market with adverse selection by becoming experts in the field and signaling the quality of the venture.[178] A seller that lives only for one period has little incentive to reveal the quality of his firm truthfully.[179] Buyers usually conclude one or at best a few transactions, i.e. they have little incentive to acquire the skills necessary to assess product quality. The intermediary, on the other hand, has an infinite time horizon, i.e. he has an incentive to undertake a large investment in "quality-detecting" skills and place a greater value on being known for selling high-quality firms or for reporting quality truthfully.[180] Because investment bankers are focused on building reputation capital, they will avoid misrepresentations and their involvement is a credible signal in a repeat-business environment.[181] Since the intermediary has a greater incentive than the seller does to truthfully report the quality of the selling firm, he increases the efficiency of the market. Biglaiser (1993) formulates two hypotheses based on his findings as follows:

> *"(1) In markets where middlemen are present, both the average price and the quality of goods will be higher if they are sold through a middleman rather than through direct sales and (2) middlemen are more likely to be present in markets if it is difficult to judge a good's quality, if it is costly to become an expert in determining a good's quality, or if switching costs are low."*[182]

A theoretical model that examines the role of the investment banker dealing with the hidden information issue between buyer and seller is introduced in chapter 5. To conclude this chapter on capital market imperfections, the next section introduces ex post information asymmetries and applies this theoretical principle to mergers and acquisitions. Specifically, moral hazard in investment banking with bankers as agents and bidders or sellers as principals is discussed.

---

177 Lizzeri (1999), p. 215.
178 Biglaiser (1993), p. 212.
179 See Grossman (1981) for the case of no intermediary and a seller, who can costless certify the quality of his products.
180 Biglaiser and Friedman (1999), p. 2; and Biglaiser and Friedman (1994). Beatty and Ritter (1986) show for initial public offerings that investment banks lose market share if they price IPOs poorly.
181 Shen and Reuer (2005), p. 398. Carter and Manaster (1990) empirically show that investment bankers draw benefits from their reputation and strive at protecting them.
182 Biglaiser (1993), p. 223.

3.2.2.3 *Ex-post Information Asymmetries*

3.2.2.3.1 Hidden Action or Moral Hazard

The second kind of information asymmetry is examined ex post and is called hidden action or moral hazard. An agency relationship arises, if the principal delegates work to the agent. Division of labor results in the agent being better informed or more skilled than the principal is (in a particular field). The agent is supposed to use this knowledge advantage in performing a service on the principal's behalf.[183] However, the strategy maximizing the principal's utility may not simultaneously maximize the utility of the agent. Separation of ownership and control may lead to excessive conservatism in investment decisions, excessive consumption of perquisites, pursuit of net present value negative projects, and managerial entrenchment.

Interests may also diverge because the principal bears all the risk, while the agent undertakes the income-generating actions. Because the principal has less knowledge than the agent does, he cannot observe the agent's actions (hidden action), specifically the exerted effort, potential consumption on the job, etc.[184] Therefore, the agent may take an action that furthers his own interest but is against the interest of the principal. This problem is called moral hazard and includes the keywords 'consumption on the job', 'shirking', and 'empire building'.

Ideally, agent and principal should design a complete contract that assigns control rights for all states of the world. Yet such complete contracts are not possible, since many future contingencies are hard to describe and predict. Rather, residual control rights exist, which imply the right to make decisions in those residual circumstances not specified by the contract.[185] If managers possess more expertise than shareholders do, they are endowed with residual rights, have considerable discretion about how to allocate investors' funds, and can expropriate them.[186] Agency costs include the costs of structuring, monitoring, and bonding a set of contracts among agents with conflicting interests, plus the residual loss, which represents the reduction in welfare due to the divergence between the agent's decisions and the principal's welfare maximizing decisions.[187]

---

183 Jensen and Meckling (1976), p. 308.
184 Fama (1980), p. 304; Holmström (1979), p. 74.
185 Shleifer and Vishny (1997), p. 741; Grossman and Hart (1986); Hart and Moore (1990).
186 Potential means of expropriation by managers are expanding the firm beyond what is rational or entrenching themselves and staying on the job even if they are not competent or qualified enough to manage the firm. See Williamson (1964); Jensen (1986); and Shleifer and Vishny (1989).
187 Jensen and Meckling (1976), p. 308; Fama and Jensen (1983), p. 327; Neus (1989), p. 473.

The most common application of the agency problem is to common stock residual claims. The problem arises due to the separation of ownership (residual risk bearing) and control (decision functions). Common solution approaches here are (1) decision hierarchies, (2) board of directors, (3) incentive structures that promote mutual monitoring among decision agents, (4) the outside managerial labor market, (5) the outside market for control (i.e. takeovers). [188]

In mergers and acquisitions, moral hazard can occur between the managers (or agents) of a firm and its stockholders (principals). Managers of the bidding firm may engage in value destroying-acquisitions due to empire building. Jensen (1986) showed that managers might seek acquisitions that maximize their own utility rather than shareholder value, if monitoring devices do not function effectively. This agency conflict is lessened in mergers & acquisitions mediated by investment bankers, because the investment bankers perform an outside valuation of the acquisition opportunity. Furthermore, managers of the target firm may resist shareholder value maximizing hostile takeovers, e.g. by implementing expensive golden parachute or poison pill rules to safeguard their position. These problems are certainly interesting but not directly connected to the information flow during the mergers and acquisitions process. Therefore, these issues are not discussed in detail. Instead the focus is on the agency conflict between the investment banker and the buyer or seller.

Restating from the last chapter, investment bankers provide a solution to (or mitigate) ex ante information asymmetry or hidden information between buyer and seller. In respect to ex post information asymmetry or hidden action between investment banker and buyer or seller, the involvement of investment bankers may pose a moral hazard problem. The short-term relationship between the investment banker and the potential buyer or target may result in the investment banker courting a company as an acquisition target that they previously had as a bidder client.[189] Additionally, investment bankers may be in the stronger position in the agency relationship with corporate clients, because they operate in an oligopolistic industry and merger deals are becoming more frequent and increasingly more complex.[190] Because of the uneven information and expertise distribution between investment bankers and corporate clients, monitoring and assessing the investment banker's performance may be difficult for corporate clients. If agency costs were sufficiently high, the agency problem would limit the

[188] Fama and Jensen (1983), p. 331; Fama (1980), p. 294.
[189] Bowers and Miller (1990), p. 35.
[190] Kosnik and Shapiro (1997), p. 9.

usefulness of investment bankers as a tool to decrease information asymmetry. The existence of this agency problem and possible solution approaches are discussed in the next section.

3.2.2.3.2 Moral Hazard between Investment Banker and Buyer or Seller

Merger gains relate positively to investment bank fees and proxies for investment bank effort, which indicates that on average investment bankers are acting in the interest of their principals.[191] Typical investment banking contracts provide incentives that are consistent with basic firm objectives. Bidding firms usually use share-based fees, which are contingent on offer outcome, specifically on the number of shares purchased, and induce the investment banker to complete the transaction.[192] Target firms typically use value-based fees, which are contingent on both the number of shares acquired and the price paid.[193] Total-value fees motivate investment bankers of the seller to both complete the initial offer and to seek out competing higher bids. Incremental value fees require the investment banker to achieve an increase in offer price before closing.[194]

However, McLaughlin (1990, 1992) finds that while contingent contracts motivate agents to act in the principal's interest, some incentive features of investment banking contracts create conflicts of interest between an investment banker and his client.[195] A widely discussed agency problem arises between the investment banker (agent) working for the bidding firm (principal), if the agent's compensation increases with a higher offer price.[196] That is, the investment banker receives a higher compensation, even though his performance is less effective for the client. In 95% of investment banking contracts with bidder clients, the investment banker's fee increases with a successful takeover. This may induce investment bankers to suggest higher bids to complete the deal. The banker is only motivated to increase the probability of the acquisition[197], rather than maximizing the expected value of surplus to

---

[191] Hunter and Walker (1990), p. 1129.
[192] McLaughlin (1990), p. 221. Approximately 80% of bidding firms use shares-based fees as contractual incentive to the investment banker.
[193] McLaughlin (1990), p. 221. Approximately 73% of target firms use value-based fees as contractual incentive to the investment banker.
[194] Only fixed fees provide no incentives to the banker since they are independent of the offer price. Fixed fees are used infrequently (9.7% of seller representation and 5.7% of bidder representation). McLaughlin (1990), pp. 221, 227.
[195] McLaughlin (1990), p. 210.
[196] McLaughlin (1990), p. 227.
[197] With a higher price, the probability of being the successful bidder will increase. The investment banker may also be induced to base his valuation of the target on assumptions that support a higher offer, which may exacerbate the problem of the winner's curse. McLaughlin (1990), p. 230.

the bidding firm. Similarly, an engagement in which the investment banker is paid on an hourly basis if there is no acquisition but receives a percentage of the offer price if a transaction is closed may result in more mergers that are less advantageous to the client than if the interests of buyer and investment banker were more perfectly aligned.[198] An additional conflict of interest may arise because investment bankers have a short-term view, i.e. the closing of a transaction and receiving a fee income, versus the long-term profit-oriented view of the buy-side client.

On the selling side, the agency problem is usually less pronounced than on the buy-side. Interests of seller and investment banker are aligned because the investment banker's fee income increases with the eventual sale price. Problems may arise, however, if the investment banker does not solicit all potential buyers for offers. This may be the case if the investment banker values potential repeat business from a particular buyer higher than the one-time increase in fee income through a higher purchase price for the selling firm. Additionally, the marginal utility for the investment banker derived from a higher fee at a certain level falls below his marginal cost of investing considerably more time, effort, and resources for the negotiation of a higher purchase price.[199] Therefore, the generally used Lehman formula for determination of the investment banker's fee income may not provide the agent with sufficient incentive to extend additional effort at the end to receive a slightly higher offer price.

Conflicts of interest may also be present if the seller has an initial (low) tender offer and the investment banker is compensated on a total value basis. The investment banker has superior information based on his industry-specific expertise about the number of other potential bidders and likely bidding ranges. Since fees are on average 5 times greater for a closed deal, the investment banker may recommend acceptance of the initial low bid to close the transaction, even if this does not create maximum value for shareholders.[200] A different conflict of interest is created with compensation based on incremental value. Under this compensation scheme, the investment banker receives the contingent fee only if the deal is closed at a higher offer price. This may induce the banker to reject the initial bid too frequently in favor of uncertain additional offers. Conversely, if the probability of acquisition decreases with a rejection of the initial bid, the investment banker may accept the initial bid with a lower ex-

---

[198] Kosnik and Shapiro (1997), p. 8; and McLaughlin (1996), p. 136. Commonly, the investment banker's fee structure is tied to successfully closing the deal and to the resulting offer price.

[199] This may especially be the case for hard-to-sell businesses, e.g. financially distressed or stagnating firms.

[200] McLaughlin (1996), p. 140. The investment banker representing the seller has an incentive to accept a hostile offer to complete the transaction and receive a certain and high fee.

pected increase in offer price, if the probability of acquisition was sufficiently high. This may not be in the interest of value-maximizing shareholders, who may prefer no transaction to a transaction with a low offer price and would in absence of the banker, reject that bid.[201]

3.2.2.3.3 Possible Solutions

Solution approaches for this moral hazard problem are fee contracts that establish appropriate incentives for the agent and align the interests of principals and agents.[202] The target firm may design a total-value contract that awards the same pay if the acquisition is completed or if there is no acquisition.[203] Investment bankers could be dissuaded from closing resisted offers by restricting the payment of contingent fees to acquisitions approved by the board.[204] An alternative fee contract for small, private sellers draws on the reverse Lehman Formula[205], which provides the investment banker with a high incentive to work hard to achieve an additional million in purchase price, because of the increasing fee percentages. Additionally, a "cost plus"[206] fee structure would compensate the investment banker adequately for smaller deals and provide him with an incentive to work hard to generate the highest price possible. Bidding firms could introduce a fee that is decreasing in offer price, i.e. a 'reverse' total-value fee.

However, McLaughlin (1992) shows that the effects of different fee structures on offer outcomes are limited.[207] This implies that the agency conflict cannot be solved solely by creating appropriate incentive-based fee contracts, but must be influenced by other factors as well. Other means may more easily control investment bankers. The 'reputation' effect for instance influences contract selection and offer outcome. McLaughlin (1996) provides numerical examples for which potential losses to target firms linked to contract incentives ac-

---

[201] McLaughlin (1996), p. 141.

[202] Jensen and Meckling (1976), p. 308; Shleifer and Vishny (1997), p. 744.

[203] This approach eliminates conflicts of interest in offer evaluation, yet it may have a negative effect on effort incentives.

[204] McLaughlin (1990), p. 230.

[205] The reverse Lehman formula inverts the traditional Lehman formula, resulting in a fee structure that provides the investment banker with 1% on the first million dollars transaction volume, 2% on the second million, 3% on the third million, 4% on the fourth million, and 5% on everything thereafter (i.e. above $4 million).

[206] A cost plus fee structure is a combination of a fixed minimum fee for a minimum acceptable selling price (MASP) specified in the engagement letter between the selling client and the investment banker, and an increasing percentage fee over any million beyond MASP. Mergers & Acquisitions: The Dealmaker's Journal (2000), p. 16.

[207] McLaughlin (1992), p. 259.

count for up to 16.7% of the initial offer value. With the mitigating effect of reputation however, losses can be greatly reduced to 3.4% or less of the initial offer value.[208]

The role of reputation has been studied in initial public offerings by, e.g., Beatty and Ritter (1986), Booth and Smith (1986), and Neus and Walz (2005). Carter and Manaster (1990) show empirically that investment bankers strive to protect their reputations, since high-quality investment banks can charge higher fees than low-quality ones.[209] An investment banker's value of reputation may decline significantly, if he is perceived to be violating his fiduciary duty and acting in his own interest at the expense of his client. This loss of future rents because of diminished reputation capital can provide a strong incentive to the banker to act in his client's interest.[210] For instance, the investment bank Wasserstein Parella was shown to have lost market share because of perceived opportunistic behavior.[211] Bowers and Miller (1990) show that larger total wealth gains result if a first-tier investment bank assists the bidder or the target, which emphasizes the importance of the advisor's reputation or credibility in acquisitions.[212] In respect to offer outcomes, acquiror shareholders alone do not perform better if they employ the services of a first-tier investment bank. Bowers and Miller (1990) do not find any evidence that first-tier banks bring superior bargaining expertise to acquisition negotiations. Servaes and Zenner (1996) and Rau (2000), p. 315, do not find any relation between the tier of the advisor and abnormal returns to the bidder, respectively. If a long-term investment banking relationship exists, Saunders and Srinivasan (2001) find that acquirors pay a 'relationship' fee premium, which is highest for top tier advisors.[213] Assuming that merger fees are determined competitively, a certification effect may explain this relationship fee premium. Hereby, investment bankers that possess superior private information on their client obtained during the long-term relationship receive rents.

McLaughlin (1992) shows empirically that reputation has a significant effect on contract choice. Bidding firm's contracts are designed with larger incentives for low-reputation bankers. For target firms, reputation shows a signaling/selection effect on contract choice. High-quality investment bankers prefer fees that are greatly contingent on the outcome, since they are able to maximize payoffs based on their superior expertise and information. Addi-

[208] McLaughlin (1996), p. 151.
[209] Bowers and Miller (1990), p. 36.
[210] McLaughlin (1996), p. 142.
[211] Wall Street Journal, February 11, 1991.
[212] Bowers and Miller (1990), p. 43. The following investment banks are categorized as first-tier: First Boston, Goldman Sachs, Merrill Lynch, Morgan Stanley, and Salomon Brothers.
[213] Saunders and Srinivasan (2001), p. 3.

tionally, contingent fees allow high-quality investment bankers to signal their quality.[214] That implies that high-quality bankers will self-select incremental-value fee contracts when representing a target and total-value fee contracts when representing bidders. McLaughlin (1992) accordingly finds that strong incentive-based contracts are associated with high-reputation investment bankers; that is contract selection is more determined by signaling than incentive reasons.

Because it was determined in the prior section that investment bankers may be a mitigating factor in information asymmetries in mergers and acquisitions, this chapter explored the hidden action or moral hazard issue in respect to investment bankers as intermediaries. As potential solution approaches to decreasing agency costs, incentive-based fee contracts, reputation of the investment banker, and signaling and self-selection components were discussed. Even though some of the discussed solution approaches create new incentive alignment problems, several beneficial solution approaches exist. Additional research opportunities exist in respect to identifying influential components besides incentive contracts and reputation.

3.3 Chapter Summary

Considering imperfect markets, intermediaries may exist to reduce transaction costs and to mitigate information asymmetries. Transaction costs include search costs, negotiation costs, and enforcement costs. A bidder or a seller will engage an intermediary, if benefits (i.e. the reduction in transaction costs) outweigh the costs (i.e. the fee payable to the intermediary). In markets with information asymmetry and no intermediaries, the adverse selection problem may completely disrupt trade. Investment bankers as experts in the field signal the quality of the venture and validate it. Since, the sellers only live one period, i.e. they have little incentive to truthfully reveal the quality of their firm. Buyers usually only conclude one or at best a few transactions, i.e. they have little incentive to acquire the skills necessary to assess product quality. The intermediary, on the other hand, has an infinite time horizon, i.e. he has an incentive to undertake a large investment in "quality-detecting" skills and place a greater value on being known for selling high-quality firms or for reporting quality truthfully. Because investment bankers are focused on building reputation capital, they avoid misrepresentations and their involvement is a credible signal in this repeat-business environment. Since the interme-

214 McLaughlin (1992), pp. 233, 247. Rau (2000), p. 295, shows that for lower-quality investment banks contingent fees account for a significantly smaller proportion of total fees than for high-quality banks.

diary has a larger incentive than the seller does to truthfully report the quality of the selling firm, he increases the efficiency of the market.

Other solution approaches to the information asymmetry problem in addition to the investment banker include earnouts, common stock, equity stake, and collaborative agreements. These approaches all mitigate the hidden information issue to varying degrees. However, they all have disadvantages, which limit their use as a mitigating tool. Monitoring difficulties and contracting costs hamper earnouts as a tool. The use of common stock as an instrument is limited by financing and tax considerations, and the use of equity stakes is hampered by control and risk issues. Collaborative agreements can also not be used freely as a tool, as coordination costs, tax policies, and local legal requirements play an important role. The mitigating role of investment bankers is hampered by agency costs that arise because of differing interests of agent (investment banker) and principal (bidder or seller). The agency conflict that is certainly an issue may be mitigated through incentive-based fee contracts and reputation. The agency conflict between investment banker and buyer or seller has not been extensively researched yet, i.e., no conclusions can be drawn. However, it seems that the incentives of investment banker and client are sufficiently aligned, so that agency costs are a minor disadvantage.

In the next chapter, the central information asymmetry problem in mergers and acquisitions will be discussed in detail. Additionally, it will be determined how much information different companies are required to report, and buyers will be categorized according to their information need.

4 Information Asymmetry between Buyer and Seller

4.1 Reporting Regulations

Information asymmetry in mergers and acquisitions can be reduced from the outset because companies have to report a certain degree of company information publicly. This implies that the buyer might already have a minimum level of information, on which to base his valuation of the target. In this section, the specific reporting requirements for different firms in Germany and the US are examined.

4.1.1 German Reporting Requirements

Empirically it can be shown that German corporations are reluctant to provide company information to creditors or the investing public.[215] However, as corporations become larger and require outside capital, they are required to provide such information, which can be regarded as a necessary counterweight to the limited liability privilege such corporations enjoy.[216] The kind of information that has to be provided is categorized according to the size and legal form of the company.

German law broadly differentiates between "Personengesellschaften" and "Kapitalgesellschaften" as business forms. "Personengesellschaften", which are particularly tied to their owners or partners can be further divided into „Einzelkaufmann"[217], "Offene Handelsgesellschaft"[218], and "Kommanditgesellschaft". Sole proprietorships and partnerships are usually exempt from reporting company information. According to §1-(1) PublG, only large sole proprietorships and partnerships that have at least two of the following three features, must publicly report company information: (1) total assets of more than €65 million, (2) revenues of more than €130 million, and (3) more than 5000 employees.[219] In line with the newly enacted KapCoRiLiG[220], "Personengesellschaften" in which no partner has unlimited liability have to adhere to the more extensive reporting regulations for "Kapitalgesellschaften"[221].

---

[215] Neus (2005), p. 154.
[216] Bundesrat Drucksache (1999), pp. 33 et sqq.
[217] Equivalent to sole proprietorships.
[218] Similar to partnerships.
[219] Coenenberg (2003), p. 30.
[220] The "Kapitalgesellschaften- und Co-Richtlinie-Gesetz" was enacted on March 9, 2000 and affects about 100,000 Personengesellschaften (Bundesrat Drucksache, 1999, p. 30). See Winkeljohann and Schindhelm (2000), pp. 1-6 and Schindhelm and Stein (2000), pp. 190-209 for more information.
[221] §§325 et sqq. HGB

"Kapitalgesellschaften"[222] are not tied to specific partners or owners, formed for a longer time, and generally report more information than "Personengesellschaften". Small[223] "Kapitalgesellschaften" report less information than large companies do, specifically they may provide an abbreviated balance sheet[224] and abbreviated notes[225]. Generally, notes must satisfy the following conditions:

1. Present information about the basis for preparation of the financial statements and the specific accounting policies used
2. Disclose any information required by IFRS that is not presented on the face of the balance sheet, income statement, statement of changes in equity, or cash flow statement
3. Provide additional information that is not presented on the face of the balance sheet, income statement, statement of changes in equity, or cash flow statement that is deemed relevant to an understanding of any of them.[226]

Small "Kapitalgesellschaften" are only required to report abbreviated notes, which do not include any income information.[227] This implies that the buyer of a small German "Kapitalgesellschaft" has some initial information about the target, however is still exposed to a large degree of information asymmetry. The limited degree of information disclosure and specifically the lack of income information translate into little information that is useful to a buyer. This information asymmetry is widened, if the tendency of German companies not to comply with reporting regulations is taken into account. According to a study by the "Wirtschaftsprüferkammer", only 3.6% of all GmbHs in Germany reported their annual information.[228] Even though this percentage should gradually increase due to the stricter sanctions under the recently enacted KapCoRiLiG, the buyer's information problem with a German GmbH or any other company that has to comply with reporting requirements will be exacerbated by this attitude towards compliance.

[222] Here, a distinction into "Gesellschaft mit beschränkter Haftung" and „Aktiengesellschaft" can be made.
[223] According to § 267 (1) HGB, companies are categorized as small if they fulfill at least two of the three following criteria: (1) total assets of less than 3.438.000 euros, (2) revenues of less than 6.875.000 euros in the twelve months before the balance sheet date, and (3) less than 50 employees on average throughout the year.
[224] §266 (1)-3 HGB, §274a (1) HGB.
[225] §288 HGB.
[226] International Accounting Standards (IAS) 1.103.
[227] §326 (2) HGB.
[228] Wirtschaftsprüferkammer (1998), A 50, Nr. 130. Note that other studies find slightly higher overall compliance rates. All studies find that most companies that did not comply with reporting requirements can be categorized as small GmbHs. Mid-sized and large GmbHs, on the other hand, have somewhat higher compliance rates. For more details see Jansen (1999), p. 1490.

Medium-sized[229] "Kapitalgesellschaften" report more information with abbreviated annual statements including an abbreviated balance sheet[230], income statement, notes[231], and other information[232]. Large "Kapitalgesellschaften"[233] must report full annual statements as well as other information as defined above.[234] Apart from the above defined size criteria, a "Kapitalgesellschaft" is according to §267 (3-2) HGB always considered large, if stocks or other securities are listed at a European exchange or traded at an organized market. Regardless of the legal form of the company, large companies[235] have to report the same information as large "Kapitalgesellschaften"[236], with some lessening of requirements for sole proprietors and "Personengesellschaften.[237] Listed companies also have to fulfill the reporting requirements of the BörsG, BörsZulV, and "ad hoc" reporting regardless of their size.

This implies that the buyer of a medium-sized or large German "Kapitalgesellschaft" has access to a reasonable amount of information about the target company, before the buyer even engages in negotiations. However, most of the information is based on historic data, which is of course a necessary and important foundation for analysis, yet it remains questionable if future predictions can simply be extrapolated from such data. The above-mentioned "Lagebericht"[238] is highly relevant to prospective buyers, as it is required to contain predictions about business developments. However, such predictions generally only include cursory statements, which may not be of much use to the buyer.[239] In addition, the reported information was not composed for valuation purposes, which diminishes the value of such data to the buyer. The buyer has only book values available, further complicating his valuation of the target.[240] A crucial part of the "Lagebericht" is the "Risikobericht", which is intended to pro-

---

[229] According to § 267 (2), HGB, companies are categorized as medium-sized if they fulfill at least two of the three following criteria: (1) total assets between 3.438.000 and 13.750.000 euros, (2) revenues between 6.875.000 and 27.500.000 euros in the twelve months before the balance sheet date, and (3) between 50 and 250 employees on average throughout the year.
[230] § 325 (1) HGB, § 327 (1) HGB.
[231] No information with respect to §285 (2), (5), (8a), (12) HGB has to be reported.
[232] Specifically, a "Lagebericht", "Bestätigungs- oder Versagungsvermerk", „Bericht des Aufsichtsrates", „Jahresergebnis", and „Vorschlag und Beschluß über Ergebnisverwendung" have to be additionally reported.
[233] According to § 267 (3), HGB, companies are categorized as large if they fulfill at least two of the three following criteria: (1) total assets over 13.750.000 euros, (2) revenues over 27.500.000 euros in the twelve months before the balance sheet date, and (3) over 250 employees on average throughout the year.
[234] § 325 (1), (2), (4), (5) HGB; § 328 HGB; § 9 (1)-1 PublG.
[235] § 1 PublG defines companies as large if they fulfill at least two of the three following criteria: (1) total assets over 65 million euros, (2) revenues over 130 million euros in the twelve months before the balance sheet date, and (3) over 5000 employees on average throughout the year.
[236] § 5 PublG, § 9 PublG, §§ 265-278 HGB.
[237] § 9 (2) PublG.
[238] § 289 HGB.
[239] Ballwieser (1997), pp. 172-182.
[240] Strasser (2000), p. 47.

vide investors and other stakeholders with sufficient information about the riskiness of a given company.[241] Empirical analysis shows however that risk assessments are rather general in content and do not inform sufficiently about possible repercussions or the importance of specific risk factors.[242]

That means that even though the buyer may have access to a large degree of information, he can satisfy his need for information only to some extent. In addition, legislators realize the need for companies to keep certain sensitive information private. This implies that even large companies could avoid reporting competitively sensitive information. The statement of affairs can be kept to a rather general nature, which will for instance allow the company not to report sensitive information from which pricing information could be deduced.[243]

Most of the companies in Germany can be categorized as small or medium sized.[244] This implies that most German companies do not need to report company information and that the buyers of most companies are exposed to a large degree of information asymmetry. Additionally, as has been shown above, even large companies can avoid reporting competitively sensitive information. This implies for the buyer of large public companies, that there would still be a certain degree of information asymmetry, though admittedly less so than in the case of small Personengesellschaften.

4.1.2 U.S. Reporting Requirements

In contrast to the German creditor-oriented reporting system, the American reporting system aims at protecting the investor. This implies that there is no obligation for Kapitalgesellschaften, Personengesellschaften, or sole proprietorships to issue an annual report. Such an obligation only arises if (1) the company is subject to federal or state exchange authorities (such as the SEC) that require audited reports, or (2) the company's by-laws or creditors demand audited reports.[245] Therefore, only listed American firms are required to report company information, whereas the many private small and medium-sized firms are not required to do so.

---

[241] The explicit duty to risk reporting was introduced as part of the "Lagebericht" in 1998 and further detailed in standard DRS 5 in May 2001.
[242] Kajüter and Winkler (2003), p. 226.
[243] Der Betrieb (2004), pp. 2414 et sqq; Der BetriebsBerater (2004), pp. 2459-2460.
[244] Neus (2005), p. 154.
[245] Haller (2000), p. 20.

Eventually most companies must access equity markets to ensure continued growth and market penetration. At that point, company information has to be reported to the investing public, because such information could not be generated otherwise. This means that stockholders are in a weaker position, so that they have to be protected and provided with company information to allow them to make an informed investment decision. Creditors, on the other hand, could force the company to provide them with information they need for a well-founded investment decision, simply because they are in the contractual position to demand such information to be provided. Therefore, the American system is oriented towards protecting investors not creditors.

Publicly traded companies are required to provide audited financial statements, which consist of balance sheet, income statement, cash flow statement, statement of changes in stockholder's equity, and notes.[246] In respect to information asymmetry, this implies that the buyer of a publicly traded firm has a large degree of information available. Obviously, the degree of information asymmetry for a public firm would be much less than for the case of a private firm. Yet information asymmetry still exists even for large publicly traded firms because of the same aspects discussed under German reporting regulations. Information asymmetry for private firms may even be exacerbated in many cases, because annual statements of private firms may not be audited and thus less reliable for the buyer. This implies that the model developed in chapter 5 is certainly applicable to the large number of small and midsized U.S. and German companies, and, although to a lesser degree, to large publicly traded companies as well.

4.2 Information Categories

A major component of mergers & acquisitions negotiations is the determination of the offer price. In order to value the selling firm's operations, the buyer needs to assess the expected future free cash flows and discount them at the appropriate rate. Free cash flow is defined as the after-tax operating earnings of the company, plus non-cash charges, less investments in operating working capital, property, plant and equipment, and other assets.[247] The fundamental drivers of free cash flow and consequently of a company's value are 1) return on invested

[246] KPMG (2003), pp. 18 et sqq.
[247] Copeland, Koller, and Murrin (2000), p. 134.

capital[248] (relative to weighted cost of capital) and 2) growth rate of revenues, profits, and capital base.[249] The first step in valuing a company is analyzing its historical performance focused on the two key value drivers. Second, the weighted average cost of capital (WACC) used to discount future free cash flows for all investors must be estimated. Then, the buyer needs to forecast future performance of the selling firm based on the above two value drivers. To estimate equity value, future free cash flows are discounted at the WACC, the discounted value of nonoperating assets is added, and the market value of all debt, hybrid securities, minority interest, or other claims is subtracted.

In order to perform a valuation of the target, the buyer has to be provided with private information on the selling company. Information can be categorized into verifiable and unverifiable information. Information is verifiable if an independent party besides the seller can attest to the truthfulness of such information and can penalize the seller if the information is found to be untruthful.[250] Examples for such verifiable information are historical financial accounting statements certified by accountants, the seller's customer list, and pricing information. Unverifiable information on the other hand cannot be attested by a third party. Therefore, it cannot be the basis for a contract, because any such contract would not be enforceable. Examples for unverifiable information are information on budgets and forecasts and information on pending patents and new proprietary products and technologies. If the seller discloses such unverifiable information, the buyer cannot assess the truthfulness of the disclosed information.

Private information may also be categorized into critical and uncritical company information. This categorization is more appropriate for this paper than the categorization into verifiable and unverifiable information. A distinction into verifiable and unverifiable information is necessary if the information disclosure issue during the negotiation phase is approached from an accounting point of view. Here, a categorization of information into critical and uncritical information is appropriate because this distinction allows the assessment of the financial effect of the disclosure action on the market value of the target company. Even though all information that is conveyed during negotiations is of proprietary nature, only critical proprietary information has the potential for negative effects.[251] After disclosure of pro-

[248] Return on invested capital (ROIC) equals the net operating profits of the selling company divided by the amount of invested capital.
[249] Copeland, Koller, and Murrin (2000), p. 137.
[250] Wagenhofer (2000), p. 61.
[251] Wagenhofer (2000), p. 57.

prietary information, the buyer may decide not to acquire the target firm and remain a competitor in the product market. Then, the buyer may use the critical proprietary information for better decision making in the product market, thereby negatively influencing the competitive position of the selling firm. In contrast, the disclosure of uncritical proprietary information cannot harm the seller competitively, because the buyer cannot use this information for his own benefit.

Uncritical proprietary information includes detailed machinery and equipment appraisals and real estate appraisals. That information only facilitates an evaluation by the buyer, but does not possess the potential for misappropriation. Similarly, information about the selling company's established products, product lines, and markets is uncritical. From a financial point of view, accounting statements[252] and information on leases and loans are uncritical. Accounting statements are mostly sufficiently general in nature, so that key drivers of the business do not have to be disclosed. Information on leases and loans is important to the buyer, because he may be able to finance the operations at lower cost after the acquisition, increasing his valuation of the target firm. Yet such information does not carry any potential for misappropriation. Additionally, general information about alliances or joint ventures is uncritical. The buyer cannot easily break-up an existing alliance and enter into it himself, especially since the existence of such alliances is usually well known among competitors. In addition, the appropriate discount rate or weighted average cost of capital for the valuation of the target firm is important proprietary information. Yet such information is not critical, since the buyer cannot misappropriate the information and use it for his own benefit. Consequently, non-critical proprietary information may be disclosed without taking the risk of competitively harming the target company.

Critical proprietary information is information that if disclosed could be used by the buyer and has the potential to negatively affect the competitive position of the seller. For instance information about the customer base of the selling firm and the respective volume of revenues may be critical. Once buyers are aware of customer names and revenue figures, they can approach those customers and offer them similar products at a lower introductory price. Similarly, information about key employees of the seller and compensation details could be used by the buyer to access valuable human capital by offering a higher compensation. Critical information is certainly also information about prototypes, products in development, pend-

[252] For detailed financial disclosure requirements please recall the discussion from the prior section.

ing patents, and additional market potential. Likewise, information about unit costs, mark-ups for different products and sale prices is critical. Forecasting information may also be critical, if for instance a pending patent is expected to increase sales significantly. Naturally, the degree of information that can be categorized as critical depends on the nature of the business for sale, as well as on its business cycle and industry cycle.

The model that is developed in chapter 5 reflects this categorization of information by assuming that the seller has critical private information on unit costs. This critical information has the potential to influence the target's competitive position negatively, if disclosed. In addition, financial buyers are assumed to have private information on cost of capital, which represents uncritical information. This private information is uncritical, since the buyer cannot benefit from using information that does not influence the production quantity decision.

Having discussed the different information categories, different buyer types will be discussed next. There is a link between buyer types and information, because the degree of information asymmetry and required information varies with buyer types.

4.3 Buyer types

Information asymmetry arises due to the differing level of information of the seller to the buyer. Both buyer and seller can either have a high level of information or a low level. Ragotzky (2003) categorizes buyer and sellers accordingly into four categories (see Table 4-1):

<table>
<tr><td></td><td></td><td colspan="2">Seller</td></tr>
<tr><td></td><td></td><td>Insider</td><td>Outsider</td></tr>
<tr><td rowspan="2">Buyer</td><td>Outsider</td><td>(1)</td><td>(2)</td></tr>
<tr><td>Insider</td><td>(3)</td><td>(4)</td></tr>
</table>

Table 4-1: Information Asymmetry of Buyer and Seller depending on Degree of Involvement in the Selling Company's Management[253]

Generally with mergers and acquisitions, the seller has a higher level of information than the buyer does (cases 1 and 2 in Table 4-1). If the Seller manages the company himself, he has a considerable information lead (case 1). A Seller that does not manage the company (case 2) has less of an information lead. The degree of this information lead depends on the degree of the seller's control and information rights. If the target is sold to an insider buyer,

[253] Ragotzky (2003), p. 16.

the information lead reverses. When both buyer and seller are well informed (case 3), then there may not be any information asymmetry. Alternatively, the level of information asymmetry may be insignificant or even reciprocal (depending on the involvement of the seller in the management). Reciprocal information asymmetry may arise because insider buyers may know more about their specific operations, while the managing owner may know more for instance about the history of the company. In the special case of inside managers as buyers and an outside seller (case 4), the information asymmetry reverses and the inside buyer has an information lead on the seller.[254] Especially in case 4 inside managers can be much better informed than sellers, because they become aware of certain information during their management duties that non-managing, outside owners do not know.

The four scenarios described above can be understood as basic scenarios of information distribution. Because of the great number of value-driving information parameters, an infinite number of scenarios with differing degrees of information asymmetry results. Yet Akerlof's case of the buyer being less informed than the seller is most commonly observed in practice. For that reason, the model developed in chapter 5 focuses on case 1 of this table, which is the case of an outside buyer combined with a manager-owner of the selling firm.

Independently of their information level, buyers may also be categorized according to their acquisition motives. On the one hand there are strategic buyers, which are interested in the target mainly due to value-driving factors, such as economies of scale, economies of scope, reduction of transaction costs, and a more dominant market position. Strategic buyers operate in the same industry as the target and are competitors, suppliers, or customers of the target. If competitors as strategic buyers acquire the target, the acquisition is called horizontal, since both buyer and seller operate and compete in the same kind of business activity. In vertical acquisitions, both buyer and seller also operate in the same industry, yet they focus on different parts of the production process. An acquisition of the target by its customer or its supplier would therefore be called a vertical acquisition.

Besides strategic buyers, there are financial buyers who are interested in the target due to financial motives.[255] The goal of financial buyers is to generate value through the acquisition. That can be accomplished by acquiring an undervalued target or by generating value after the acquisition, e.g. through more efficient management. Financial buyers can be indi-

---

[254] For more information on inside buyers or management buy-outs (case 3 and 4), see Niemann (1995) and Ragotzky (2003), Chapter 4.
[255] Häcker (2005), p. 223.

viduals or firms with financial motives, institutional investors, or leveraged buyout (LBO) firms. Individuals or firms may be interested in a target based on financial motives, e.g. for conglomerate or personal management reasons. LBO firms look for acquisition targets with a low debt ratio to highly leverage and then to profitably divest them.[256] Generally, LBO firms target companies that have a stable cash flow and that can service future debt payments, and have a large tangible asset base that can be used as collateral are targeted.

Depending on the type of buyer, the degree of information asymmetry between seller and buyer varies. A financial buyer with a portfolio of totally unrelated businesses will be entirely unfamiliar with the target's industry, thus information asymmetries will be largest in this case. A strategic buyer will have a smaller degree of information asymmetries because he operates in the same industry. No information asymmetry exists in the case of a management buy-out (MBO). In this special case the current management and the buyer are one; thus no information asymmetries can exist.[257]

The different buyer types also have a bearing on the disclosure of private company information. The disclosure of private information to a financial buyer is unproblematic because the financial buyer is not active in the industry. If the acquisition is not completed, the financial buyer cannot influence the seller negatively based on the disclosed information. In respect to strategic buyers however, the disclosure of private information is problematic. If the acquisition fails the strategic buyer may use the disclosed proprietary and critical information to his advantage and may harm the target's competitive position. Therefore, the seller has to consider potential competitive damages in his disclosure decision about critical private information. In the next section, confidentiality agreements are introduced. Such agreements are industry standard and aim at preventing the described misappropriation of private information by buyers.

4.4 Confidentiality Agreements

Regulatory instruments can mitigate the problem of the buyer misappropriating competitively sensitive information that was disclosed during the acquisition process. The main instrument in the field is called confidentiality (or non-disclosure) agreement.[258] The objective of the confidentiality agreement is to ensure that the buyer does not disclose proprietary information

---

[256] Azarmi and Häcker (2003), p. 1367.
[257] Niemann (1995), p. 2.
[258] Picot (1998), pp. 29 et sqq.

received during the acquisition process to third parties and does not use such information for his own good. The mere acknowledgement that an acquisition is being discussed may lead to economic losses or loss of reputation for the target firm.[259] Customers, banks, suppliers, and other stakeholders may demand a premium or may lower their purchases because they are concerned about the target not being able to fulfill the guarantee obligations or to provide spare parts. Similarly, key employees may question the security of their positions and may transfer to a competitor. That is why the confidentiality agreement also prevents the disclosure of the mere fact that an acquisition is being discussed. The agreement typically states what information is to be provided, how this information is to be provided, who will have access to the information, and under what circumstances the information can be passed along to third parties[260]. In addtion, an assurance will be included in the confidentiality agreement that the informational material will not be used for any purpose other than evaluating the proposed transaction. Since many buyers withdraw from acquisitions and negotiations do break down, there is a need to specifying a mechanism for returning the confidential material in case that negotiation ceases.[261]

Even though the confidentiality agreement is a highly useful instrument regulating the handling of proprietary information in the field of acquisitions, it lastly does not prevent the buyer from misusing confidential information. Ramifications based on confidentiality agreements can be considered more psychological than legal in nature.[262] In case of a violation of the agreement, proof has to be brought by the seller, who naturally finds it difficult to assess if the buyer is abiding by the signed agreement and even more so to actually prove that the buyer is not. Even harder yet is to quantify the amount of damage that was caused by the breach of the agreement. German law permits the so-called "Vertragsstrafe"[263], which mitigates the enforcement problem to a certain degree. Once specified in a confidentiality agreement, this fixed penalty does not require a proof of damage; however it still has to be shown by the seller that the buyer breached the confidentiality agreement. Therefore, even if the combination of confidentiality agreement plus "Vertragsstrafe" is considered, this instrument currently does not guarantee adequate enforcement of its rules. Especially if one bears in mind

[259] Jansen (2001), p. 183.

[260] Third parties that may receive the private information are attorneys, accountants, etc, who are involved in the transaction.

[261] Strasser (2000), p. 166.

[262] Jansen (2001), p. 183; and Hölters (2002), p. 35.

[263] §340 BGB and the respective comments.

that in many cases of breach of a confidentiality agreement the resulting amount of damage potentially could not be atoned for anyhow.[264]

4.5 Information Disclosure Dilemma for the Seller

In Chapter 3 the hidden information problem that exists between the seller and the buyer of a company during the M&A process was introduced. During acquisition negotiations the seller has to disclose extensive private company information to the buyer. If relevant information is withheld, the buyer assumes that the information is unfavorable[265] and purchase price is influenced negatively. Therefore, the seller should disclose the private information in order to maximize his acquisition proceeds. However, he also runs a risk when he discloses private information to a potential buyer. The buyer could terminate the acquisition, and use the private information for his own benefit. For instance, the buyer may use disclosed pricing and customer information to pursue the seller's most important client and offer him conditions that are more favorable. This problem becomes especially severe, if the prospective buyer is a current competitor of the firm, because potential damage from the misuse of information could be limitless. Indeed, a large number of acquisition negotiations break off unsuccessfully every year.[266]

The common solution approach to prevent competitive damages is the use of confidentiality agreements. In the last section it was shown that confidentiality agreements might not be a sufficient instrument to safeguard the seller's interest regarding the disclosure of private company information, because they may not always be enforceable. Therefore, the seller also has to consider in his disclosure decision that the disclosed private information may negatively influence his competitive position. As a result, full disclosure of private information may not be optimal for the seller at all times if potential competitively harmful side effects are considered.[267] Since the seller aims at dissuading the buyer from exploiting the provided proprietary information, he would be induced to reveal only unfavorable information, if any, in order to minimize competitively harmful effects.[268] Not revealing favorable informa-

264 Jansen (2001), p. 183.
265 Milgrom (1981), p. 382.
266 According to Berman (2004) in the Wall Street Journal "Today, caution rules the boardroom.(...). Directors are demanding months of due diligence, and even then only about one in 10 would-be combinations reach fruition."
267 The problem arising from competitive damages may be especially severe if the prospective buyer is a direct competitor of the firm.
268 Wagenhofer (1990), p. 346.

tion would however decrease the purchase price that buyers will be willing to pay. Thus, the ultimately resulting degree of information disclosure will be a trade-off between the two forces (1) purchase price and (2) potential for competitive damages, and will depend on the degree of uncertainty about the buyer's intentions. In addition, the degree of information disclosure depends on the type of buyer.[269]

Determining whether the seller should disclose his private information to the buyer is highly relevant from a financial point of view. Once the expected gain from a buyer's offer to the seller under disclosure and non-disclosure is determined, the seller chooses the buyer and the disclosure strategy that maximizes his expected return. In the following chapter, these information-related issues are theoretically modeled. The investment banker is modeled as the intermediary who provides the seller with access to different buyer categories and formulates a financial sale decision parameter.

[269] In Chapter 5 it will be shown that more information can be disclosed to financial buyers than to strategic buyers.

5 <u>Information Disclosure Model</u>

5.1 Introduction

5.1.1 Overview

This section of the dissertation theoretically analyzes hidden information in mergers and acquisitions within a modeled economy. Suppose that there is an owner who would like to sell his firm and multiple prospective buyers willing to buy it. The parties to this selling process have differing degrees of information. The seller is aware of proprietary financial information, budgets, information about his customers, markets, product development, technology, capability of management, etc. The buyer on the other hand expects to be provided with such proprietary information during the evaluation period to decide whether to acquire the firm. The classical problems inherent in the information disclosure literature are exacerbated if the buyer is a strategic buyer, i.e. a competitor of the selling firm, or a supplier or customer of the selling firm. That is, if private information is released to a buyer, who eventually does not acquire the selling firm, that buyer could use the proprietary information against the seller. Therefore the standard recommendation in investment banking is that the seller should not reveal his proprietary information for as long as possible, as the acquisition might not be completed. Negative effects of disclosure may be reduced with the use of confidentiality agreements or prevented by the use of contingency payments, e.g. earn-out agreements. These two instruments and their limitations were discussed before. This section theoretically analyzes disclosure strategies in a model with incomplete information.

To remain as realistic as possible, the model presents a seller, an investment banker as intermediary, a horizontal strategic buyer or competitor, multiple suppliers as vertical buyers, multiple customers as vertical buyers, and various financial buyers in an auction. One of these financial buyers (the financial buyer) emerges as the winner of an auction held by the investment banker amongst financial buyers. Modeling reality, financial buyers are assumed only accessible through investment bankers. The proprietary information is modeled with two variables: cost of capital (K) and variable unit costs (k). The unique contribution of this model is that it differentiates between different kinds of private information and attributes the knowledge about the information to different players. While the private information on unit costs is known by the seller, the private information about cost of capital has two components, 1) the cost of capital of the selling company K_S known by the seller and 2) the differential cost of new capital ΔK for a firm of the same risk as the one offered for sale, which is known by the financial buyers as a whole. That is, an auction amongst financial buyers serves a price discovery function by revealing the differential cost of capital through the price.

The private information about cost of capital cannot competitively harm the seller if it is disclosed, because it is only relevant if the acquisition is completed. Therefore, the seller can make his disclosure decision about cost of capital depending merely on the expected value of the target firm as assessed by the strategic buyer, and entirely ignore potential negative competitive effects arising from disclosure of this information. The disclosure recommendation to the seller resulting from this model will be full disclosure of the financial buyer's private information on cost of capital to all buyers.

The private information on unit costs on the other hand may harm the seller competitively, since in the event that the acquisition fails the strategic buyer may adjust his production quantity in the product market by exploiting the disclosed information. Therefore, the probability of the strategic buyer acquiring the target company has to be taken into account. Depending on the probability of acquisition and on the level of unit costs, the seller will 1) not disclose any information, or 2) partially disclose information, or 3) fully disclose his private information on unit costs.

Another contribution of this model is that the involvement of the investment banker and the financial buyer strengthen the bargaining position of the seller. Through the involvement of the investment banker, the seller now has access to a completely new class of buyers, which provides the seller with more selling options. Additionally, the involvement of the investment banker allows the seller to separate the private information into two different components. The cost of new capital component of private information is only relevant if the acquisition materializes, while the unit cost component of private information also has the potential to harm the seller competitively if the acquisition fails. Thus, different disclosure issues are considered for the two components of private information.

Negotiations between seller and buyer in acquisitions and the inherent private information issues have rarely been examined in literature. Several papers in literature consider information disclosure from an accounting point of view.[270] Wagenhofer (2000), who employs a model that is technically similar to my approach, also has an accounting point of view. Specifically, he examines verifiable and unverifiable information in respect to the optimal

[270] See for instance Crawford and Sobel (1982); Verrecchia (1983); Dontoh (1989); Farrell and Gibbons (1989); Verrecchia (1990); Wagenhofer (1990); Gigler (1994); Penno (1997); and Korn (2004).

disclosure strategy. In contrast, I take a financial point of view that regards disclosure strategies merely as a tool to achieve maximum sale price in mergers & acquisitions for the selling company. That is, this model explores the mergers & acquisitions process with different kinds of players and their respective valuations, and models an investment banker that makes a disclosure recommendation to the seller depending on the acquirer's valuation of the selling firm. The seller's perspective is modeled in that the investment banker is an intermediary of the seller and will recommend a sale strategy that maximizes the seller's expected pay-off.

	Wagenhofer	**Häcker**
Seller	Yes	Yes
Investment Banker	No	Yes

Buyer	One type
	• Strategic (horizontal)
		Three types
		• Strategic (horizontal)
		• Strategic (vertical)
		  o Supplier
		  o Customer
		• Financial

Private information	1 dimension (y)	2 dimensions (K and k)
Costs	Unit Costs	Unit costs and cost of capital
Profit	Gross Profit	EVA

Table 5-1: Differences between Wagenhofer (2000) and Häcker (2007)

Table 5-1 summarizes the main differences between Wagenhofer (2000) and this model. In both papers the seller is modeled similarly (first row of Table 5-1). The first difference arises out of the introduction of the investment banker as an intermediary in the mergers & acquisitions process (row 2). While Wagenhofer (2000) does not have an intermediary in his model, this model introduces an investment banker. The existence of an investment banker models reality closely, since virtually every mergers & acquisition transaction is assisted by investment bankers. Their inclusion is also important, because they have access to a wide inventory of potential financial and strategic buyers, which the seller could not access by himself.

The introduction of the investment banker also allows this paper to model two additional buyer categories. While Wagenhofer (2000) models only the competitor as a horizontal strategic buyer, this article models the horizontal buyer, two different vertical strategic buyers and the financial buyer (row 3). The extension with the financial buyer is important, since the financial buyer, as an industry outsider is not in the position to use disclosed private information against the seller if the acquisition is not completed. That is, through the inclusion of the financial buyer the major disadvantage of disclosure can be avoided. In addition, the modeled mergers & acquisitions process becomes closer to practice, since generally both financial and strategic buyers bid on a target firm. The inclusion of vertical strategic buyers is also important because they combine the advantages of horizontal strategic buyers and financial buyers. Like horizontal buyers, vertical buyers also have synergies arising from the acquisition. Moreover, like the financial buyers, vertical buyers cannot directly influence the production decision and use the disclosed private information against the seller if no acquisition materializes. In contrast to the financial buyer, however, there may be a secondary effect arising from the disclosure of private information to vertical buyers.

If the supplier as a vertical buyer was aware of the private information on the seller's unit costs, his bargaining power in the product market might increase if the acquisition fails. A supplier that receives more information has a better bargaining position. Especially if there is limited competition among suppliers, the seller's supplier could raise the prices for his products, thereby increasing the costs of the seller. Similarly, a customer as vertical buyer might realize upon disclosure of the private information on unit costs that the seller's unit costs are lower and therefore his margins higher than expected. This is especially significant if the customer has a large order volume and therefore a strong bargaining position. If the acquisition fails, he may then demand a lower price from both the seller and the horizontal buyer. Alternatively, the customer may simply replace the seller's product with a more economical substitute product, if possible. The customer may on the other hand decide to have his product manufactured abroad, e.g. in a developing country with much lower labor costs. Any of these measures could decrease the profit of the seller through lower demand.

Concerning the private information that underlies the disclosure decision, Wagenhofer (2000) has one parameter (y) for private information, which summarizes the private information on demand and on cost (row four in Table 5-1). This model is a two-dimensional extension of Wagenhofer (2000) that works with two private information parameters: 1) unit cost and 2) cost of capital. Additionally, unit costs (k) in this model are defined differently from Wagenhofer's costs (row 5 and 6). Wagenhofer includes production costs in k, while setting fixed costs to zero. That definition of k results in gross profit, which certainly disregards a fair share of costs. In contrast, the definition of unit costs applied in this model includes cost of goods sold, selling, general, and administrative expenses, and interest and tax expenses. Cost of capital is then deducted in the profit function, which is similar to the deduction of fixed costs. Therefore, the resulting profit is Economic Value Added (EVA), which also takes the opportunity cost of the invested capital into account. Since EVA is an estimate of the amount that earnings fall short or exceed the required rate of return by lenders or shareholders at comparable risk, both operating and capital costs are considered for the acquisition.

Wagenhofer (2000) models the disclosure decision of private and competitively sensitive information to the strategic buyer in detail. Instead of focusing on the disclosure decision for one specific buyer type, this model provides a comprehensive overview of the mergers & acquisitions process and all its participants. All the potential buyers of a target firm with their unique characteristics as well as the investment banker are captured in the model. Another important contribution of this model is that it links the price discovery function of financial buyers with information about cost of capital and asset valuation in an economy. With an auction among financial buyers, with the competitor, and with the supplier and customer of the target firm, investment banking market valuation during the acquisition process is modeled. The financial point of view of the mergers & acquisition process allows the model's results to be interpreted into sale recommendations. The investment banker makes sale recommendations depending on the valuation of the respective buyers. The milestones of the selling process are graphed in Table 5-2.

1	S engages IB
2	IB identifies potential buyers (FB, HB, VB)
3	IB receives bid from FB
4	IB derives ΔK from bidding price and discloses it to S
5	S discloses ΔK to HB and VB
6	Depending on the acquisition probability, the IB recommends disclosure or non-disclosure of k
7	HB and VB make an offer based on their valuations
8	S maximizes his expected gain from buyers' offers

Table 5-2: Milestones of the Selling Process

The first milestone in the selling process is that the seller (S) engages the investment banker (IB) as the intermediary in the sale.[271] The investment banker proceeds with identifying suitable potential buyers for the seller. Potential buyers are financial buyers, horizontal strategic buyers, and vertical buyers. In particular, the investment banker can access financial

[271] Typically, buyers also engage an investment banker as intermediary. Here, the perspective of the seller is taken, since that point of view has not been widely researched before.

buyers (FB), who play a special role since buyers who buy for financial gain possess private information about cost of capital. In a third step, the investment banker runs an auction, from which the winning financial bidder emerges with the highest price (p_{FB}). This price then implicitly reveals the differential cost of new capital (ΔK) that the financial buyer expects for the target. The investment banker passes this information along to the seller. It will be shown within the model that it will always be optimal for the seller to disclose this private information on cost of new capital to all buyers in a fifth step.

As a sixth step, the seller has to decide whether to disclose his private information on unit costs to the buyers. The disclosure decision here is more complex, because with disclosure the buyer may competitively harm the seller in the product market if the acquisition is not completed. Therefore, the disclosure decision of the seller primarily depends on the probability (ϕ) of the buyer acquiring the selling firm, and secondarily depends on the level of unit costs (k). Depending on the nature of the buyer, i.e. competitor, supplier, or customer, the derived disclosure recommendation varies. A common finding among all buyers, however, is that for a high probability of acquisition a high degree of unit cost information is disclosed. In a seventh step, all strategic buyers submit an offer price, either with full information or depending on their expected value of the private information given non-disclosure. In a last step, the investment banker recommends a sale decision to the seller, which is based on the differing bids of the buyers, their respective acquisition probability, and their particular potential for competitive damages.

The next section develops the assumptions for the model and explains the different players and their roles extensively. In the following sections, the milestones in the acquisition process as described in Table 5-2 are modeled. After having determined disclosure recommendations to the seller for differing levels of probability of the acquisition, a sale recommendation to the seller can finally be made.

5.1.2 Model Assumptions and Role of Players

This model may be viewed as an extension of Wagenhofer's (2000) information disclosure model. The model adds an investment banker as intermediary to Wagenhofer's model, and introduces three different types of buyers who are classified as horizontal and vertical strategic buyers and financial buyers. My assumptions are as follows:

1. *One-Period Model Assumption.*

The model is in discrete time with the investment banker (intermediary), the seller, the horizontal strategic buyer (competitor), two different vertical strategic buyer types (suppliers and customers), and financial buyers, all of which live only one period.

2. *Separability Assumption: The buyers do not exchange information amongst each other.*

The horizontal buyer, the two vertical buyer types, and financial buyers are separate players, i.e. it is assumed that they do not exchange private information that was disclosed to them amongst each other. For instance, the financial buyer will not pass along his private information on cost of new capital directly to the horizontal buyer, which would circumvent the selling firm. However, since the intermediary is the agent of the selling firm, private information is shared between the investment banker and the seller.

3. *Duopoly Assumption: Seller and competitor operate in a Cournot-duopoly.*

The selling firm (S) is operating in a Cournot-duopoly with a competitor or horizontal strategic buyer (HB), who is interested in acquiring the selling firm.[272]

4. *Homogeneous Products Assumption: Seller and competitor produce homogeneous products.*

The two firms operate in the same product market and produce homogeneous products or close substitutes.

5. *Non-triviality Assumption:*
    - *Non-zero output*
    - *Profitable firms*
6. *Rational Expectations Assumption: Both S and HB in the Cournot duopoly hold rational expectations.*

The model assumes that both firms (S and HB) in the Cournot duopoly produce and sell products (non-zero output), are profitable, and hold rational expectations.

One of the players in the model is the investment banker (IB), who is in the unique position to induce financial buyers (FB) to bid on the target. This assumption reflects the practice, as in practice it is virtually impossible for the selling firm to establish contact and credi-

[272] Here a Cournot duopoly is chosen to better show the effects of information disclosure on resulting price. The choice of a Cournot duopoly is standard in this literature (see e.g. Wagenhofer (2000)). An extension of the model to more than two competing firms is feasible and straightforward.

bly communicate and market the firm to financial buyers without the services of an investment banker.

7. *Accessibility Assumption: Only the investment banker has access to financial buyer* Because of the intermediary's role as expert, it is relatively easy and cheap for him to locate financial buyers that are interested in the target. The investment banker is able to gain access to financial buyers through his industry-specific expertise, superior information, and access to his personal network and to his extensive private equity databases with detailed individual investment profiles. Here, these facts are simplified by assuming that only the investment banker has access to the financial buyer. Therefore, the investment banker plays an important role in the acquisition process. He can access financial buyers and acts as a market maker, bringing together multiple financial buyers in an auction for the sale of the target firm. The auction has a price discovery function, in that the appropriate market value of the target firm based on full information but without any synergy value is derived. Additionally, the introduction of the investment banker enriches the model by reflecting the reality of the mergers & acquisition process more accurately.

The second player is the financial buyer. The introduction of a financial buyer into the mergers & acquisition process reflects reality closely. It allows access to a completely new buyer category, which increases the options of the seller. Information disclosure to the financial buyer is unproblematic, since he does not operate in the same industry as the target and cannot use the provided information to harm the target's competitive position.[273] Therefore, the seller may disclose all private information to the financial buyer without fearing negative competitive effects. The investment banker with his access to financial buyers holds an auction with multiple financial buyers. Financial buyers mimic the open market in that they have a price discovery role. That is, each financial buyer evaluates the target company and bids a price for it. From this auction, one financial buyer (the financial buyer) emerges as the highest bidder by providing the highest value assessment. Through the financial buyer's valuation, his assessment of the appropriate risk premium for the acquisition can be concluded.

[273] This assumes that the seller's industry has at least moderate entry barriers. If entry barriers were low and the disclosed information was positive, the financial buyer could decide not to acquire the firm but to enter the duopoly market. This would lead to a decrease in price and thus a decrease in profit for the seller and the strategic buyer. In a duopoly market the existence of entry barriers can safely be assumed, since a duopoly could not persist and competitors would enter the market if there were no entry barriers.

The risk premium for the acquisition is given by the cost of new capital, one of the proprietary information parameters.[274] Since the cost of new capital for the target firm is only incurred if the acquisition is completed, its disclosure cannot competitively harm the seller. The financial buyer possesses proprietary information on cost of new capital, and he reveals his assessment of the appropriate cost of new capital through his bid at the auction. Since the cost of new capital varies with industries and economic cycles, it can only be accurately assessed by the FB within a competitive auction.

8. *Valuation Assumption: Only the financial buyer can accurately assess the cost of new capital for the target firm.*
9. *Cost of Capital Assumption: The financial buyer offering the highest price is applying the "accurate" cost of capital.*

Neither the seller nor any strategic buyer is able to assess the cost of new capital for the target firm. The financial buyer is the only player who can accurately assess the cost of new capital through an auction, because of his investment expertise in purchasing firms for financial gain.[275] That is, the financial buyer possesses private information on the cost of new capital, which can only be utilized when the seller involves the investment banker and the financial buyer in the acquisition process. For horizontal and vertical strategic buyers, information on the cost of new capital for buying and selling a similar asset in the market for firms as determined by financial buyers is important private information.

Since the seller discloses all relevant information to financial buyers who do not have any synergy benefits, the cost of new capital is the only component of the financial buyer's bid that is unknown to the seller. Therefore, the private information on the appropriate cost of new capital (ΔK) as assessed by the financial buyer is revealed through his bid. Additionally, the highest financial bidder is assumed to accurately estimate the cost of capital. This is a reasonable assumption, because financial buyers as market insiders that derive no value from synergies will determine practically the same cost of capital for the target firm. By going to the market for sale of firms - a market intermediated by the investment banker (market maker role) - the seller receives information on his firm's cost of new capital required for buying equity ownership in the selling firm.

---

[274] The two proprietary information categories that exist with acquisitions are summarized in assumption 18.

[275] For example, when financial buyers provide a valuation for a pharmaceutical firm with a product (that may cure aids) that is twice the current valuation known to the competitor, then they are incorporating their financial knowledge as to the current value of that medicine to the society. That value and the cost of capital for this firm change over time.

The investment banker also offers the target for sale to the horizontal strategic buyer. If that horizontal buyer acquired the selling firm, he would operate in a monopoly and the arising synergies from the acquisition would be captured by the monopoly surplus.

10. HB Synergy Assumption: Synergies for the horizontal strategic buyer are captured by the monopoly surplus.

The maximum that the horizontal buyer would be willing to pay is the expected profit of the target after the acquisition plus the gain from the acquisition. The gain from the acquisition corresponds to synergies that exist if a strategic buyer acquires the target firm. In the case of the duopoly, those synergies are captured by the monopoly surplus.[276]

However, synergies must not necessarily be positive. Considering symmetric Cournot markets with homogenous products and linear demand and cost, Salant, Switzer, and Reynolds (1983) showed that bilateral mergers are never profitable, unless a Cournot duopoly becomes a monopoly through the merger.[277] The term "merger puzzle" originating from the Salant, Switzer, and Reynolds (1983) paper accordingly questions the rationale behind mergers. There are numerous studies that show that acquiring shareholders' stock prices decrease upon acquisition announcements. The recent Moeller, Schlingemann, and Stulz (2005) study on acquiring-firm returns in the recent merger wave shows empirical evidence of such negative synergies. Moeller, Schlingemann, and Stulz find that acquiring-firm shareholders lost $240 billion from 1998 through 2001 in the aggregate.[278]

Accordingly, synergies for strategic buyers may be either positive or negative. With negative or sufficiently low synergies, the seller would generate maximum price if he sold to the financial buyer. Therefore, the magnitude of synergies for different buyer types is highly relevant for the eventual sale decision of the target firm.

11. VBS Synergy Assumption: Synergies for the supplier as a vertical buyer are captured by a reduction in unit costs.

Suppliers of the target are potential buyers, whose synergy gain is based on their vertical relationship. This synergy is assumed to increase with a decrease in unit costs.

12. VBC Synergy Assumption: Synergies for the customer as a vertical buyer are captured by an increase in demand.

---

[276] Modeling synergy by monopoly surplus is standard in this literature (e.g. see Wagenhofer (2000)).

[277] Salant, Switzer, and Reynolds (1983), p. 196.

[278] Note that his aggregate result was dominated by a small number of acquisitions with negative synergy gains and coincided with extremely high valuations of acquiring firms, since the studied time frame is within the so-called "internet bubble" period.

Customers of the seller are potential buyers whose synergies are assumed to base on an increase in demand. The increase in demand may arise because the customer will supply his entire product need from the target firm after the acquisition, instead of also buying products from the competing firm.

13. No Bargaining Game Assumption: Seller captures the entire gain from acquisition.

Since the decision who to sell to at what price and when to disclose what kind of private information is the focus of this paper, the non-trivial bargaining game about sharing the gain from the acquisition will not be modeled in detail.[279] Rather, the seller is expected to capture the entire gain from the acquisition, which results in the highest possible offer price for the target firm.

14. Maximum Bid Assumption: All buyers will offer their highest price in the auction.

All strategic and financial buyers are assumed to offer the highest price in the auction that they are willing to pay. This assumption reflects reality, in that the competitive auction environment and orchestration of the bids through the investment banker as a third party induces every participant to submit his highest possible bid. Generally, a winner's curse[280] could arise in that the winning bidder is likely to have overestimated the value of the target. Since the perspective of the selling company rather than the bidder's perspective is taken in this model, the problem of the winner's curse is not considered.

15. Unit Cost Assumption: The seller possesses private information on unit costs, with $k \in [1; 2]$. It is common knowledge that k is identically distributed.

The seller possesses private information on variable unit costs, which is relevant to both firms in the Cournot duopoly. Both the horizontal buyer and the vertical buyers do not know the seller's private information on unit costs (k). If the seller does not disclose his private information on unit cost, the buyer values the target based on his expected value of unit costs.

16. The Expected Unit Cost Assumption: All buyers expect the same unit costs.

The seller possesses private information on unit costs. Since all buyers hold rational expectations, they are all assumed to estimate the same expected unit costs.

17. Stochastic Independence Assumption:

- *Unit costs k and cost of capital K are stochastically independent.*

---

279 For standard results see Nash (1953) for cooperative bargaining games and Rubinstein (1982) or Sutton (1986) for non-cooperative games.

280 See Capen, Clapp, and Campbell (1971), Giliberto and Varaiya (1989), and Varaiya (1988) for a detailed discussion of the winner's curse phenomenon.

- *Unit costs k and synergy benefits "s" for the supplier are stochastically independent.*
- *Unit costs k and competitive damages "c" for the supplier are stochastically independent.*

The two variables on which private information exists are assumed stochastically independent. That is, if unit costs, which relate to production, increase, there is no related effect on cost of capital. The development of cost of capital is of a financial nature and therefore independent of the change in unit costs. In addition, unit costs and synergy benefits as well as unit costs and competitive damages for the supplier are independent random variables.

With acquisitions, two proprietary information categories exist:

18. Proprietary Information Assumption:

a. Proprietary information that may harm the seller if disclosed to the buyer is given by the unit cost parameter k.

b. Proprietary information that cannot competitively harm the seller if disclosed is given by the cost of new capital parameter ΔK.

Depending on the nature of the proprietary information, the seller's disclosure decision may vary. The disclosure of proprietary information on cost of new capital cannot harm the seller. If the strategic buyer does not acquire the seller, he only has the sunk cost of his firm's old cost of capital and not the cost of new capital. However, if the strategic buyer acquires the seller, he will have to recover the cost of new capital from unit sales. If the cost of new capital is not recoverable from future unit sales, the acquisition is not financially justifiable. If the cost of old capital increases but is not recovered from unit sales, owners of the target firm experience a reduction in their wealth. Therefore, the private information of the financial buyer on cost of new capital is only relevant information for the strategic buyer if he acquires the target firm. Additionally, the private information on cost of capital does not influence the production decision of seller or strategic buyer. That is, if the private information on cost of new capital is disclosed and the strategic buyer does not acquire the seller, this information cannot competitively harm the seller in the product market.

In contrast to the cost of new capital case, disclosure of private information on unit costs may result in negative competitive effects for the seller (profit effect). If the private information on unit costs is disclosed to the horizontal strategic buyer and the acquisition fails, the competitor might adjust his production quantity decision. If the disclosed private information is favorable, the horizontal buyer will increase his production quantity, thereby decreasing the seller's profit. On the other hand, the disclosure of such information has a valuation effect reflected in the offer price of the horizontal buyer (price effect). If favorable private information is disclosed, the buyer will offer a higher price for the target company. The price effect and the profit effect are negatively correlated, which results in different disclosure recommendations for differing levels of probability of acquisition. For instance, if the probability of acquisition by the competitor is high, the price effect outweighs the profit effect.

The same disclosure issue applies to vertical buyers. Since vertical buyers as suppliers and customers are upstream and downstream in channels of distribution from the target company, they cannot influence the production process in the Cournot duopoly directly. However, they could indirectly change the production decision of the target company if the acquisition failed by influencing demand or unit costs of the target. Therefore, the disclosure decision of the seller in respect to vertical buyers has to consider potential competitive damages as well.

19. Probability of Acquisition Assumption: The probability ϕ of a strategic buyer acquiring the target is exogenous and constant. The probability function is common knowledge.

Since many acquisition negotiations break off, it is uncertain whether a strategic buyer will actually acquire the seller. This uncertainty is built in the model through the parameter $\phi \in [0, 1]$, which gives the probability of the strategic buyer eventually acquiring the seller. In this model, different levels of ϕ will be examined and ϕ will be considered exogenous.[281]

20. Vertical Buyers Synergy and Damages Assumption: Synergy and competitive damage parameters of vertical buyers are assumed to be known to all players.

The information asymmetry that exists with acquisitions is assumed to be fully captured by the two cost parameters (assumption 18). The possible extension of incorporating uncertain synergy and competitive damages parameters of vertical buyers is not undertaken. This extension would only complicate matters and distract from the main information asymmetry issue. Instead, synergy and competitive damages parameters of vertical buyers are assumed to be known to all players.

21. Demand Assumption: Both seller and competitor have the same information about total demand (δ), and total demand is assumed greater than or equal to 2.5.

Total demand is assumed not trivially small. The non-triviality assumption (assumption 5) implies that both seller and his competitor produce products (non-zero output) and that profit

[281]The reason for not endogenizing the acquisition probability will be discussed in depth in section 5.5.1.

is positive. From equation (5.3) it can then be inferred that the difference between total demand, unit costs and quantities produced must be positive. Since unit costs are $k \in [1; 2]$, $x_S > 0$, $x_{HB} > 0$, and $K_i > 0$, total demand is assumed to be greater than or equal to 2.5. This assumption ensures that the profit of seller and competitor does not become trivially small.

22. Linearity Assumption: The inverse demand function is assumed linear.

Both seller and strategic buyer have the same information on δ, which is the demand parameter indicating the size of the market and is assumed greater than or equal to 2.5. Demand is modeled by an inverse demand function, which is assumed linear.

5.1.3 The Basic Model

There is an owner intending to sell his firm (S) and a horizontal strategic buyer willing to buy it (HB). The two firms are competing in a Cournot duopoly (duopoly assumption) in a one-period model (one-period model assumption). Demand is modeled by an inverse linear demand function (linearity assumption). The price p of the product depends on demand and the total quantity offered and sold by the seller (x_S) and the strategic buyer (x_{HB})

$$p = \delta - (x_S + x_{HB}) \tag{5.1}$$

With p = price of product

δ = demand parameter indicating size of the product market

x_S = quantity produced by the seller

$x_S + x_{HB}$ = total supply in a duopoly market

Hereby, the selling firm and the strategic buyer produce homogeneous goods (homogeneous products assumption) and set their production quantity concurrently.[282] Unit costs k are constant, linear in quantity, and equal for S and HB.

[282] In a Cournot duopoly, firms forecast the competitor's produced quantity and then choose their own quantity so that their profit is maximized. Then, taking into account demand, the price is set so that all products are sold. In Bertrand competition, an alternative to the Cournot set-up, both firms set their prices and meet the resulting demand afterwards. Cournot competition is chosen for this model, because it allows better modeling of information asymmetry. Additionally, if Bertrand competition were chosen with homogeneous products, there would be no profit for seller or strategic buyer.

5.1.3.1 *Symmetrical Information on Unit Costs*

With symmetrical information distribution among seller and strategic buyer, the respective profit is as follows,

$$\pi_i = (p - k) \cdot x_i - K_i \tag{5.2}$$

Here, π_i = profit for firm i

k = unit costs

x_i = quantity produced by firm i

K_i = cost of capital for firm i

Each party knows its own cost of capital K_i, however neither the seller nor horizontal or vertical strategic buyers know the cost of new capital in the acquisition case (ΔK). The financial buyer can determine the cost of new capital relevant for the acquisition case, and therefore has private information on the market cost of capital required for the acquisition of the target firm (valuation assumption). Demand (δ) is known by both seller and competitor (demand assumption). The profit for firm i then reads

$$\pi_i = (\delta - k - \underbrace{x_S - x_{HB}}_{\text{total supply}}) \cdot x_i - K_i \tag{5.3}$$

Equation (5.3) results from substituting equation (5.1) into (5.2).

Let us model a basic case that allows the derivation of different offer prices for different buyer types. This basic case assumes that the seller has private information on unit costs, i.e. the competitor (HB) will make his production decision based on the expected value of unit costs. The optimal production quantity of the seller (x_S) can be derived by setting the first derivative of π_S with respect to x_S equal to zero,

$$\pi_S = (\delta - k - x_S - x_{HB}) \cdot x_S - K_S \rightarrow \max! \tag{5.4}$$

$$\frac{\partial \pi_S}{\partial x_s} = \delta - k - 2x_S - x_{HB} \overset{!}{=} 0$$

$$x_S(k) = \frac{\delta - k - x_{HB}}{2} \tag{5.5}$$

Likewise, one obtains

$$x_{HB}(k) = \frac{\delta - k - x_S}{2} \tag{5.6}$$

5.1.3.2 Asymmetrical Information on Unit Costs

The seller is assumed to have private information on unit costs (unit cost assumption) that is relevant for both firms. The seller possesses the private information on unit costs, while the competitor only knows that the seller knows k, a fact that is common knowledge. Since the private information of the seller on unit costs is unknown to the competitor, he will make his production decision based on the expected production quantity of seller.

$$x_{HB}(k) = \frac{\delta - E[k] - E[x_S]}{2} \tag{5.7}$$

Substituting (5.5) into (5.7) results in

$$x_{HB}(k) = \frac{\delta - E[k] - \frac{\delta - E[k] - x_{HB}(k)}{2}}{2} \Rightarrow$$

$$x_{HB}(k) = \frac{\delta - E[k]}{3} \tag{5.8}$$

Hereby, $x_{HB}(k)$ represents the optimal production quantity of the horizontal buyer HB if the private information on unit costs is unknown to him. Similarly, the optimal production quantity of the seller (x_S) can be derived. Substituting equation (5.8) into (5.5) results in

$$x_S(k) = \frac{\delta - k - \frac{\delta - E[k]}{3}}{2}$$

This simplifies to

$$x_S(k) = \underbrace{\frac{\delta - k}{3}}_{\substack{\text{“regu-} \\ \text{lar”quantity}}} - \underbrace{\frac{k - E[k]}{6}}_{\substack{\text{information} \\ \text{effect}}}$$

$$\text{or} \quad x_S(k) = \frac{1}{3}\delta - \frac{1}{2}k + \frac{1}{6}E[k] \tag{5.9}$$

The information effect shows that if the competitor underestimates unit costs, i.e. if the competitor expects unit costs to be lower than they actually are, the seller produces less than in the "regular" case. Conversely, if the competitor overestimates unit costs, i.e. if the competitor expects unit costs to be higher than they actually are, the seller produces more than in the "regular" case.

The profit of the seller if the strategic buyer does not know the private information on unit costs can be derived by entering equation (5.8) and (5.9) into equation (5.4):

$$\pi_S(x_S(k);x_{HB}(k);k)=\left(\delta-k-\left(\frac{1}{3}\delta-\frac{1}{2}k+\frac{1}{6}E[k]\right)-\left(\frac{\delta-E[k]}{3}\right)\right)\cdot\left(\frac{1}{3}\delta-\frac{1}{2}k+\frac{1}{6}E[k]\right)-K_S$$

$$\pi_S(x_S(k);x_{HB}(k);k)=\left(\frac{1}{3}\delta-\frac{1}{2}k+\frac{1}{6}E[k]\right)^2-K_S \tag{5.10}$$

Since the model is a one-period model, the profit of the seller is the basis for the value assessment of potential buyers. In contrast to financial buyers, strategic buyers reap additional value or synergy benefits in excess to the profit of the seller from an acquisition. These synergy benefits vary with the source of respective synergy. In the next section, the individual value assessments for financial buyers, the horizontal strategic buyer, and finally for the two types of vertical buyers are derived.

5.2 Offering Price of Non-Strategic Buyer

When the investment banker is engaged by the seller, the investment banker will also solicit financial buyers as potential buyers for the target firm. Information disclosure to financial buyers is unproblematic, since they do not operate in the same industry as the target and cannot use the provided information to harm the target's competitive position. Therefore, the seller may disclose all private information to the financial buyer without fearing negative competitive effects.

The investment banker is the only player able to gain access to financial buyers (accessibility assumption) through his industry-specific expertise, superior information, his extensive private equity databases with detailed individual investment profiles, and his personal network. The investment banker with his access to financial buyers holds an auction with multiple financial buyers. The number of financial buyers is denoted with n = 1, ..., N. Modeling reality, those financial buyers may have slightly differing information on the cost of new capital, which is tied to the market value of the seller. The price discovery role of financial buyers mimicking the open market means that they evaluate the target company and each bid a price for it. Hereby, it is assumed that all buyers will offer their highest price in the auction (maximum bid assumption). From this auction, one financial buyer (the financial buyer) emerges as the highest bidder by providing the highest value assessment.

Recall that neither the seller nor the strategic buyers are able to accurately assess the cost of new capital for the target firm. The financial buyer is the only player who can correctly assess the cost of new capital because of his industry expertise. For simplicity, it is assumed that the highest bidder is applying the "accurate" cost of new capital (cost of capital assumption). Since the estimates for cost of capital by financial buyers who are industry insiders are rather uniform, the above assumption is not simplistic. Additionally, financial buyers do not derive any value from synergies and will therefore only vary in their valuations in respect to the cost of new capital.

The financial buyer's private information about cost of new capital ΔK can be understood as the differential cost of capital that the buyer will incur with the acquisition of the target. ΔK will be positive if the acquisition requires the buyer to raise additional capital at a higher cost than historical cost of capital (K_S). It is also possible that ΔK becomes negative, for example based on a decrease in riskiness of the firm in relation to the portfolio of all assets in a dynamic economy that the buyer may benefit from.

The seller fully discloses all relevant information about the target company to financial buyers, who do not have any synergy benefits. Financial buyers have private information on the cost of new capital, which is tied to the market value or EVA of the seller. That is, financial buyers possess private information on the cost of new capital, which can only be utilized when the seller involves the investment banker and financial buyers in the acquisition process. By going to the market for sale of firms - a market intermediated by the investment banker (market maker role) - the seller receives information on his firm's market-valued current cost of capital.

The offer price of the financial consists of two components,

$$p_{FB} = \pi_S - \Delta K$$

Because the seller's information was fully disclosed to the financial buyer, the only component of the financial buyer's bid that is unknown to the seller is the differential cost of new capital (ΔK). The private information on the cost of new capital as assessed by the financial buyer is revealed through his bid to the investment banker. From the financial buyer's valuation, his assessment of the appropriate risk premium for the target firm can be concluded. The cost of new capital varies over industries and over the economic cycles. It can only be accurately assessed by the FB (valuation assumption).

Since the financial buyer is not a direct competitor of the seller, the seller can disclose all sensitive information to the financial buyer. That is, the seller will disclose his private information about unit costs as well as all other relevant information to the financial buyer. Hereby, the separability assumption precludes the financial buyer from circumventing the seller and disclosing private information directly to strategic buyers. The financial buyer now knows the level of unit cost and the appropriate new cost of capital (ΔK), while the strategic buyer knows neither unit costs nor ΔK.

The competitor HB of the seller will base his production decision on his expected value of unit costs,

$$x_{HB}(k) = \frac{\delta - E[k]}{3} \tag{5.11}$$

Since both firms select their production quantities simultaneously, the seller will then produce

$$x_S(k) = \frac{1}{3}\delta - \frac{1}{2}k + \frac{1}{6}E[k] \tag{5.12}$$

and will make a profit of

$$\pi_S(x_S(k); x_{HB}(k); k) = \left(\frac{1}{3}\delta - \frac{1}{2}k + \frac{1}{6}E[k]\right)^2 - K_S \tag{5.13}$$

Given that the model is a one-period model, the maximum price (p_{FB}) that the financial buyer is willing to pay for the seller is the selling firm's profit adjusted for the new cost of capital (ΔK) that is incurred with the acquisition (equation (5.14)).

$$p_{FB} = \left(\frac{1}{3}\delta - \frac{1}{2}k + \frac{1}{6}E[k]\right)^2 - (K_S + \Delta K) \tag{5.14}$$

The strategic buyer's expected value of unit costs influences the target's profit and therefore the offer price of the financial buyer because of the Cournot duopoly set-up and because no private information was disclosed to the strategic buyer.

Considering that both vertical and horizontal strategic buyers have synergy potential while the financial buyer does not, the offer price of the financial buyer should not be the highest if synergies are positive. However, even for positive synergies the seller may be better off selling to the financial buyer as an industry outsider, if the potential for competitive damages in case that the acquisition fails is sufficiently large. The seller is thus able to access a new buyer category with the help of the investment banker. Additionally, the involvement of investment banker generates access to the private information of the financial buyer on cost of new capital. The seller now possesses additional acquisition-relevant private information about cost of new capital made available by the financial buyer and investment banker. The seller may disclose this cost of new capital to buyers and provide them with an additional decision-relevant parameter that was objectively appraised by the market.

5.3 Disclosure Decision about Private Information on Cost of Capital

The private information examined in this model can be categorized into private information on 1) cost of capital and 2) on unit cost. The unique characteristic of cost of capital is that there are no proprietary costs associated with its disclosure. In contrast, proprietary costs exist for the disclosure of private information on unit costs. Therefore, the disclosure recommendations for the two information categories can be explored separately (stochastic independence assumption). First, the private information on cost of capital will be explored.

Cost of capital can be categorized into two components, 1) the seller's cost of capital K_S and 2) the cost of new capital ΔK incurred with the acquisition. The seller knows his own old cost of capital (K_S), which may differ from the cost of capital of the horizontal strategic buyer (K_{HB}) depending on firm size and risk characteristics. The cost of new capital can be derived from the financial buyer's offer price. For horizontal and vertical strategic buyers, the cost of new capital for buying and selling a similar asset in the market for firms determined by the financial buyers is important private information. This private information can only be obtained through the involvement of the investment banker who is in the unique position to access financial buyers. However, should the investment banker recommend the disclosure of the private information to the seller?

Because of the fixed-cost characteristic of cost of capital, the disclosed information is only relevant for the acquisition case. If the acquisition failed and information on cost of capital had been disclosed, no negative competitive effect would result. The reason for this is that the strategic buyer's production decision is not influenced by cost of capital concerns, i.e. the competitor and thus the seller would produce the same quantities, both under disclosure and non-disclosure of the information on cost of capital. From a proprietary cost point of view, the seller may disclose all cost of capital information to any buyer.

Since there are no competitive damages that the seller needs to consider, he should disclose the private information on cost of capital to a buyer, if the buyer's price under disclosure is higher than the price under non-disclosure. If the expected value of cost of new capital that the buyer estimates is higher than the actual cost of capital as determined by the financial buyer, the buyer's valuation of the target under non-disclosure of cost of new capital is lower than under disclosure. The buyer expects the acquisition to be too expensive and therefore his offer price would be too low and could be increased by the disclosure. Similarly, if the expected level of cost of new capital were lower than the actual level of that cost of capital as revealed by the financial buyer, the buyer's valuation of the target under non-disclosure would be higher than under disclosure. That means that the seller should disclose information on ΔK if $E[\Delta K] > \Delta K$ and not disclose information if the buyer underestimates the cost of new capital, i.e. if $E[\Delta K] < \Delta K$.

The problem with this disclosure mechanism is that it neglects the reaction of the buyer to the non-disclosure of the private information. Upon observing non-disclosure, a buyer with rational beliefs (rational expectation assumption) will realize that his estimate of the cost of new capital is too low. He would then correct $E[\Delta K]$ upward and induce the seller to disclose all ΔK to the buyer, that are below the revised estimate of $E[\Delta K]$. If the seller did not disclose any private cost of new capital information upon observing the higher $E[\Delta K]$, the buyer again would conclude that his estimate was too low and increase his expected cost of new capital even further. This unraveling principle will lead to full disclosure of cost of new capital information.[283]

This first disclosure issue can be concluded by recommending the seller to disclose the private information on cost of new capital to any horizontal or vertical strategic buyer for all levels of ΔK. Next, the offer prices of the horizontal strategic buyer and the two vertical buyers are derived. These offer prices are based on full information about cost of capital. The investment banker now needs to consider if the second private information component, i.e.

[283] See Milgrom (1981) for voluntary disclosure of verifiable information and Crawford and Sobel (1982) and Gigler (1994) for voluntary disclosure of unverifiable information.

unit costs, should be disclosed to buyers. Private information on unit costs will be disclosed if the expected gain to the seller taking into account the probability of the buyer acquiring the firm is higher for the disclosure of private information than for its non-disclosure. The investment banker will recommend the disclosure strategy, which offers the highest expected gain to the seller. In the following sections, the disclosure of private information on unit costs is explored in detail for all strategic buyers and disclosure recommendations are provided to the seller.

5.4 Offering Price of Strategic Buyers

5.4.1 Horizontal Buyer's Offering Price

In addition to financial buyers, the investment banker will also solicit the horizontal strategic buyer as potential buyer. The horizontal strategic buyer in the Cournot duopoly is the competitor of the selling firm, abbreviated with HB. Since the buyer is a direct competitor of the seller, a disclosure trade-off in respect to private information on unit costs arises.

Recall that the disclosure issue with private information on cost of capital was unproblematic, because the private information did not influence the production decision and therefore did not possess the potential to hurt the seller competitively. With private information about unit costs, on the other hand, a disclosure trade-off exists. Empirically it can be shown that acquisitions fail frequently.[284] If the private information on unit costs was disclosed to the horizontal strategic buyer and the acquisition failed, the knowledge about the private information would influence the production decision of the strategic buyer, which would in turn have an effect on the profit of the seller in the product market.

The seller generally strives at disclosing favorable private information on unit costs, because there is a positive price effect. However, if the acquisition failed, the disclosed favorable information would lead to a negative profit effect for the seller in the Cournot duopoly. The strategic buyer would adjust his production quantity upward based on the favorable private information on unit costs, thereby reducing the produced quantity of the seller (strategic substitutes) and lowering his profit. With unfavorable private information on unit costs, the situation is reversed. With unfavorable information there is a negative price effect in the case of acquisition and a positive profit effect if the acquisition fails, because the strategic buyer

[284] For instance the failed merger between Deutsche Bank and Dresdner Bank in 2000.

would adjust his production quantity downward. The balance between those countervailing effects determines the disclosure strategy that will be recommended to the seller.

Next, the offer price of the horizontal buyer under non-disclosure of the private information on unit costs is determined. Hereby, the cost of new capital is considered as given, since the seller will always disclose the financial buyer's assessment of cost of new capital to all buyers. Because the model is set up as a Cournot duopoly, synergies inherent in the acquisition for the horizontal strategic buyer can be captured by the monopoly surplus (HB synergy assumption). The monopoly surplus (MS) is the excess profit of the unified firm after the acquisition (π_M) over the combined pre-acquisition profit of the seller and the horizontal buyer.

$$MS = \pi_M - (\pi_S + \pi_{HB}) \tag{5.15}$$

If the horizontal buyer acquires the seller, the Cournot duopoly becomes a monopoly (M). The inverse demand function now reads,

$$p = \delta - x_M \tag{5.16}$$

The cost of capital in the monopoly case consists of the seller's cost of capital (K_S), the horizontal buyer's costs of capital (K_{HB}), and the differential cost of new capital arising from the acquisition (ΔK). The monopoly profit then reads

$$\pi_M = (p - k) \cdot x_M - (K_S + K_{HB} + \Delta K) \Rightarrow$$ [285]

$$\pi_M = (\delta - x_M - k) \cdot x_M - (K_S + K_{HB} + \Delta K) \quad \rightarrow \max! \tag{5.17}$$

$$\frac{\partial \pi_M}{\partial x_M} = \delta - k - 2x_M = 0 \Rightarrow$$

$$x_M = \frac{\delta - k}{2} \tag{5.18}$$

The optimal monopoly profit is derived by inserting (5.18) into (5.17)

$$\pi_M = \left(\delta - \frac{\delta - k}{2} - k\right)\left(\frac{\delta - k}{2}\right) - (K_S + K_{HB} + \Delta K) \Rightarrow$$

---

[285] Hereby, unit costs k are not the lesser of S or HB unit costs, but rather the (expected) unit costs of the seller. Since the private information of the seller on unit cost is relevant to both S and HB, unit costs are the k of the seller.

$$\pi_M = \frac{1}{4}(\delta - k)^2 - (K_S + K_{HB} + \Delta K) \tag{5.19}$$

The optimal monopoly production quantity is given by equation (5.18) and the monopoly profit by equation (5.19). Hereby, monopoly unit costs k are the unit costs of the seller, who possesses private information on the "appropriate" level of unit costs. The horizontal buyer however does not know the seller's private information on unit costs ex ante, i.e. the expected value of the horizontal buyer about the level of unit costs has to be derived. Based on equation (5.19),

$$E[\pi_M] = \frac{1}{4}E[\delta^2 - 2\delta k + k^2] - (K_S + K_{HB} + \Delta K) \Rightarrow$$

$$E[\pi_M] = \frac{1}{4}(\delta^2 - 2\delta \cdot E[k] + E[k^2]) - (K_S + K_{HB} + \Delta K) \tag{5.20}$$

The horizontal buyer pays at most the expected profit of the seller in case of the acquisition, which includes the gain from acquisition, i.e. the monopoly surplus.

$$\begin{aligned} p_{SB}(\delta; k; K_S; \Delta K) &= E[\pi_M - \pi_{HB}] = \\ &\frac{1}{4}(\delta^2 - 2\delta \cdot E[k] + E[k^2]) - (K_S + K_{HB} + \Delta K) - \pi_{HB}(k) \end{aligned} \tag{5.21}$$

Hereby, the level of unit costs that the horizontal buyer expects varies with the disclosure strategy of the seller. For instance would the horizontal buyer with rational expectations adjust his unit cost expectations upward upon observing non-disclosure of the seller's private information for high acquisition probability.

The strategic buyer's profit in the Cournot duopoly may be calculated from equation (5.3) as follows,

$$\pi_{HB}(k) = (\delta - k - \underbrace{x_S}_{(5.9)} - x_{HB}) \cdot \underbrace{x_{HB}}_{(5.8)} - K_{HB} \Rightarrow$$

$$\pi_{HB} = \left(\delta - E[k] - \left(\frac{1}{3}\delta - \frac{1}{2}E[k] + \frac{1}{6}E[k]\right) - \left(\frac{\delta - E[k]}{3}\right)\right) \cdot \left(\frac{\delta - E[k]}{3}\right) - K_{HB} \Rightarrow$$

$$\pi_{HB} = \left(\frac{\delta - E[k]}{3}\right)^2 - K_{HB} \tag{5.22}$$

Inserting equation (5.22) into (5.21) it follows that,

$$p_{HB}(\delta;k;K_S;\Delta K)=\frac{1}{4}\left(\delta^2-2\delta\cdot E[k]+E[k^2]\right)-\left(K_S+K_{HB}+\Delta K\right)-\left(\left(\frac{\delta-E[k]}{3}\right)^2-K_{HB}\right)\Rightarrow$$

$$p_{HB}(\delta;k;K_S;\Delta K)=\frac{1}{4}\left(\delta^2-2\delta\cdot E[k]+E[k^2]\right)-\frac{1}{9}\left(\delta-E[k]\right)^2-\left(K_S+\Delta K\right) \qquad (5.23)$$

Equation (5.23) gives the price that the strategic buyer is willing to offer to the seller in order to acquire his firm if he does not know the private information on unit costs. This determined price assumes that the seller is able to capture the entire gain from acquisition (no bargaining game assumption).

5.4.2 Vertical Buyers' Offering Prices

In addition to financial buyers, the investment banker will also solicit vertical buyers as potential buyers. This addition of vertical strategic buyers models reality, in that all potential buyers for a target firm, i.e. financial buyers, horizontal strategic buyers, and vertical strategic buyers are now present in the model. Vertical buyers are either suppliers (VBS) or customers (VBC) of the target firm. Since vertical strategic buyers operate on a different production stage than the target, synergies may arise from the control over an additional production stage.

Synergies for the target's suppliers may arise due to a unit cost reduction (VBS synergy assumption). If the supplier acquires the target, the supplier's distribution channel becomes secured. The supplier then can for instance undergo investments in specific and larger machinery specifically tailored to the target, thereby reducing the unit cost for the target. Synergies for the target's customers, on the other hand, may arise due to an increase in demand (VBC synergy assumption). The customer may have only purchased a portion of his production line from the target and after the acquisition will receive all his products from the target.

Depending on the nature of the vertical strategic buyer, the factors demand and unit costs will change, in turn influencing the production quantity of the seller and the strategic buyer. With different production quantities the profit of the seller will also change, resulting in different offering prices of vertical buyers for the selling firm.[286] Each vertical strategic buyer will estimate the same unit costs for the seller (expected unit cost assumption). Each

[286] After the acquisition of the seller by a vertical buyer, the production quantity and profit of the horizontal buyer may change. The horizontal buyer could thus decide to further raise his offer price to prevent the vertical buyer from the acquisition. This effect can reasonably be neglected in the following, since all buyers are assumed to offer their highest possible price (maximum bid assumption).

vertical buyer will submit a different offering price depending on his source and magnitude of synergy.

5.4.2.1 Offering Price of Suppliers

The source of synergies for the supplier (as a vertical buyer) in an acquisition is the economies of scale that are captured as a unit cost reduction item. If the supplier acquires the seller, the acquired company's unit costs will be decreased by the synergy factor "s". Unit costs that the vertical buyer as supplier would incur after acquiring the seller are captured by $(1-s)k$.

The profit of the target firm based on equation (5.4) can be written as

$$\pi_S = (\delta - (1-s)k - x_S - x_{HB}) \cdot x_S - K_S \Rightarrow \max! \tag{5.24}$$

and the seller's profit maximizing production quantity based on equation (5.5) is

$$x_S = \frac{\delta - (1-s)k - x_{HB}}{2} \tag{5.25}$$

Based on equation (5.6), the strategic buyer finds his profit maximizing production quantity accordingly with

$$x_{HB} = \frac{\delta - k - x_S}{2} \tag{5.26}$$

Note that the strategic buyer's unit costs remain at level k and are not reduced to (1–s)k. Again, the strategic buyer makes his production decision based on the expected production quantity of the seller.

$$x_{HB}(\delta;k) = \frac{\delta - E[k] - E[x_S]}{2} \tag{5.27}$$

With the stochastic independence assumption, substituting (5.25) into (5.27) leads to

$$x_{HB}(\delta;k;s) = \frac{\delta - E[k] - \frac{\delta - (1-s)E[k] - x_{HB}}{2}}{2}$$

This results in the following equation,

$$x_{HB}(\delta;k;s)=\frac{\delta-(1+s)\cdot E[k]}{3} \tag{5.28}$$

Hereby, s stands for the synergies that the supplier will obtain with the acquisition of the seller. The supplier's synergy benefits influence the horizontal buyer's production quantity because of the Cournot duopoly set-up. Equation (5.28) shows that with higher synergy effects for the supplier, i.e. lower unit costs for the seller, the horizontal buyer produces less in comparison to the basic case.

Similarly, the optimal production quantity of the seller (x_S) can be derived. Substituting equation (5.28) into (5.25) results in

$$x_S(\delta;k;s)=\frac{\delta-(1-s)k-\frac{\delta-(1+s)\cdot E[k]}{3}}{2}\Rightarrow$$

$$x_S(\delta;k;s)=\frac{1}{3}\delta-\frac{(1-s)}{2}k+\frac{1}{6}(1+s)\cdot E[k] \tag{5.29}$$

Comparing equation (5.29) with equation (5.9) shows that the selling firm produces more after the acquisition because the synergy benefits reduce unit costs and because the competitor (HB) produces less. The profit of the seller based on equation (5.24) is derived as

$$\pi_S(x_S(\delta;k;s);x_{HB}(\delta;k;s);\delta;k;s)=\left(\delta-(1-s)k-\left(\begin{matrix}\frac{1}{3}\delta-\frac{(1-s)}{2}k+\\ \frac{1}{6}(1+s)\cdot E[k]\end{matrix}\right)-\left(\frac{\delta-(1+s)\cdot E[k]}{3}\right)\right)$$
$$\cdot\left(\frac{1}{3}\delta-\frac{(1-s)}{2}k+\frac{1}{6}(1+s)\cdot E[k]\right)-K_S\Rightarrow$$

$$\pi_S(x_S(\delta;k;s);x_{HB}(\delta;k;s);\delta;k;s)=\left(\frac{1}{3}\delta-\frac{(1-s)}{2}k+\frac{1}{6}(1+s)\cdot E[k]\right)^2-K_S \tag{5.30}$$

Comparing equation (5.30) with equation (5.10) shows that with higher synergy effects "s", i.e. lower unit costs of the target after acquisition by the supplier, the seller produces more and has a higher profit in comparison to the basic case. The supplier as vertical buyer pays at most the expected profit of the seller in case of the acquisition, which includes the synergy benefits from acquisition, i.e. the reduction of unit costs.[287] Based on the no bargaining game assumption and maximum bid assumption, the supplier will offer this maximum price. The number of suppliers as vertical buyers is denoted with m = 1, ..., M. Suppliers as vertical buyers and the horizontal strategic buyer do not know the unit cost "k" of the seller. It is assumed that all buyers expect unit costs to be at the same level (expected unit cost assumption). The offering price function based on equation (5.30) for suppliers (as vertical buyers) under non-disclosure can thus be written as follows,

$$p_{VBS,m}\begin{pmatrix}\delta; s_m; k; \\ K_S; \Delta K\end{pmatrix} = \begin{pmatrix}\frac{1}{3}\delta - \frac{(1-s_m)}{2}E[k] \\ +\frac{1}{6}(1+s_m)\cdot E[k]\end{pmatrix}^2 - (K_S + \Delta K) \Rightarrow$$

$$p_{VBS,m}(\delta; s_m; k; K_S; \Delta K) = \left(\frac{\delta - (1-2s_m)\cdot E[k]}{3}\right)^2 - (K_S + \Delta K) \tag{5.31}$$

5.4.2.2 Offering Price of Customers

Having determined the offering prices of different suppliers as vertical strategic buyers, the offer price of the target's customers as vertical buyers will be examined next. A customer of the seller may obtain all of his products either from the seller, or from the horizontal buyer, or both from the seller and horizontal buyer. Such a customer may now decide to acquire the selling firm. Customers as vertical buyers (VBC) derive their synergies from an increase "d" in the seller's demand (VBC synergy assumption). This increase in demand is generated, because the customer will obtain all of his products from the seller if he acquires the target. If the customer already obtained all his products from the seller, his synergies ceteris paribus would be d = 0. However, if any portion of his products was obtained from the horizontal buyer before and is now ordered from the seller instead, then $d > 0$. Since the competing firms are operating in a Cournot duopoly, they each should satisfy half of total demand. If some of the seller's demand is now customer-specific, his "share" of total demand will increase by "d", while the horizontal buyer's share of total demand will decrease by "d".

[287] Note that the supplier has a separate stand-alone profit, which is not influenced by the level of his synergy benefits in respect to the target company.

The seller has private information on unit costs, while the customer as a buyer is not aware of the private information on unit costs. The profit of the target firm based on equation (5.4) can be written as

$$\pi_S = (\delta - k - (x_S - d\delta) - x_{HB}) \cdot x_S - K_S \Rightarrow \max! \tag{5.32}$$

$$\frac{\partial \pi_S}{\partial x_s} = (1+d)\delta - k - 2x_S - x_{HB} \overset{!}{=} 0$$

In addition, the seller's profit maximizing production quantity based on equation (5.5) is

$$x_S = \frac{(1+d)\delta - k - x_{HB}}{2} \tag{5.33}$$

Based on equation (5.3), the horizontal buyer finds his profit maximizing production quantity accordingly.

$$\pi_{HB} = (\delta - k - x_S - (x_{HB} + d\delta)) \cdot x_{HB} - K_{HB} \Rightarrow \max!$$

$$\frac{\partial \pi_{HB}}{\partial x_s} = (1-d)\delta - k - x_S - 2x_{HB} \overset{!}{=} 0$$

$$x_{HB} = \frac{(1-d)\delta - k - x_S}{2} \tag{5.34}$$

Since the horizontal buyer holds rational expectations, he knows that if his customer acquires the target company, his share of total demand will decrease by "d". The horizontal buyer then makes his production decision based on the expected production quantity of the seller, depending on the expected level of unit costs. Substituting equation (5.33) into (5.34) and considering the private information of the seller on unit costs results in

$$x_{HB}(\delta, d, k) = \frac{(1-d)\delta - E[k] - \frac{(1+d)\delta - E[k] - x_{HB}}{2}}{2} \Rightarrow$$

$$x_{HB}(\delta, d, k) = \frac{(1-3d)\delta - E[k]}{3} \tag{5.35}$$

This means that with higher synergy effects, i.e. a higher share of total demand for the seller, the horizontal buyer produces much less in comparison to the basic case, because his share of total demand has decreased, while the seller's share of total demand has increased.

Similarly, the optimal production quantity of the seller (x_S) can be derived. Substituting equation (5.35) into (5.33) results in

$$x_S(\delta,d,k)=\frac{(1+d)\delta-k-\frac{(1-3d)\delta-E[k]}{3}}{2}\Rightarrow$$

$$x_S(\delta,d,k)=\frac{1}{3}(1+3d)\delta-\frac{1}{2}k+\frac{1}{6}E[k] \tag{5.36}$$

Comparing equation (5.36) with equation (5.9) shows that the selling firm produces more after the acquisition to take advantage of the synergy benefits and the lower production of the competitor. The profit of the seller based on equation (5.32) is

$$\pi_S\begin{pmatrix}x_S(\delta,d,k);\\ x_{HB}(\delta,d,k);\\ \delta;d;k\end{pmatrix}=\left((1+d)\delta-k-\begin{pmatrix}\frac{1}{3}(1+3d)\delta\\ -\frac{1}{2}k+\frac{1}{6}E[k]\end{pmatrix}-\frac{(1-3d)\delta-E[k]}{3}\right)\cdot\begin{pmatrix}\frac{1}{3}(1+3d)\delta\\ -\frac{1}{2}k+\frac{1}{6}E[k]\end{pmatrix}-K_S$$

$$\pi_S(x_S(\delta,d,k);x_{HB}(\delta,d,k);\delta;d;k)=\left(\frac{1}{3}(1+3d)\delta-\frac{1}{2}k+\frac{1}{6}E[k]\right)^2-K_S \tag{5.37}$$

This means that with higher synergy effects, i.e. a higher share of total demand for the seller, the seller produces much more and has a higher profit than in the basic case. Meanwhile, the competitor's profit is much lower, because his share of total demand was decreased and the production quantity of the seller increased. The customer as vertical buyer offers at most the expected profit of the seller in case of the acquisition, which includes the gain from acquisition, i.e. the increase in demand. Based on the no bargaining game and maximum bid assumption, the customer will offer this maximum price. The number of suppliers as vertical buyers is denoted with i = 1, ….., I. Neither customers as vertical buyers nor the horizontal buyer know the unit cost "k" of the seller. It is assumed that all buyers expect unit costs to be at the same level (expected unit cost assumption). The offering price function based on equation (5.37) for customers (as vertical buyers) under non-disclosure can thus be written as follows,

$$p_{VBC,i}(\delta;d_i;k;K_S;\Delta K)=\left(\frac{1}{3}(1+3d_i)\delta-\frac{1}{2}E[k]+\frac{1}{6}E[k]\right)^2-(K_S+\Delta K)\Rightarrow$$

$$p_{VBC,i}(\delta;d_i;k;K_S;\Delta K)=\left(\frac{(1+3d_i)\delta-E[k]}{3}\right)^2-(K_S+\Delta K) \qquad (5.38)$$

5.4.3 Summary

The offer prices of strategic buyers depend on the level of demand, old cost of capital of the selling firm, on the new cost of capital, and on the buyer's estimate of unit costs, and the offer prices differ with the synergies of each buyer. Equation (5.23), (5.31), and (5.38) describe the offering prices of different types of strategic buyers,

$$p_{HB}(\delta;k;K_S;\Delta K)=\frac{1}{4}\left(\delta^2-2\delta\cdot E[k]+E[k^2]\right)-\frac{1}{9}(\delta-E[k])^2-(K_S+\Delta K)$$

$$p_{VBS,m}(\delta;s_m;k;K_S;\Delta K)=\left(\frac{\delta-(1-2s_m)\cdot E[k]}{3}\right)^2-(K_S+\Delta K)$$

$$p_{VBC,i}(\delta;d_i;k;K_S;\Delta K)=\left(\frac{(1+3d_i)\delta-E[k]}{3}\right)^2-(K_S+\Delta K)$$

With higher demand or with higher synergies, the offering price of strategic buyers increases. And with lower unit costs, lower cost of capital of the selling firm, and lower differential cost of new capital, the price of strategic buyers increases. Generally, the strategic buyer with the highest synergy or with the lowest differential cost of new capital will offer the highest price.

The offer prices derived above are based on non-disclosure of the seller's proprietary information about unit costs. The investment banker must decide now if the seller should fully disclose this proprietary information on unit costs to a particular buyer, or if he should sell to that buyer under non-disclosure. That is, the disclosure issue discussed in the next section only refers to the disclosure of proprietary information to a particular buyer, and not to the mandatory reporting of company information to the investing public. In the next section disclosure recommendations will be derived that depend on the probability of acquisition and the absolute level of the private information on unit costs.

5.5 Expected Gains

5.5.1 Probability of the Strategic Buyer Acquiring the Seller

To be able to make a disclosure recommendation for the private information on unit costs, let unit costs k be restricted to k = [1; 2]. Since the private information is cost information, a level of k = 1 is favorable private information, while a level of k = 2 reflects unfavorable private information. A look at the profit function (equation (5.3)) shows that profit is ceteris paribus highest for the lowest level of k, i.e. k = 1. It is common knowledge a priori that k is identically distributed (unit cost assumption), i.e. f(k) = 1 for all k. While the seller possesses private information on unit costs k, the strategic buyers only know that the seller knows k (which is common knowledge). The private information is both relevant for the price that the strategic buyer will bid on the selling firm and for the production quantity of both firms in the Cournot duopoly if the acquisition fails.

With information disclosure there is a trade-off between the two value components of the target company. If the acquisition is successful, the seller will disclose favorable private information on unit costs to increase the buyer's offer price. If acquisition negotiations between the seller and horizontal buyer break off, the seller and horizontal buyer will remain competitors in the duopoly. Information that the horizontal buyer acquired during the negotiation process will now influence his production decision.[288] The disclosed favorable information on unit costs would negatively influence the target in the product market, since the horizontal buyer would adjust his production quantity upward, thereby decreasing the profit of the seller. If the horizontal buyer was not aware of the private information on unit costs, the seller could exploit the uninformed and too low quantity decision of his competitor. This tradeoff of the two value components exists vice versa for unfavorable information. Full disclosure of unfavorable information would lower the selling price. If the acquisition failed however, the profit of the seller would be increased because the horizontal buyer would adjust his production quantity downwards. Similarly, there is a secondary effect for vertical buyers. Therefore, the seller should not simply sell to the highest bidder determined in the prior section. Rather, potential competitive damages to the seller in the product market if the acquisition fails but

[288] Note that the horizontal buyer in the duopoly setting cannot be prevented from using the private information on unit costs that he received during the negotiation process for his own benefit, i.e. to adjust production quantities accordingly. This predicament is circumvented if the private information is disclosed to the financial buyer. Regardless of the probability of the financial buyer eventually acquiring the firm, the profit of the seller will not be negatively influenced by any change in production quantities (provided that no leakage occurs).

the private information was disclosed must be considered. Therefore, the probability of the strategic buyer acquiring the target (ϕ) has to be taken into account to derive the expected gain to the seller.

Since many acquisition negotiations break off unsuccessfully, it is uncertain whether the strategic buyer will actually acquire the seller. Following Wagenhofer (2000), this uncertainty is built in the model through the parameter $\phi \in [0, 1]$, which gives the probability of a strategic buyer eventually acquiring the seller. The probability function is common knowledge. In this model, different levels of ϕ will be examined and ϕ will be considered exogenous (probability of acquisition assumption). Even if ϕ was endogenous and resulted from a particular decision that the buyer faced during the acquisition process, ϕ would still be exogenous at an earlier point of the acquisition process. This means that at the outset of the acquisition process, the strategic buyer has a probability of acquiring the target that is exogenous and influenced by many factors.

Table 5-3, which is not intended to be comprehensive, identifies some important strategic, financial, and other factors that influence the probability of an acquisition from the outset.[289]

Strategic Aspects • Attractiveness of the industry with its level of competition, life cycle, and entry barriers • Market share and market position of the target • Range of products and patents of the target • Key employees and intangible goods of the target • Organizational structure and company culture • Number of alternative targets for the strategic buyer
Financial Aspects • Profitability of the target • Target's financial structure and possibility to lever the firm or cut fixed costs • Required purchase price by seller • Financial means available to the buyer
Other Aspects • Number of potential buyers and the resulting level of competition • Terms of the acquisition as defined in the purchase agreement

Table 5-3: Factors Influencing the Acquisition Probability from the Outset

[289] Jansen (2001), p. 107, pp. 165 et sqq., pp. 175 et sqq. ; and Kierulff (1981), p. 66.

At the beginning of the acquisition process, the buyer decides whom to buy and in which industry to buy. All the factors mentioned above play a role in determining the probability of the buyer actually acquiring the target firm. That is, at an early stage in the acquisition process, ϕ is exogenous. Then the buyer engages in the acquisition process and, as he learns more about the private information on unit costs, this new information may influence his probability of acquiring the target.

For instance, the terms of the acquisition are a major determinant for a mutually satisfactory purchasing agreement. The probability of the potential buyer actually acquiring the target may be influenced by the private information on unit costs, because favorable unit cost information can foster the bargaining position of the seller or vice versa. A better bargaining position of the seller may decrease the probability of the buyer acquiring the target. As an example, private information about a new, more cost-efficient production process would (all else constant) advance the bargaining position of the seller, leading to a purchasing agreement with more seller-friendly terms. This reasoning would imply that the probability $\phi(\cdot)$ decreases with a lower level in k, as the bargaining position of the seller increases with a lower level in k.[290]

Another example would be the number of alternatives that the strategic buyer has. If, for instance, a higher level of the private information on unit costs means that the selling company has not succeeded in producing a more cost efficient product, the alternative acquisition opportunities, i.e. the main competitors of the target company, become more attractive since their market share is not endangered. This implies that the probability $\phi(\cdot)$ ceteris paribus decreases with an increasing level of k as the desirability of the alternatives increases.

As has been shown, the actual level of private information on unit costs could influence the level of ϕ. However, such endogenous factors may somewhat offset each other and may not be critically important because there are so many additional exogenous reasons for driving mergers. Therefore, it seems to be a reasonable assumption to regard ϕ as exogenous and constant.[291]

---

[290] Note that this example only examines one effect on the probability of acquisition. It neglects the positive effect of a favorable (low) level of unit costs on the expected market position of the target and does not examine this mitigating effect on the decrease in ϕ.

[291] The results of this model would naturally be stronger if ϕ was endogenous, however this question has yet been unanswered in literature. See Wagenhofer (2000), p. 59. This issue is left here as a research challenge for the future, because endogenizing ϕ would technically be very difficult and is not central to the results.

In the next section, the expected gain that the seller derives from the offering price made by the strategic buyer and the seller's profit in the market if the acquisition fails is determined, for both disclosure and non-disclosure of the private information on unit costs. The major difference to the private information case with cost of new capital before is that with private information on unit costs the uncertainty about the strategic buyer's intention to acquire the selling firm has to be taken into account. That means that the expected gain to the seller from a strategic buyer's offer consists of two components. The first component is the price that the strategic buyer will bid to acquire the seller, times its probability. The second component is the profit of the seller in the product market if the acquisition fails, times its probability.

5.5.2 Expected Gain to the Seller from Horizontal Buyer's Bid

Since the horizontal buyer is a direct competitor of the seller, the effect of disclosure of unit cost information on the seller's position in the product market if the acquisition fails is important. Therefore, the probability of the horizontal buyer acquiring the target (ϕ) has to be taken into account. With uncertainty about the intentions of the horizontal buyer, the seller has counterbalancing incentives in respect to the disclosure of private information on unit costs. If the horizontal buyer did acquire the target firm, the seller would want to disclose favorable private information on unit costs to increase the price offered by the horizontal buyer, while not disclosing negative private information. If the horizontal buyer however did not acquire the firm and remained a competitor, the seller would want to disclose unfavorable information to adjust the horizontal buyer's production quantity downward. He would however not disclose favorable information on unit costs, because the overestimation of the actual level of unit costs by the horizontal buyer and the consequentially low quantity decision would increase the profit of the seller. In addition to the effect of the probability of acquisition on the disclosure decision, the conclusions that the horizontal buyer draws from non-disclosure must be considered.

The expected gain to the seller based on the offer price of a strategic buyer will be determined next, which takes into account the uncertainty about the strategic buyer's intention to acquire the selling firm. That means that the expected gain to the seller based on the strategic buyer's offer consists of two components, reflecting either the fact that the acquisition can be successful or it can fail. The first component of the seller's expected gain is the price that the strategic buyer will bid to acquire the seller, times its probability. The second component is the profit of the seller in the product market if the acquisition fails, times its probability.

$$g_n = \phi \cdot p_n + (1-\phi)\pi_S \qquad \text{with } n = \begin{cases} SB \\ VBS \\ VBC \end{cases} \tag{5.39}$$

Here, ϕ = probability of the strategic buyer acquiring the selling firm[292]

Equation (5.39) shows the gain that the seller expects from a horizontal buyer's bid given the probability of the acquisition, the offer price of the horizontal buyer (p_{HB}), and the profit of the seller in the product market π_S if the acquisition fails. The offer price of the horizontal buyer under non-disclosure is given by equation (5.23). The profit of the seller in the product market if the acquisition fails and the private information on unit costs was not disclosed is given by equation (5.10) in the basic model. The expected gain to the seller derived from the horizontal buyer's offering price based on equation (5.39) can thus be written as

$$g_{HB}(k) = \phi \cdot \begin{bmatrix} \frac{1}{4}\left(\delta^2 - 2\delta \cdot E[k] + E[k^2]\right) \\ -\frac{1}{9}\left(\delta - E[k]\right)^2 - \left(K_S + \Delta K\right) \end{bmatrix} + (1-\phi) \cdot \left[\left(\frac{1}{3}\delta - \frac{1}{2}k + \frac{1}{6}E[k]\right)^2 - K_S\right] \Rightarrow$$

$$\begin{aligned} g_{HB}(k) = {} & \frac{\phi}{36} \cdot \left[9\left(\delta^2 - 2\delta \cdot E[k] + E[k^2]\right) - 4\left(\delta - E[k]\right)^2\right] + \frac{(1-\phi)}{36}\left[\left(2\delta - 3k + E[k]\right)^2\right] \\ & - \left(K_S + \phi \cdot \Delta K\right) \end{aligned} \tag{5.40}$$

Equation (5.40) shows the expected gain to the seller based on the offering price of the horizontal buyer and on non-disclosure of the private information on unit costs.

If the private information on unit costs k were disclosed, the expected gain to the seller under full disclosure would be

$$g_{HB} = \frac{\phi}{36} \cdot \left[9\left(\delta^2 - 2\delta \cdot k + k^2\right) - 4\left(\delta - k\right)^2\right] + \frac{(1-\phi)}{36}\left[\left(2\delta - 3k + k\right)^2\right] - \left(K_S + \phi \cdot \Delta K\right) \Rightarrow$$

---

[292] The probability ϕ of a strategic buyer acquiring target may vary among buyers. To reduce clutter in the following equations, the subscripts indicating a particular buyer (e.g. ϕ_{HB}) have been omitted. The subscripts will be added again in the final equations to consider different acquisition probabilities for different buyers.

$$g_{HB} = \frac{1}{36}(\phi + 4)(\delta - k)^2 - (K_S + \phi \cdot \Delta K) \quad (5.41)$$

Equation (5.41) shows the expected gain to the seller based on the offering price of the horizontal buyer and on full disclosure of the private information on unit costs. In the next section, the expected gain to the seller based on the vertical buyers' bids will be determined.

5.5.3 Expected Gain to the Seller from Vertical Buyers' Bids

In contrast to the case with the horizontal strategic buyer, there is no immediate effect on the profit of the seller in the product market if the private information on unit costs is disclosed to a vertical buyer. Since the vertical buyer is in a different stage of the production process, he cannot influence the seller's production quantity directly. However, there may well be a secondary effect. If the vertical customer of the seller knew the cost information of the seller, he could use this information to his advantage in negotiations about his price of the product if the acquisition failed. Similarly, cost and pricing information may lead the vertical supplier of the seller to use this knowledge to his advantage in negotiations about his price of the product. Such effects may result either in a decrease of the seller's profit or in a decrease in his share of total demand, if the supplier or customer switched to the horizontal buyer. Because of this potential secondary effect based on the disclosure of competitively sensitive private information, the probability of the vertical buyer acquiring the firm also has to be taken into account. First, the expected gain to the seller based on the bid of a supplier as vertical buyer will be determined. After that, the expected gain to the seller based on the bid of a customer as vertical buyer is derived.

5.5.3.1 Expected Gain to the Seller from Supplier's Bid

The expected gain to the seller based on a supplier's offering price and under non-disclosure of private information can be determined from equation (5.39). Recall that the expected gain to the seller from a supplier's offer consists of two components, reflecting either the fact that the acquisition can be successful or it can fail. Therefore, both the gain to the seller in case of the acquisition and the gain to the seller if the acquisition fails have to be considered. The first component of the seller's expected gain is the price that a supplier will bid to acquire the target times its probability. The second component is the profit of the seller in the product market if the acquisition fails times its probability.

If a supplier as vertical buyer acquires the firm, the offering price under non-disclosure of the private information on unit costs is given by equation (5.31). In addition, the seller's profit in the product market when there is no acquisition and private information on unit costs are not disclosed, is derived based on equation (5.10) of the basic model. Thereby, all players know the level of the supplier's synergies and competitive damages (vertical buyers synergy and damages assumption). The expected gain to the seller derived from a supplier's offering price under non-disclosure based on equation (5.39) can thus be written as

$$g_{VBS,m}(k)=\phi\cdot\left[\left(\frac{\delta-(1-2s_m)\cdot E[k]}{3}\right)^2-(K_S+\Delta K)\right]+(1-\phi)\cdot\left[\left(\frac{1}{3}\delta-\frac{1}{2}k+\frac{1}{6}E[k]\right)^2-K_S\right]\Rightarrow$$

$$g_{VBS,m}(k)=\phi\cdot\left[\left(\frac{\delta-(1-2s_m)\cdot E[k]}{3}\right)^2\right]+(1-\phi)\cdot\left(\frac{1}{3}\delta-\frac{1}{2}k+\frac{1}{6}E[k]\right)^2-(K_S+\phi\Delta K) \quad (5.42)$$

Equation (5.42) shows the expected gain to the seller based on the offering price of a supplier and on non-disclosure of the private information on unit costs. Synergies for the supplier arise through economies of scale. These synergies are captured in a unit cost reduction by the synergy factor "s". Unit costs that the vertical buyer as supplier would incur after acquiring the seller are captured by $(1-s)k$.

If the private information on unit costs k were disclosed to suppliers, the offer price of a supplier based on equation (5.30) would be

$$p_{VBS,m}=\left(\frac{1}{3}\delta-\frac{1}{2}(1-s_m)k+\frac{1}{6}(1+s_m)\cdot E[k]\right)^2-(K_S+\Delta K) \quad (5.43)$$

If the private information on unit costs was disclosed to a supplier and the acquisition failed, the seller's unit costs in the product market could increase due to the greater bargaining power of the supplier. That is, if the supplier eventually did not acquire the seller, he might misuse his knowledge of the private information on unit costs. Through the higher information level, the supplier's negotiating position is strengthened, which may enable him to raise the prices for his products. That is, unit costs to the seller if the supplier does not acquire the target may be increased by the parameter "c" to $(1+c)k$.

The production quantity of the seller if the acquisition with the supplier fails based on equation (5.5) and the production quantity of the horizontal buyer based on equation (5.6) now reads

$$x_S = \frac{\delta - (1+c)k - x_{HB}}{2} \tag{5.44}$$

$$x_{HB} = \frac{\delta - k - x_S}{2} \tag{5.45}$$

The horizontal buyer makes his production decision based on how much he expects the seller to produce. Inserting equation (5.44) into equation (5.45) yields

$$x_{HB} = \frac{\delta - E[k] - \frac{\delta - E[(1+c)k] - x_{HB}}{2}}{2} \Rightarrow$$

$$x_{HB} = \frac{\delta - (1-c)\cdot E[k]}{3} \tag{5.46}$$

That is, the competitor produces more than in the basic case, because of the competitive damages to the seller. Taking the production quantity of the horizontal buyer in account and putting equation (5.46) into (5.44), one may show that the seller then produces

$$x_S = \frac{\delta - (1+c)k - \frac{\delta - (1-c)\cdot E[k]}{3}}{2} \Rightarrow$$

$$x_S = \frac{1}{3}\delta - \frac{1}{2}(1+c)k + \frac{1}{6}(1-c)\cdot E[k] \tag{5.47}$$

Recall that the number of suppliers as vertical buyers is denoted with m = 1, ..., M. Based on equation (5.47) and on the basic profit function (5.4), the seller's profit in the product market under full disclosure of k if the acquisition by a supplier fails will be

$$\pi_{S,m}(\text{Disclosure VBS}) = \left(\frac{1}{3}\delta - \frac{1}{2}(1+c_m)k + \frac{1}{6}(1-c_m)\cdot E[k]\right)^2 - K_S \tag{5.48}$$

The seller produces less and has a lower profit than in the basic case, because the supplier increased his unit costs and because his competitor in the duopoly now produces more.

Hereby, the extent of the seller's profit decrease depends on the magnitude of competitive damages "c".

Taking into account the probability of the supplier acquiring the seller, the expected gain to the seller under full disclosure of the private information consists of two components (equations (5.43) and (5.48)) and reads

$$g_{VBS,m} = \phi \cdot \left[\begin{pmatrix} \frac{1}{3}\delta - \frac{1}{2}(1 - s_m)k \\ + \frac{1}{6}(1 + s_m) \cdot E[k] \end{pmatrix}^2 - (K_S + \Delta K) \right] + (1 - \phi) \cdot \left[\begin{pmatrix} \frac{1}{3}\delta - \frac{1}{2}(1 + c_m)k \\ + \frac{1}{6}(1 - c_m) \cdot E[k] \end{pmatrix}^2 - K_S \right] \Rightarrow$$

$$\begin{aligned} g_{VBS,m} = {} & \phi \cdot \left[\left(\frac{1}{3}\delta - \frac{1}{2}(1 - s_m)k + \frac{1}{6}(1 + s_m) \cdot E[k] \right)^2 \right] \\ & + (1 - \phi) \cdot \left[\left(\frac{1}{3}\delta - \frac{1}{2}(1 + c_m)k + \frac{1}{6}(1 - c_m) \cdot E[k] \right)^2 \right] - (K_S + \phi \Delta K) \end{aligned} \tag{5.49}$$

Equation (5.49) shows the expected gain to the seller based on the offering price of the supplier and on full disclosure of the private information on unit costs. Depending on whether the supplier's bid results to a higher expected gain to the seller under disclosure (equation (5.49)) of the private information on unit costs or its non-disclosure (equation (5.42)), the investment banker makes a disclosure recommendation about the private information on unit costs. Before this disclosure recommendation is derived, the expected gain to the seller based on the bids of customers will be determined in the next section.

5.5.3.2 Expected Gain to the Seller from Customer's Bid

Having determined the expected gain to the seller derived from different suppliers' bids, the expected gain to the seller based on different customers' bids will be now be obtained. Customers as vertical buyers (VBC) derive their synergies from an increase in their share of total demand by "d". A customer of the seller may obtain all of his products either from the seller, or from the horizontal buyer, or both from the seller and horizontal buyer. Such a customer may now decide to acquire the selling firm. The customer will obtain all of his products from the seller if he acquires the target. Since the target usually will have multiple customers and since customers as horizontal buyers generally acquire a supplier, who is responsible for a large share of the customer's supplies, a likely interval for synergy benefits of $d = [0; 0.5]$ is set.

Based on equation (5.39), the expected gain to the seller based on a customer's offering price and under non-disclosure of private information can be determined. Recall that the expected gain to the seller from a customer's offer consists of two components, reflecting the fact that the acquisition can either succeed or fail. If a customer as vertical buyer acquires the firm, the offering price under non-disclosure of the private information on unit costs is given by equation (5.38). If the customer does not acquire the selling firm, the seller will reap a profit in the product market. That profit is his gain in the event that the acquisition fails. If no private information on unit costs was disclosed to the customer, the customer cannot influence the target's production decision, and the profit of the seller will be given by equation (5.10). Recall that the number of customers as vertical buyers is denoted with i = 1, ….., I. The expected gain to the seller derived from a customer's offering price under non-disclosure based on equations (5.39), (5.38), and (5.10) can thus be written as

$$g_{VBC,i}(k) = \phi\left(\frac{(1+3d_i)\delta - E[k]}{3}\right)^2 + (1-\phi)\left(\frac{1}{3}\delta - \frac{1}{2}k + \frac{1}{6}E[k]\right)^2 - (K_S + \phi\Delta K) \tag{5.50}$$

Synergies for the supplier captured in equation (5.50) arise through an increase in his share of total demand by synergy factor "d" and a simultaneous decrease in share of total demand by "d" for the strategic buyer.

On the other hand, if the private information on unit costs k were disclosed to customers, the offer price of a customer would be given by equation (5.37) as

$$p_{VBC,i}(Discl) = \left(\frac{1}{3}(1+3d_i)\delta - \frac{1}{2}k + \frac{1}{6}E[k]\right)^2 - K_S$$

If the acquisition fails and private information on unit costs was disclosed, the customer may influence the seller's production decision negatively. For instance could the margins of the seller be higher and the unit costs lower than the customer expected. He may then demand a lower price both from the seller and from the horizontal buyer. Alternatively, the customer may simply replace the seller's product with a more economical substitute product, if possible. The customer may also decide to have his product manufactured abroad, e.g. in a developing country with much lower labor costs. These measures could decrease the profit of the seller and the horizontal buyer through lower demand. Since the seller is operating in a Cournot duopoly, a customer will generally have limited alternatives and not a very strong bargaining position. Therefore, competitive damages arising from the disclosure of information to the customer should be smaller in this setting than for suppliers. Therefore, competitive damages "h" for the customer are assumed to be defined by $h = (0; 0.2]$ and the lower demand is assumed equal for both seller and horizontal buyer. Based on equation (5.8) and (5.9), the horizontal buyer and seller will then produce

$$x_{HB} = \frac{(1-h)\delta - E[k]}{3}$$

and $x_S = \frac{1}{3}(1-h)\delta - \frac{1}{2}k + \frac{1}{6}E[k]$.

The profit of the seller would be

$$\pi_S(VBC) = \left(\frac{1}{3}(1-h)\delta - \frac{1}{2}k + \frac{1}{6}E[k]\right)^2 - K_S \tag{5.51}$$

if the private information on unit costs was disclosed and the acquisition failed. That means that the higher the loss in demand due to the disclosure of private information, the lower is the profit of the seller.

Taking into account the probability of a customer acquiring the seller, the expected gain to the seller under full disclosure consists of two components (equations (5.37) and (5.51)) and reads

$$g_{VBC,i} = \phi \cdot \left[\left(\frac{1}{3}(1+3d_i)\delta - \frac{1}{2}k + \frac{1}{6}E[k]\right)^2 - (K_S + \Delta K)\right]$$
$$+ (1-\phi) \cdot \left[\left(\frac{1}{3}(1-h_i)\delta - \frac{1}{2}k + \frac{1}{6}E[k]\right)^2 - K_S\right] \Rightarrow$$

$$g_{VBC,i} = \phi \cdot \left(\frac{1}{3}(1+3d_i)\delta - \frac{1}{2}k + \frac{1}{6}E[k]\right)^2$$
$$+ (1-\phi) \cdot \left(\frac{1}{3}(1-h_i)\delta - \frac{1}{2}k + \frac{1}{6}E[k]\right)^2 - (K_S + \phi \cdot \Delta K) \tag{5.52}$$

Equation (5.52) shows the expected gain to the seller based on the offering price of a customer "i" and on full disclosure of the private information on unit costs to the customer. Hereby, "h" denotes the competitive damages from the misappropriation of the disclosed information on unit costs by the customer if the acquisition fails. Since the horizontal buyer does not know the seller's private information on unit costs, his expected value of unit costs is denoted with E[k]. Depending on the level of the expected gain to the seller from the customer's bid under disclosure or non-disclosure of the private information on unit costs, the investment banker makes a disclosure recommendation about the private information on unit costs.

In the following sections a disclosure recommendation about private information on unit costs will be derived, first based on the offer price of the horizontal strategic buyer and then on the offer prices of vertical buyers.

5.6 Disclosure of Private Information on Unit Costs

5.6.1 Disclosure to the Horizontal Buyer

5.6.1.1.1 Disclosure Decision

When giving a recommendation about the disclosure of private information on unit costs to the seller, the investment banker will base his decision on the expected gain from an offer. That is, the investment banker will recommend the disclosure of private information on unit costs, if the expected gain from the horizontal buyer's offer is higher under disclosure than under non-disclosure of the private information.

Generally, if favorable private information on unit costs is disclosed, there is a positive effect on purchase price and a negative effect on competition in the product market of the Cournot duopoly if the acquisition fails, because the horizontal buyer will adjust his production quantity upward upon receiving favorable private information. With unfavorable private information on unit costs, the situation is reversed. With unfavorable information there is a negative effect on purchase price and a positive competition effect in the product market, because the horizontal buyer would adjust his production quantity downward if he did not acquire the seller. The balance and trade-off between those two countervailing effects determines the disclosure strategy of the seller.

The private information on unit costs should be disclosed to the horizontal strategic buyer, if the expected gain to the seller is greater under disclosure than under non-disclosure, i.e. if $g_{HB}(\text{Disclosure}) > g_{HB}(\text{Non}-\text{Disclosure})$, or equation (5.41) > (5.40).

$$\frac{1}{36}(\phi+4)(\delta-k)^2-(K_S+\phi\cdot\Delta K)>\frac{\phi}{36}\cdot\left[9\left(\delta^2-2\delta\cdot E[k]+E\left[k^2\right]\right)-4(\delta-E[k])^2\right]$$
$$+\frac{(1-\phi)}{36}\left[(2\delta-3k+E[k])^2\right]-(K_S+\phi\cdot\Delta K)\Rightarrow$$

$$(\phi+4)(\delta-k)^2>\phi\cdot\left[9\left(\delta^2-2\delta\cdot E[k]+E\left[k^2\right]\right)-4(\delta-E[k])^2\right]+(1-\phi)[2\delta-3k+E[k]]^2 \qquad (5.53)$$

Equation (5.53) considers both the gain to the seller in case of the acquisition, and the profit of the seller in the product market if the acquisition fails. Depending on the probability of the horizontal strategic buyer acquiring the firm and the level of the private information on unit costs, different disclosure strategies result. Taking into account the probability of the strategic buyer acquiring the firm, the investment banker can make a disclosure recommendation for different levels of acquisition probability.

5.6.1.1.2 Theorem 1

Theorem 1: Given that

1) *The seller has private information about his unit costs k;*
2) *The competitor as a horizontal strategic buyer is able to derive synergies from an acquisition of the seller, which are captured by the monopoly rent;*
3) *The seller may incur competitive damages if the private information was disclosed to the horizontal strategic buyer and the acquisition failed;*
4) *The probability of acquisition "ϕ" is a constant and demand is denoted with δ; then*

(i) *A full disclosure equilibrium of the private information on unit costs k exists for low and high probability of acquisition, i.e. if* $\phi<\frac{4\delta-9}{2(7\delta-12)}$ *or* $\phi>\frac{4\delta-3}{2(7\delta-9)}$.

(ii) *If only a partial disclosure equilibrium of the private information on unit costs k exists, then* $N=[1;k_1]\cup[k_2;2]$

(iii) *A non-disclosure equilibrium of the private information on unit costs k exists if*

$$\frac{-112\delta^2+336\delta-267+3\sqrt{5\left(32\delta^2-96\delta+77\right)}}{2\left(-196\delta^2+588\delta-471\right)}<\phi<\frac{-112\delta^2+336\delta-267-3\sqrt{5\left(32\delta^2-96\delta+77\right)}}{2\left(-196\delta^2+588\delta-471\right)}$$

The proof is in the Appendix. Note that N denotes the subset of private information on k, which is not disclosed in equilibrium. In the partial disclosure equilibrium from Theorem 1(ii), k_1 and k_2 are those values of $k = [1; 2]$, for which $T = 0$.[293] For an illustration of the results of Theorem 1 see Figure 5-1 and 5-2.

The seller should fully disclose his private information on unit costs if the probability of the horizontal buyer acquiring the firm is sufficiently small or sufficiently large, i.e. full disclosure if

$\left(\phi < \frac{4\delta - 9}{2(7\delta - 12)}\right) \cup \left(\phi > \frac{4\delta - 3}{2(7\delta - 9)}\right)$, given $\delta \geq 2.5$ and $\phi \in [0; 1]$. The seller should not disclose his private information on unit costs, if the probability of the strategic buyer acquiring the firm is average, i.e. the seller will not disclose for

$$\frac{-112\delta^2 + 336\delta - 267 + 3\sqrt{5(32\delta^2 - 96\delta + 77)}}{2(-196\delta^2 + 588\delta - 471)} < \phi < \frac{-112\delta^2 + 336\delta - 267 - 3\sqrt{5(32\delta^2 - 96\delta + 77)}}{2(-196\delta^2 + 588\delta - 471)}.$$

If the seller only partially discloses the private information on unit costs, he should disclose average information, while not disclosing extremely positive and negative private information on unit costs.[294]

If the probability of the horizontal strategic buyer acquiring the target firm is sufficiently low, full disclosure results because the positive profit effect outweighs the negative price effect. If there were non-disclosure, the strategic buyer would expect private information on unit costs to be favorable, i.e. $N = \{1\}$ (rational expectations assumption). This is the worst outcome if the Cournot competition in the product market continues. If the competitor underestimated the actual level of unit costs he would overproduce, thereby lowering the profit of the seller in the product market. Therefore, disclosure has a positive effect on the seller's profit in the product market for the case that the acquisition fails (profit effect). The horizontal strategic buyer would produce less, thereby increasing the seller's profit. On the other hand, there is a negative effect on the purchase price upon disclosure (price effect), if the strategic buyer underestimates the true level of k. Since for a low probability of the strategic buyer acquiring the seller, i.e. for $\phi < \frac{4\delta - 9}{2(7\delta - 12)}$, the positive profit effect of disclosure outweighs the

---

293 Partial disclosure equilibriums are derived and discussed in detail in section 5.6.1.1.3.

294 See the illustrative example in the next section for a more detailed discussion of partial disclosure equilibria.

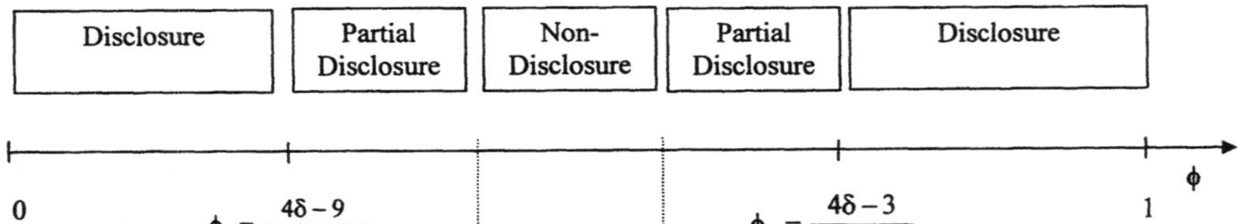

$$\phi_1 = \frac{4\delta - 9}{2(7\delta - 12)} \qquad \phi_4 = \frac{4\delta - 3}{2(7\delta - 9)}$$

$$\phi_2 = \frac{-112\delta^2 + 336\delta - 267 + 3\sqrt{5(32\delta^2 - 96\delta + 77)}}{2(-196\delta^2 + 588\delta - 471)} \qquad \phi_3 = \frac{-112\delta^2 + 336\delta - 267 - 3\sqrt{5(32\delta^2 - 96\delta + 77)}}{2(-196\delta^2 + 588\delta - 471)}$$

Figure 5-1: Lower and Upper Bounds of Disclosure, Partial Disclosure, and Non-Disclosure Equilibrium Intervals for Different Levels of Probability of Acquisition and as a Function of Demand

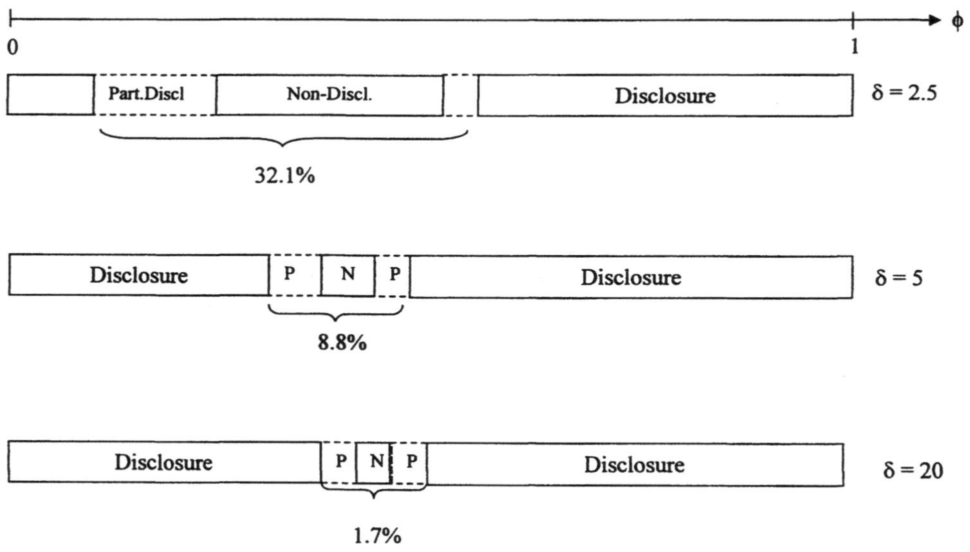

Figure 5-2: Upper and Lower Bounds of Disclosure, Partial Disclosure, and Non-Disclosure Equilibrium Intervals for Differing Levels of Demand

negative price effect, the seller should fully disclose his private information on unit costs for a low level of ϕ.

If the probability of the horizontal strategic buyer acquiring the firm is sufficiently high, full disclosure results because the positive price effect outweighs the negative profit effect. If there were non-disclosure, the horizontal buyer would expect the private information on unit costs to be unfavorable, i.e. $N = \{2\}$ (rational expectations assumption). That is the worst outcome if the acquisition is completed, because the horizontal buyer would offer a lower purchase price based on his overestimation of the actual level of unit cost. Upon disclosure of the private information on unit costs, a positive price effect results. However, based on the disclosure of the better than expected information on unit costs the horizontal buyer will increase his production quantity in the product market if the acquisition fails, thereby decreasing the profit of the seller. This negative profit effect is outweighed by the positive price effect for a sufficiently large probability of the horizontal buyer acquiring the firm. That is, for $\phi > \frac{4\delta - 3}{2(7\delta - 9)}$ the seller is induced to full disclosure of his private information on unit costs.

Figure 5-3 graphs the gain that the seller expects from the strategic buyer HB for a low level of demand ($\delta = 2.5$) and for different values of unit costs k. For $\delta = 2.5$, the upper full disclosure interval based on Figure 5-1 becomes $\phi = (0.4118; 1]$. That is, for both $\phi = 45\%$ and $\phi = 90\%$ the seller should fully disclose the private information on unit costs. Figure 5-3 shows that the expected gain curves are downward sloping. That is, the worse the private information on unit costs, the lower the gain that the seller can expect from a strategic buyer. Also, the higher the HB's acquisition probability for a given level of unit costs, the higher will be the expected gain from the HB.

If neither the price effect nor the profit effect clearly dominates, equilibria besides full disclosure may result. In such partial disclosure equilibria, very favorable private information and very unfavorable private information on unit costs is generally concealed because of the trade-off between the price effect and the profit effect. That is, with partial disclosure only average private information on unit costs is disclosed, because the very high and very low levels of private information have an increasingly negative effect, while the positive effect increases more gradually. The net result is a concave function, with negative effects most distinct at the upper and lower boundary of the unit cost interval.[295]

[295] Section 5.6.1.1.3 illustrates the properties of a partial disclosure equilibrium in detail.

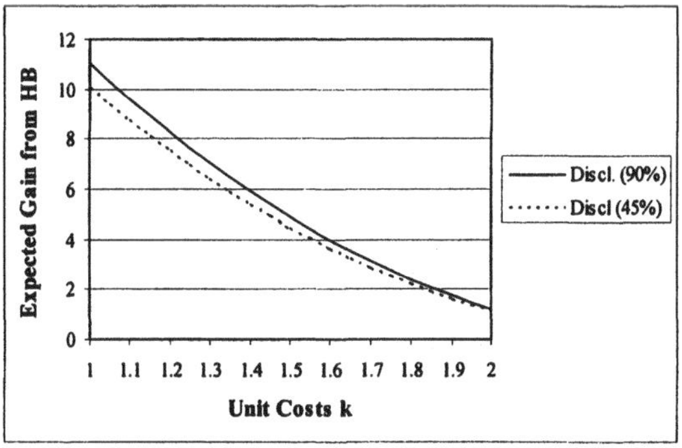

Figure 5-3: Expected Gain from HB based on Full Disclosure and for $\delta = 2.5$, $\phi = 0.9$, and $\phi = 0.45$

	Upper bound of the					
Demand	Discl. Interval ϕ_1	Part.Discl. Interval ϕ_2	Non-Discl. Interval ϕ_3	Part. Discl. Interval ϕ_4	% Disclo-sure	% Non-Discl. or Part. Discl.
2.5	0.0910	0.1907	0.3712	0.4118	67.9	32.1
5	0.2391	0.2578	0.3126	0.3269	91.2	8.8
20	0.2773	0.2805	0.2909	0.2938	98.3	1.7

Table 5-4: Upper and Lower Bounds of Disclosure, Partial Disclosure, and Non-Disclosure Equilibrium Intervals for Differing Levels of Demand

The last part of Theorem 1 shows that non-disclosure equilibria exist for average levels of ϕ. Depending on the level of demand, the disclosure recommendation for the seller changes for different levels of probability of acquisition (see Table 5-4 and Figure 5-2). For a low level of demand, the seller's private information on unit costs is an important criterion. For a low-level $\delta = 2.5$, 32% of the time there is either partial disclosure of average information or non-disclosure of the private information on unit costs. With increasing demand, the full disclosure equilibrium interval increases. For infinitely high demand all bounds of disclosure, partial disclosure, and non-disclosure intervals converge to $\phi = \frac{2}{7}$. Therefore, the seller should disclose his private information on unit costs for all levels of ϕ for a very high level of demand.

Figure 5-4 graphs the gain that the seller expects from the strategic buyer HB for a low level of demand (δ = 2.5) and for different values of unit costs k. For δ = 2.5, the non-disclosure interval based on Figure 5-1 becomes $\phi = (0.1907; 0.3712)$. Figure 5-4 graphs the expected gain curve for $\phi = 0.3$. Again, the expected gain curve is downward sloping, because the expected gain from the HB decreases with more unfavorable private information, i.e. with a higher level of unit costs k.

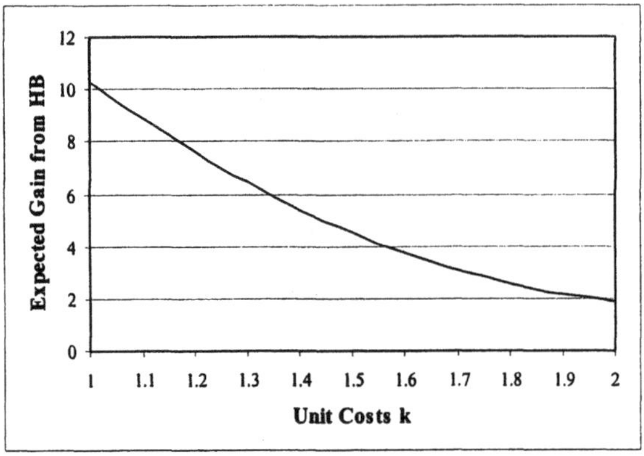

Figure 5-4: Expected Gain from HB based on Non-Disclosure and for $\delta = 2.5$ and $\phi = 0.3$

5.6.1.1.3 Illustrative Example for Partial Disclosure Equilibrium

An example can show the properties of a partial disclosure equilibrium as determined under Theorem 1(ii). Assume that the level of demand is low, with $\delta = 2.5$. Additionally, the probability of the strategic buyer acquiring the seller is low with $\phi = 0.15$. As Table 5-4 shows, the seller should partially disclose his private information for the specified acquisition probability and level of demand. To determine the upper and lower bounds of the non-disclosure regions within the partial disclosure equilibrium, the expected gain to the seller difference curve T must equal zero. Figure 5-5 shows that the non-disclosure region is $N = [1; k_1] \cup [k_2; 2]$ in equilibrium.

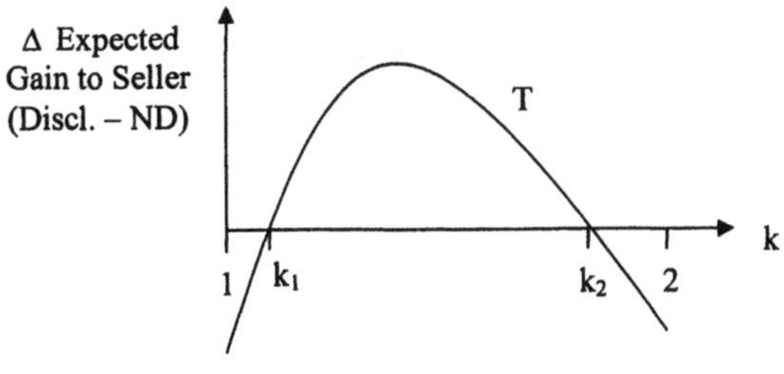

Figure 5-5: Expected Gain Difference Curve for Partial Disclosure Equilibrium

To determine k_1 and k_2, T must be equal to zero. Recall from equation (A.3) in the Appendix that T is

$$T = 5(2\phi - 1)k^2 + 2\delta(2 - 7\phi)k + 6E[k|N](1 - \phi)k + 2\delta(7\phi - 2)E[k|N]$$
$$+ (5\phi - 1)E[k|N]^2 - 9\phi E[k^2|N]$$

For $\delta = 2.5$ and $\phi = 0.15$, T becomes

$$T = -3.5k^2 + (4.75 + 5.1E[k|N])k - 4.75E[k|N] - 0.25E[k|N]^2 - 1.35E[k^2|N] \quad (5.54)$$

Upon observing non-disclosure, the strategic buyer now expects the value of the private information on unit costs k to be within $[1; k_1]$ or $[k_2; 2]$. The expected value of k given non-disclosure[296] is determined by

$$E[k|N] = \left[\frac{1}{2}k^2\right]_{k_2}^{2} \cdot \left(\frac{1}{2-k_2}\right)\left(\frac{2-k_2}{(k_1-1)+(2-k_2)}\right) + \left[\frac{1}{2}k^2\right]_{1}^{k_1} \cdot \left(\frac{1}{k_1-1}\right)\left(\frac{k_1-1}{(k_1-1)+(2-k_2)}\right) \Rightarrow$$

$$E[k|N] = \frac{2 - \frac{1}{2}k_2^2 + \frac{1}{2}k_1^2 - \frac{1}{2}}{1 - k_2 + k_1} \Rightarrow$$

$$E[k|N] = \frac{3 + k_1^2 - k_2^2}{2(1 - k_2 + k_1)} \quad (5.55)$$

Likewise, the expected value of k^2 is derived,

$$E[k^2|N] = \left[\frac{1}{3}k^3\right]_{k_2}^{2} \cdot \left(\frac{1}{2-k_2}\right)\left(\frac{2-k_2}{(k_1-1)+(2-k_2)}\right)$$
$$+ \left[\frac{1}{3}k^3\right]_{1}^{k_1} \cdot \left(\frac{1}{k_1-1}\right)\left(\frac{k_1-1}{(k_1-1)+(2-k_2)}\right) \Rightarrow$$

$$E[k^2|N] = \frac{\frac{8}{3} - \frac{1}{3}k_2^3 + \frac{1}{3}k_1^3 - \frac{1}{3}}{1 - k_2 + k_1} \Rightarrow$$

---

296 Recall that k is identically distributed, i.e. f(k) = 1 for all k.

$$E\left[k^2|N\right]=\frac{7+k_1^3-k_2^3}{3(1-k_2+k_1)} \tag{5.56}$$

Entering the expected values from equation (5.55) and (5.56) into equation (5.54) results in

$$\begin{aligned} T = &-3.5k_{1/2}^2+\left(4.75+5.1\cdot\frac{3+k_1^2-k_2^2}{2(1-k_2+k_1)}\right)k_{1/2}-4.75\cdot\frac{3+k_1^2-k_2^2}{2(1-k_2+k_1)} \\ &-0.25\cdot\left(\frac{3+k_1^2-k_2^2}{2(1-k_2+k_1)}\right)^2-1.35\cdot\frac{7+k_1^3-k_2^3}{3(1-k_2+k_1)} \end{aligned} \tag{5.57}$$

1) Find k_1 for which equation (5.57) or T equals zero.

$$\begin{aligned} T: &-3.5k_1{}^2+\left(4.75+5.1\cdot\frac{3+k_1^2-k_2^2}{2(1-k_2+k_1)}\right)k_1-4.75\cdot\frac{3+k_1^2-k_2^2}{2(1-k_2+k_1)}-0.25\cdot\left(\frac{3+k_1^2-k_2^2}{2(1-k_2+k_1)}\right)^2 \\ &-1.35\cdot\frac{7+k_1^3-k_2^3}{3(1-k_2+k_1)}=0 \qquad \Rightarrow \end{aligned}$$

$$\begin{aligned} T: &-3.5k_1{}^2+4.75k_1+\frac{7.65k_1+2.55k_1^3-2.55k_1k_2^2}{1-k_2+k_1}-\frac{7.125+2.375k_1^2-2.375k_2^2}{1-k_2+k_1} \\ &-\frac{9+6k_1^2-6k_2^2+k_1^4+k_2^4-2k_1^2k_2^2}{16(1-k_2+k_1)^2}-\frac{3.15-0.45k_2^3+0.45k_1^3}{1-k_2+k_1} \qquad \Rightarrow \end{aligned}$$

$$\begin{aligned} T: &\frac{-3.5k_1{}^2(1-k_2+k_1)^2+4.75k_1(1-k_2+k_1)^2+\left(7.65k_1+2.55k_1^3-2.55k_1k_2^2\right)(1-k_2+k_1)}{(1-k_2+k_1)^2} \\ &+\frac{\left(-7.125-2.375k_1^2+2.375k_2^2\right)(1-k_2+k_1)-\frac{1}{16}\left(9+6k_1^2-6k_2^2+k_1^4+k_2^4-2k_1^2k_2^2\right)}{(1-k_2+k_1)^2} \\ &+\frac{\left(-3.15+0.45k_2^3-0.45k_1^3\right)(1-k_2+k_1)}{(1-k_2+k_1)^2}=0 \qquad \Rightarrow \end{aligned}$$

$$T: -3.5k_1^2 + 7k_1^2k_2 - 7k_1^3 - 3.5k_1^2k_2^2 - 3.5k_1^4 + 7k_1^3k_2 + 4.75k_1 - 9.5k_1k_2 + 9.5k_1^2 + 4.75k_1k_2^2$$
$$+ 4.75k_1^3 - 9.5k_1^2k_2 + 7.65k_1 - 7.65k_1k_2 + 7.65k_1^2 + 2.55k_1^3 - 2.55k_1^3k_2 + 2.55k_1^4$$
$$- 2.55k_1k_2^2 + 2.55k_1k_2^3 - 2.55k_1^2k_2^2 - 7.125 + 7.125k_2 - 7.125k_1 - 2.375k_1^2 + 2.375k_1^2k_2$$
$$- 2.375k_1^3 + 2.375k_2^2 - 2.375k_2^3 + 2.375k_1k_2^2 - 0.5625 - 0.375k_1^2 + 0.375k_2^2 - 0.0625k_1^4$$
$$- 0.0625k_2^4 + 0.125k_1^2k_2^2 - 3.15 + 3.15k_2 - 3.15k_1 + 0.45k_2^3 - 0.45k_2^4 + 0.45k_1k_2^3 - 0.45k_1^3$$
$$+ 0.45k_1^3k_2 - 0.45k_1^4 = 0$$

$$T: -1.4625k_1^4 + (4.9k_2 - 2.525)k_1^3 - (5.925k_2^2 + 0.125k_2 - 10.9)k_1^2$$
$$+ (3k_2^3 + 4.575k_2^2 - 17.15k_2 + 2.125)k_1 \qquad (5.58)$$
$$- (0.5125k_2^4 + 1.925k_2^3 - 2.75k_2^2 - 10.275k_2 + 10.8375) = 0$$

2) Find k_2 for which equation (5.57) or T equals zero.

$$T: -3.5{k_2}^2 + \left(4.75 + 5.1 \cdot \frac{3 + k_1^2 - k_2^2}{2(1 - k_2 + k_1)}\right)k_2 - 4.75 \cdot \frac{3 + k_1^2 - k_2^2}{2(1 - k_2 + k_1)} - 0.25 \cdot \left(\frac{3 + k_1^2 - k_2^2}{2(1 - k_2 + k_1)}\right)^2$$
$$- 1.35 \cdot \frac{7 + k_1^3 - k_2^3}{3(1 - k_2 + k_1)} = 0 \qquad \Rightarrow$$

$$T: -3.5{k_2}^2 + 4.75k_1 + \frac{7.65k_2 + 2.55k_1^2k_2 - 2.55k_2^3}{1 - k_2 + k_1} - \frac{7.125 + 2.375k_1^2 - 2.375k_2^2}{1 - k_2 + k_1}$$
$$- \frac{9 + 6k_1^2 - 6k_2^2 + k_1^4 + k_2^4 - 2k_1^2k_2^2}{16(1 - k_2 + k_1)^2} - \frac{3.15 - 0.45k_2^3 + 0.45k_1^3}{1 - k_2 + k_1} \qquad \Rightarrow$$

$$T: \frac{-3.5{k_2}^2(1 - k_2 + k_1)^2 + 4.75k_2(1 - k_2 + k_1)^2 + (7.65k_2 + 2.55k_1^2k_2 - 2.55k_2^3)(1 - k_2 + k_1)}{(1 - k_2 + k_1)^2}$$
$$+ \frac{(-7.125 - 2.375k_1^2 + 2.375k_2^2)(1 - k_2 + k_1) - \frac{1}{16}(9 + 6k_1^2 - 6k_2^2 + k_1^4 + k_2^4 - 2k_1^2k_2^2)}{(1 - k_2 + k_1)^2}$$
$$+ \frac{(-3.15 + 0.45k_2^3 - 0.45k_1^3)(1 - k_2 + k_1)}{(1 - k_2 + k_1)^2} = 0 \qquad \Rightarrow$$

$$
\begin{aligned}
T: & -3.5k_2^2 + 7k_2^3 - 7k_1k_2^2 - 3.5k_1^2k_2^2 - 3.5k_2^4 + 7k_1k_2^3 + 4.75k_2 - 9.5k_2^2 + 9.5k_1k_2 + 4.75k_2^3 \\
& + 4.75k_1^2k_2 - 9.5k_1k_2^2 + 7.65k_2 - 7.65k_2^2 + 7.65k_1k_2 + 2.55k_1^2k_2 - 2.55k_1^2k_2^2 \\
& + 2.55k_1^3k_2 - 2.55k_2^3 + 2.55k_2^4 - 2.55k_1k_2^3 - 7.125 + 7.125k_2 - 7.125k_1 - 2.375k_1^2 \\
& + 2.375k_1^2k_2 - 2.375k_1^3 + 2.375k_2^2 - 2.375k_2^3 + 2.375k_1k_2^2 - 0.5625 - 0.375k_1^2 \\
& + 0.375k_2^2 - 0.0625k_1^4 - 0.0625k_2^4 + 0.125k_1^2k_2^2 - 3.15 + 3.15k_2 - 3.15k_1 + 0.45k_2^3 \\
& - 0.45k_2^4 + 0.45k_1k_2^3 - 0.45k_1^3 + 0.45k_1^3k_2 - 0.45k_1^4 = 0
\end{aligned}
$$

$$
\begin{aligned}
T: & -1.4625k_2^4 + (4.9k_1 + 7.275)k_2^3 - (5.925k_1^2 + 14.125k_1 + 17.9)k_2^2 \\
& + (3k_1^3 + 9.675k_1^2 + 17.15k_1 + 22.675)k_2 \\
& - (0.5125k_1^4 + 2.825k_1^3 + 2.75k_1^2 + 10.275k_1 + 10.8375) = 0
\end{aligned} \tag{5.59}
$$

Equations (5.58) and (5.59) can now be solved numerically for the levels of unit costs k_1 and k_2, for which the expected gain difference curve equals zero.[297] Figure 5-6 shows the expected gain curves for disclosure and non-disclosure of the private information, with the magnitude of the expected gain to the seller given on the vertical axis.

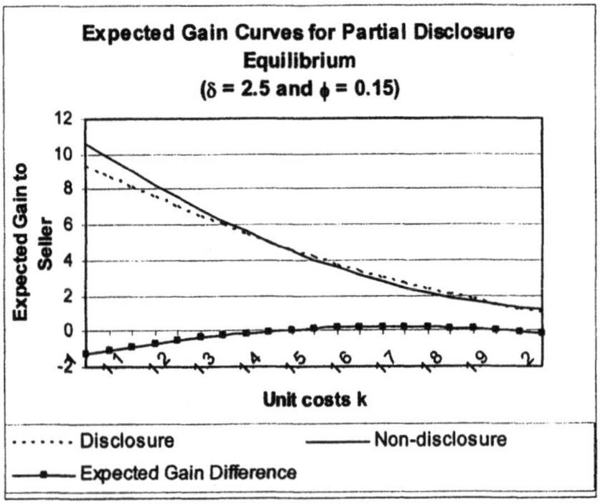

Figure 5-6: Expected Gain Curves for Disclosure and Non-Disclosure of Private Information on Unit Costs for Partial Disclosure Equilibrium ($\delta = 2.5$ and $\phi = 0.15$).

The expected gain curves are convex, and are downward sloping in k. The private information on unit costs k is given on the horizontal axis, with k = [1; 2]. The higher (or the more unfavorable) the unit costs k, the lower is the expected gain to a seller from a strategic buyer's

[297] The numerical solutions to equations (5.58) and (5.59) were derived with the MathLab program.

offer. The difference between the expected gain to the seller under disclosure and non-disclosure is depicted by the expected gain difference curve T. While both the "disclosure expected gain curve" and the "non-disclosure expected gain curve" are convex, the net effect with the expected gain difference curve T is a concave function. For $\delta = 2.5$ and $\phi = 0.15$, the respective profit functions simplify to

$$\text{Profit (Disclosure)} = 4{,}15k^2 - 20{,}75k + 25{,}9375$$

$$\text{Profit (Non-Disclosure)} = 7{,}65k^2 - 32{,}3595k + 35{,}3508$$

$$\text{T (Gain Difference)} = -3{,}5k^2 + 11{,}6095k - 9{,}4133$$

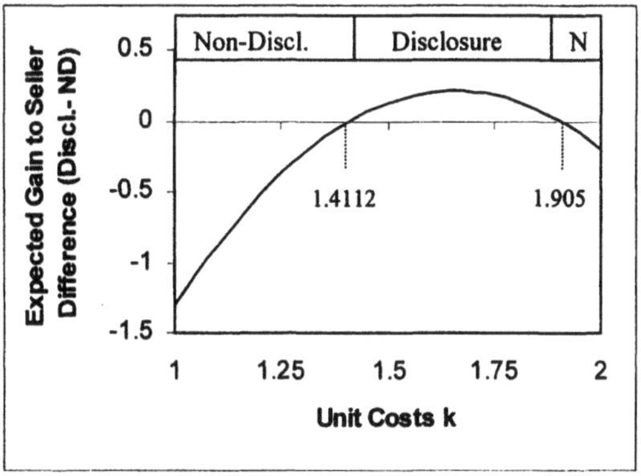

Figure 5-7: Expected Gain Difference Curve for Illustrative Example.

To study the difference in expected gain to the seller between disclosure and non-disclosure in detail, the expected gain difference curve T from Figure 5-6 is graphed separately in Figure 5-7. The vertical axis now gives the difference in expected gain to the seller between disclosure and non-disclosure of the private information. Figure 5-7 shows that the concave expected gain difference curve T crosses twice at the points $k_1 = 1.4112$ and $k_2 = 1.9057$.[298] Given that $\delta = 2.5$ and $\phi = 0.15$, the seller should disclose his private information on unit costs if such information was average to bad, i.e. for $k = (1.4112; 1.9057)$. On the other hand, the seller should not disclose his private information, if such information is

[298] The values are rounded and were derived based on equations (5.58) and (5.59) with the MathLab program.

positive or very bad, i.e. $N = [1; 1.4112] \cup [1.9057; 2]$. Upon observing non-disclosure, the strategic buyer expects the information to be $E[k|N] = 1.3450$.

In this partial disclosure equilibrium, neither the price effect nor the profit effect clearly dominates. The trade-off between those two effects results in the non-disclosure of excellent and very poor private information on unit costs, and the disclosure of average private information on unit costs. Extreme values of private information on unit costs have an increasingly negative effect, while the positive effect increases more gradually. As Figure 5-7 shows, the negative effects of information disclosure are most severe at the boundaries of the information set.

5.6.2 Disclosure to Vertical Buyers

5.6.2.1 Disclosure to the Supplier

5.6.2.1.1 Disclosure Decision

Synergies for a supplier to the seller arise through economies of scale and are captured in a unit cost reduction. If the vertical buyer acquires the seller, the acquired company's unit costs will be decreased by the synergy factor "s", while the competitor's unit costs remain at level k. Unit costs that the vertical buyer as supplier would incur after acquiring the seller are captured by $(1-s)k$ with $s = [0; 0.5]$ and $k = [1; 2]$.[299]

If the private information about the seller's unit costs is disclosed to the vertical buyer, his bargaining power as a supplier may increase. That is, if the acquisition fails, the supplier may misappropriate the private information on unit costs. Through the higher information level, the supplier has a stronger negotiating position, which may enable him to raise the prices for his products.[300] That is, unit costs to the seller if the supplier does not acquire the target but private information was disclosed may be increased by the parameter "c" to $(1+c)k$, with $c = (0; 0.2]$.[301] Again, c denotes the competitive damages "c" that the seller will

[299] Note that the specified interval for "s" has been set in this particular way to reflect plausible real-world conditions. Naturally, the interval range could easily be changed to adapt to different circumstances, while results would remain similar.

[300] This effect is especially pronounced if the supplier concentration is high, i.e. if the number of alternative suppliers for the seller is limited. Additionally, if the specificity of the seller's product is high, his switching costs should be higher and he might have to agree to a higher price by the supplier.

[301] The same reasoning as for the setting of the synergy interval applies.

incur if private information is disclosed to the supplier but the acquisition fails. Additionally, let demand be $\delta \geq 2.5$ and the probability of the supplier acquiring the seller $\phi = [0;1)$.[302]

Again, the expected gain to the seller consists of two components. The investment banker will only recommend full disclosure of private information on unit costs k to the seller if his expected gain under full disclosure is larger than the expected gain under non-disclosure, i.e. if (5.49) > (5.42).

$$\begin{aligned}&\phi\cdot\left[\begin{pmatrix}\frac{1}{3}\delta-\frac{1}{2}(1-s)k\\+\frac{1}{6}(1+s)\cdot E[k]\end{pmatrix}^2\right]+(1-\phi)\cdot\left[\begin{pmatrix}\frac{1}{3}\delta-\frac{1}{2}(1+c)k\\+\frac{1}{6}(1-c)\cdot E[k]\end{pmatrix}^2\right]-(K_S+\phi\Delta K)\\&>\phi\cdot\left[\left(\frac{\delta-(1-2s)\cdot E[k]}{3}\right)^2\right]+(1-\phi)\cdot\left(\frac{1}{3}\delta-\frac{1}{2}k+\frac{1}{6}E[k]\right)^2-(K_S+\phi\Delta K)\end{aligned}\tag{5.60}$$

The left-hand side of the inequality (5.60) shows the expected gain to the seller for the disclosure case, while the right-hand side of the inequality shows the expected gain to the seller for non-disclosure of the private information on unit costs k.[303] In the first term and on the left-hand side of the equation, the supplier knows the private information on unit costs, while the horizontal buyer (competitor) does not. In the first term on the right-hand side of the inequality, the supplier does not know the private information on unit cost (non-disclosure case). For the supplier as a buyer this the only uncertain factor. Because the supplier does not have any influence on the production decision of the seller in the non-disclosure case, the last term of the inequality gives the base profit of the seller in the product market.

Equation (5.60) simplifies to

$$\begin{aligned}&\phi\cdot\left[\left(\frac{1}{3}\delta-\frac{1}{2}(1-s)k+\frac{1}{6}(1+s)\cdot E[k]\right)^2\right]+(1-\phi)\cdot\left[\left(\frac{1}{3}\delta-\frac{1}{2}(1+c)k+\frac{1}{6}(1-c)\cdot E[k]\right)^2\right]\\&>\phi\cdot\left[\left(\frac{\delta-(1-2s)\cdot E[k]}{3}\right)^2\right]+(1-\phi)\cdot\left(\frac{1}{3}\delta-\frac{1}{2}k+\frac{1}{6}E[k]\right)^2\Rightarrow\end{aligned}$$

[302] The special case of certainty about the acquisition will be separately discussed at the end of this section.

[303] Note that in the derivation of equation (5.60) the subscript "m", which indicates that there may be multiple suppliers, was omitted. This was done to reduce the clutter in the subsequent calculations. The derived expected gain to the seller may easily be applied to multiple suppliers with different synergy potential, if necessary.

$$
\begin{aligned}
&\frac{1}{9}\phi\delta^2-\frac{1}{3}\phi\delta k+\frac{1}{3}\phi\delta sk+\frac{1}{9}\phi\delta E[k]+\frac{1}{9}\phi\delta sE[k]+\frac{1}{4}\phi k^2-\frac{1}{2}\phi sk^2+\frac{1}{4}\phi s^2k^2-\frac{1}{6}\phi E[k]k\\
&\quad-\frac{1}{6}\phi sE[k]k+\frac{1}{6}\phi sE[k]k+\frac{1}{6}\phi s^2E[k]k+\frac{1}{36}\phi E[k]^2+\frac{1}{18}\phi sE[k]^2+\frac{1}{36}\phi s^2E[k]^2\\
&\quad+\frac{1}{9}\delta^2-\frac{1}{3}\delta k-\frac{1}{3}\delta ck+\frac{1}{9}\delta E[k]-\frac{1}{9}\delta cE[k]+\frac{1}{4}k^2+\frac{1}{2}ck^2+\frac{1}{4}c^2k^2-\frac{1}{6}E[k]k\\
&\quad+\frac{1}{6}c\cdot E[k]k-\frac{1}{6}cE[k]k+\frac{1}{6}c^2E[k]k-\frac{1}{9}\phi\delta^2+\frac{1}{3}\phi\delta k+\frac{1}{3}\phi\delta ck-\frac{1}{9}\phi\delta E[k]+\frac{1}{9}\phi\delta c\cdot E[k]\\
&\quad-\frac{1}{4}\phi k^2-\frac{1}{2}\phi ck^2-\frac{1}{4}\phi c^2k^2+\frac{1}{6}\phi E[k]k-\frac{1}{6}\phi c\cdot E[k]k+\frac{1}{6}\phi cE[k]k-\frac{1}{6}\phi c^2E[k]k\\
&\quad+\frac{1}{36}E[k]^2-\frac{1}{18}c\cdot E[k]^2+\frac{1}{36}c^2E[k]^2-\frac{1}{36}\phi E[k]^2+\frac{1}{18}\phi cE[k]^2-\frac{1}{36}\phi c^2E[k]^2\\
>\;&\frac{1}{9}\phi\delta^2-\frac{2}{9}\phi\delta E[k]+\frac{1}{9}\phi E[k]^2+\frac{4}{9}\phi\delta sE[k]-\frac{4}{9}\phi sE[k]^2+\frac{4}{9}\phi s^2E[k]^2+\frac{1}{9}\delta^2-\frac{1}{3}\delta k\\
&\quad+\frac{1}{9}\delta E[k]+\frac{1}{4}k^2-\frac{1}{6}E[k]k+\frac{1}{36}E[k]^2-\frac{1}{9}\phi\delta^2+\frac{1}{3}\phi\delta k-\frac{1}{9}\phi\delta E[k]-\frac{1}{4}\phi k^2\\
&\quad+\frac{1}{6}\phi E[k]k-\frac{1}{36}\phi E[k]^2\Rightarrow
\end{aligned}
$$

$$
\begin{aligned}
&\left[9\left(\phi(1-s)^2+(1-\phi)(2+c)c\right)\right]\cdot k^2+6\begin{bmatrix}\phi(s-1)\cdot(2\delta+(1+s)\cdot E[k])\\+(1-\phi)(cE[k]-2\delta)\cdot c\end{bmatrix}k\\
&\quad+\left[3\phi(6s-5s^2-1)+c(1-\phi)(c-2)\right]\cdot E[k]^2+4\left[3(1-s)\phi\delta-(1-\phi)\delta c\right]\cdot E[k]\;>0
\end{aligned}
$$

The expected gain difference curve T that shows the difference between expected gain to the seller in the disclosure case and in the non-disclosure case can therefore be given by

$$
\begin{aligned}
T=&\left[9\begin{pmatrix}\phi(1-s)^2\\+(1-\phi)(2+c)c\end{pmatrix}\right]\cdot k^2+6\begin{bmatrix}\phi(s-1)\cdot(2\delta+(1+s)\cdot E[k])\\+(1-\phi)(cE[k]-2\delta)\cdot c\end{bmatrix}k\\
&+\left[3\phi(6s-5s^2-1)+c(1-\phi)(c-2)\right]\cdot E[k]^2+4\left[3(1-s)\phi\delta-(1-\phi)\delta c\right]\cdot E[k]
\end{aligned}
\tag{5.61}
$$

If the expected gain difference curve is positive, i.e. $T > 0$, the expected gain to the seller in the disclosure case is larger than in the non-disclosure case. Moreover, if the difference curve is negative, i.e. $T < 0$, the expected gain to the seller in the disclosure case is smaller than in the non-disclosure case.

5.6.2.1.2 Theorem 2

Theorem 2: Given that

1) *The seller has private information on unit costs k, which is unknown to the supplier and the competitor;*
2) *The supplier as a vertical buyer is able to derive synergy "s" from the acquisition of the seller;*
3) *The seller may incur competitive damages "c" if the private information on unit costs was disclosed to the supplier and the acquisition fails;*
4) *The probability of acquisition "ϕ" is a constant;*

   then

(i) There is no full disclosure equilibrium for any probability of acquisition, with $\phi = [0;1)$.

(ii) A non-disclosure equilibrium exists for low to average probabilities of acquisition, i.e. if

$$0 \le \phi \le \frac{9(9c+6-8\delta)c}{9(3(1+(3c+2)c)+(7s-10)s)+24(s-1-3c)\delta}$$

(iii) A partial disclosure equilibrium exists for average to high probabilities of acquisition, i.e. if $\frac{9(9c+6-8\delta)c}{9(3(1+(3c+2)c)+(7s-10)s)+24(s-1-3c)\delta} < \phi < 1$

The proof is in the Appendix. It is reasonable that for uncertainty, i.e. for $\phi < 1$, no full disclosure equilibrium can exist. If there are competitive damages, i.e. $c > 0$, the profit component of the expected gain of the seller is always smaller under disclosure than under non-disclosure. Therefore, there is always non-disclosure of private information for low levels of acquisition probability. Hereby, the range of the non-disclosure interval will increase with an increasing level of competitive damages. For private information to be disclosed, the probability of acquisition has to be sufficiently high so that the price effect can dominate the profit effect. The purchase price component of the expected gain to the seller based on equation (5.60) and under full disclosure reduces to

$$\phi \cdot \left[\frac{1}{6}(2\delta - 3k + E[k|N] + 3sk + s \cdot E[k|N])\right]^2 \tag{5.62}$$

and under non-disclosure to

$$\phi \cdot \left[\frac{1}{6}\left(2\delta - 2E[k|N] + 4sE[k|N]\right)\right]^2 \quad (5.63)$$

Comparing equation (5.63) with (5.62) and considering that $s = [0; 0.5]$, it can be concluded that the price component will be higher under full disclosure than under non-disclosure of the private information if $k < E[k|N]$. Given that the $E[k|N] = 1.5$ under non-disclosure for $k = [1; 2]$, small k or good private information on unit costs should be disclosed first.[304] A full disclosure equilibrium could thus only exist for a high probability of acquisition and if for k = 2 the expected gain to the seller under full disclosure was higher than under non-disclosure. Because of the competitive damages this is never the case, so no full disclosure equilibrium can exist.

Competitive damages occur if the seller discloses the private information on unit costs and the acquisition fails. Therefore the effect of disclosure on the product market is always negative. For sufficiently small probabilities of the supplier acquiring the seller, non-disclosure equilibria will exist because the profit component of the expected gain of the seller will dominate any price effect. Figure 5-8 shows an illustrative example for a non-disclosure equilibrium. Graphed is the expected gain difference curve T, which shows the difference between the expected gain to the seller under disclosure and non-disclosure. If the expected gain difference curve is negative, the expected gain to the seller is higher under non-disclosure than under disclosure. Again, unit costs are given on the horizontal axis, while the expected gain difference to the seller is given on the vertical axis.

Table 5-5 shows different scenarios for different values of the input parameters synergy "s", competitive damages "c", and demand "δ" (columns 1-3). The fourth column shows the upper bound of the non-disclosure interval, that results based on the level of the input parameters. The acquisition probability non-disclosure region is given in the last column. For no synergies, low competitive damages, and very high demand, the private information on unit costs will not be disclosed for a small number of acquisition probabilities (row 1). If the acquisition probability is larger than 2.91%, partial disclosure of the private information results.

The smallest non-disclosure region (row 1) results if synergies and competitive damages are low and demand is high. The non-disclosure region becomes largest for high synergy, high competitive damages, and high demand (rows 11-12). Thereby, the level of de-

[304] This effect can also be examined for the illustrative partial disclosure equilibrium example in the next section.

mand has only a small effect on the non-disclosure region (rows 4 and 6, and rows 9, and 11-12). In addition, the level of synergies has only a small effect on the non-disclosure region (rows 3-5 and rows 8-9). The one variable with a large effect on the non-disclosure region is the level of competitive damages (rows 1 and 7, rows 2 and 3, rows 5 and 9, and rows 6 and 10). The non-disclosure region increases with the level of competitive damages.

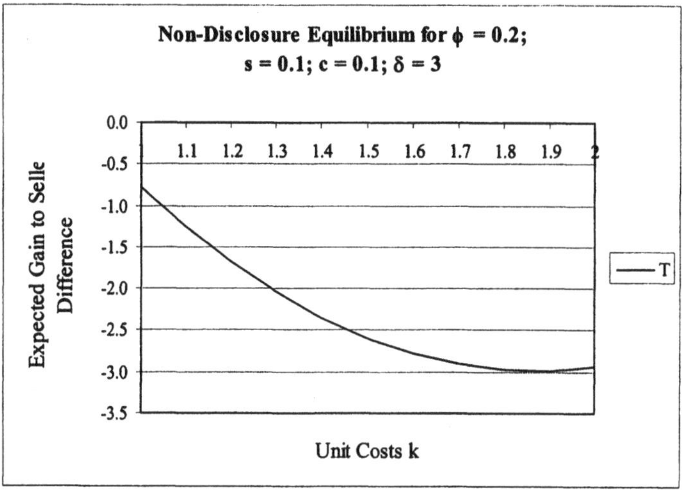

Figure 5-8: An Example of a Non-Disclosure Equilibrium for the Disclosure Decision to the Supplier

	s	c	δ	ND Interval
1	0	0.01	1000000000	ϕ = [0; 0.0291]
2	0	0.01	3	ϕ = [0; 0.0346]
3	0	0.1	3	ϕ = [0; 0.2548]
4	0.3	0.1	3	ϕ = [0; 0.2599]
5	0.5	0.1	3	ϕ = [0; 0.2869]
6	0.3	0.1	150	ϕ = [0; 0.2993]
7	0	0.2	1000000000	ϕ = [0; 0.3750]
8	0	0.2	3	ϕ = [0; 0.3932]
9	0.5	0.2	3	ϕ = [0; 0.4326]
10	0.3	0.2	150	ϕ = [0; 0.4605]
11	0.5	0.2	150	ϕ = [0; 0.5435]
12	0.5	0.2	1000000000	ϕ = [0; 0.5455]

Table 5-5: Non-Disclosure Equilibria as a Function of Synergy, Competitive Damages, and Demand

That is, for high competitive damages, there is a pronounced negative effect on profit of the seller and less disclosure will result.

For a sufficiently large probability of the supplier acquiring the seller, partial disclosure results. In the next section, an example for a partial disclosure equilibrium will be shown for a specific level of synergies, competitive damages, demand, and probability of acquisition.

5.6.2.1.3 Illustrative Examples for Partial Disclosure Equilibrium

This section gives an example that shows the properties of a partial disclosure equilibrium as determined under Theorem 2(iii) for two different cases.

First, assume that the level of competitive damages, synergies, and probability of acquisition is high, with c = 0.2, s = 0.4, and $\phi = 0.9$. Additionally, the demand is a) assumed low with $\delta = 3$ and b) assumed high with $\delta = 150$. From the expected gain difference curve in equation (5.61) its second derivative can be derived as

$$\frac{\partial^2 T}{\partial k^2} = 2\left[9\left(\phi(1-s)^2 + (1-\phi)(2+c)c\right)\right] \tag{5.64}$$

For s = 0.4, c = 0.2, and $\phi = 0.9$ equation (5.64) is positive with

$$\frac{\partial^2 T}{\partial k^2} = 6.624 > 0$$

It follows that the profit curve T is convex, and the k where T = 0 (see Figure 5-9) can be determined as follows.

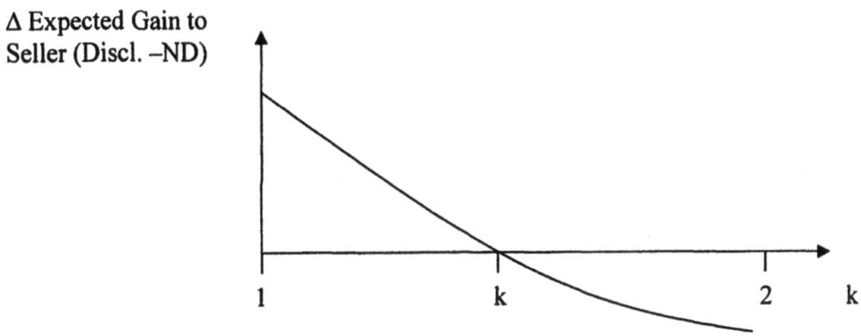

Figure 5-9: Sample Partial Disclosure Equilibrium

The expected value of unit costs k given non-disclosure must be between k and 2 and is derived as

$$E[k|N]=\left[\frac{1}{2}k^2\right]_k^2\cdot\left(\frac{1}{2-k}\right)=\frac{2-0.5k^2}{2-k} \qquad \text{with } k=[1;2]$$

Since k is identically distributed, i.e. f(k) = 1 for all k. Entering this expected value and the values for s, c, δ, and φ in equation (5.61) results in

$$T(\delta=3)=3.312k^2-\left(20.16+4.512\cdot\left(\frac{2-0.5k^2}{2-k}\right)\right)k+1.584\cdot\left(\frac{2-0.5k^2}{2-k}\right)^2 +19.2\cdot\left(\frac{2-0.5k^2}{2-k}\right) \tag{5.65}$$

$$T(\delta=150)=3.312k^2-\left(1008+4.512\cdot\left(\frac{2-0.5k^2}{2-k}\right)\right)k+1.584\cdot\left(\frac{2-0.5k^2}{2-k}\right)^2 +960\cdot\left(\frac{2-0.5k^2}{2-k}\right) \tag{5.66}$$

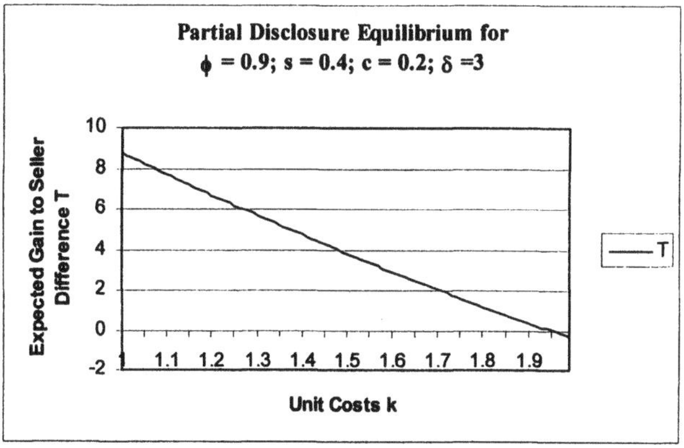

Figure 5-10: Partial Disclosure Equilibrium for High Probability of Acquisition, Synergies, Competitive Damages, and Low Demand.

Solving equation (5.65) with low demand (δ = 3) for the k for which T = 0, results in $k=1.9505$ and $E[k|N]=1.9753$ (values rounded). The partial disclosure equilibrium for this convex expected gain difference curve is graphed in Figure 5-10. For high demand ($\delta = 150$), solving equation (5.66) for the k for which T = 0, results in $k = 1.8202$ and $E[k|N] = 1.9101$ (values rounded). The partial disclosure equilibrium for this convex expected gain difference curve is graphed in Figure 5-11.

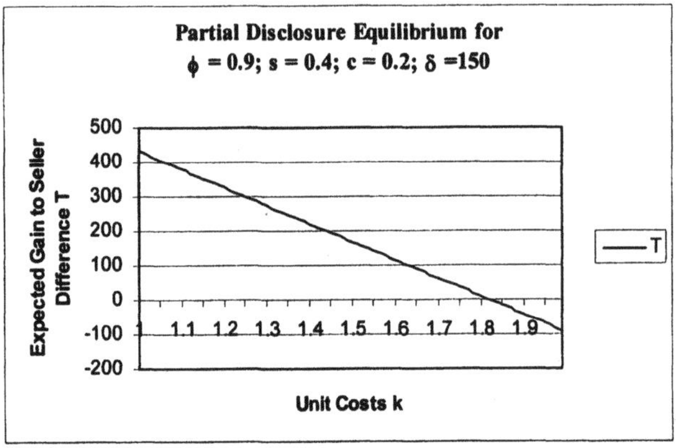

Figure 5-11: Partial Disclosure Equilibrium for High Probability of Acquisition, Synergies, Competitive Damages, and Demand.

Second, assume that the level of competitive damages, and demand is low with $c = 0.01$ and $\delta = 3$. The probability of the supplier acquiring the seller is high, with $\phi = 0.9$. Additionally, synergies are 1) assumed low with s = 0 and 2) assumed high with s = 0.4. By entering these values into the expected gain difference curve in equation (5.61) and its second derivative in equation (5.64), it can be concluded that the expected gain difference curve T is convex. For c = 0.01, $\delta = 3$, s = 0 or s = 0.4, and $\phi = 0.9$ the second derivative is positive with

$$\frac{\partial^2 T}{\partial k^2}(s = 0) = 0.0362 > 0 .$$

$$\frac{\partial^2 T}{\partial k^2}(s = 0.4) = 5.8682 > 0$$

To find the level of unit cost where T = 0 (see Figure 5-9), enter $E[k|N] = \frac{2 - 0.5k^2}{2 - k}$ and the values for s, c, δ, and ϕ in equation T. This results in

$$T(s=0.4) = 8.1181 \cdot k^2 - \left[32.4360 + 5.3999 \cdot \left(\frac{2-0.5k^2}{2-k}\right)\right]k - 2.7020 \cdot \left(\frac{2-0.5k^2}{2-k}\right)^2 + 32.3880 \cdot \left(\frac{2-0.5k^2}{2-k}\right) \quad (5.67)$$

$$T(s=0.4) = 2.9341 \cdot k^2 - \left[19.476 + 4.536 \cdot \left(\frac{2-0.5k^2}{2-k}\right)\right]k + 1.6180 \cdot \left(\frac{2-0.5k^2}{2-k}\right)^2 + 19.428 \cdot \left(\frac{2-0.5k^2}{2-k}\right) \quad (5.68)$$

Solving equation (5.67) with no synergies for the level of k for which T = 0, results in $k = 1.9942$ and $E[k|N] = 1.9971$ (values rounded). The partial disclosure equilibrium for this convex expected gain difference curve is graphed in Figure 5-12. For high synergies (s = 0.4), solving equation (5.68) for the k for which T = 0, results in k = 1.9962 and $E[k|N] = 1.9981$ (values rounded). The partial disclosure equilibrium for this convex expected gain difference curve is graphed in Figure 5-13.

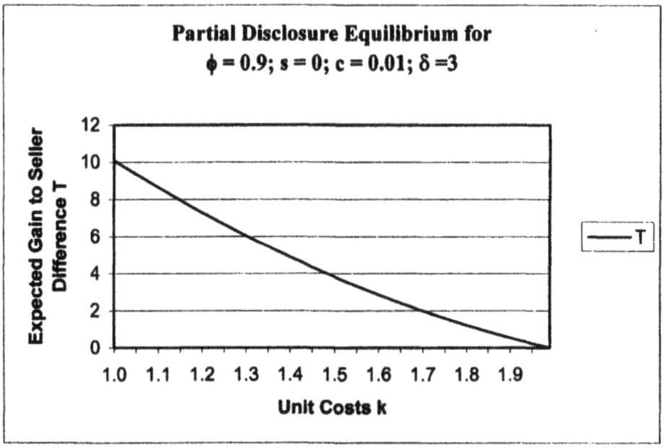

Figure 5-12: Partial Disclosure Equilibrium for High Probability of Acquisition,but for Low Synergies, Competitive Damages, and Demand.

One general inference that can be drawn for partial disclosure equilibria is that with an increase in the probability of acquisition, all else equal, the full disclosure interval within the partial disclosure equilibrium increases while the non-disclosure interval decreases. That can be explained by the fact that with a larger probability of acquisition the weight of the profit effect if the acquisition fails becomes reduced, while the price effect becomes more and more important. That is, since the effect of competitive damages becomes smaller with larger acquisition probability, the full disclosure region within the partial disclosure equilibrium increases with an increase in the probability of acquisition.

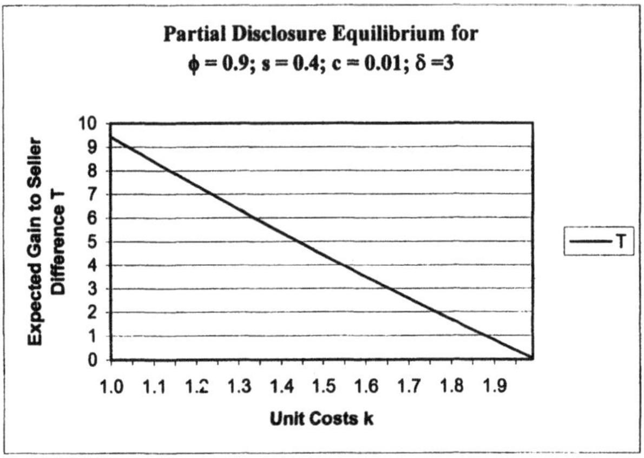

Figure 5-13: Partial Disclosure Equilibrium for High Probability of Acquisition and Synergies, but for Low Competitive Damages, and Demand.

Comparing Figure 5-10 with Figure 5-11 shows that a variation in the level of demand has an effect on the partial disclosure equilibrium.[305] The area of non-disclosure of unfavorable private information on unit costs increases with higher demand. That is, the higher the level of demand (all else equal), the smaller the full disclosure interval within the partial disclosure equilibrium. Comparing Figure 5-12 with Figure 5-13 shows that the level of synergies has a very small effect on the partial disclosure equilibrium. The effect of synergies on the partial disclosure equilibrium is especially small because the probability of acquisition is high. With lower acquisition probability, the effect of a variation of synergies might become somewhat larger.[306] In respect to competitive damages, comparing Figure 5-10 with Figure 5-13 shows that the full disclosure interval within the partial disclosure equilibrium increases

[305] Note that the exemplified variation in demand is rather large. A smaller variation in demand will lead to a smaller effect on the partial disclosure equilibrium.

[306] The effect of a variation of synergies also becomes larger, if the assumed synergy interval is extended, e.g. to s = [0; 1). However, the interval of synergy benefits with s = [0; 0.5] was set to reflect real-world conditions and could easily be extended if necessary.

with lower competitive damages. Again, this effect is likely to be especially small when the acquisition probability is large, and might become somewhat larger with a lower acquisition probability.

An additional inference is that the expected gain difference curves are downward sloping. That means that the disclosure of private information on unit costs will first be recommended for a low level of unit costs. Recall that for $k = [1; 2]$ a level of $k = 1$ implies very favorable private information about unit costs. That is, the buyer would be able to produce at a very low unit cost, thereby increasing his profit. Disclosure of that fact if the buyer overestimates actual unit costs, i.e. $E[k|N] > k$, will increase the price component upon disclosure, thereby resulting in a disclosure recommendation for a low level of unit costs for a sufficiently high acquisition probability. With an increasing probability of acquisition that full disclosure region within the partial disclosure equilibrium widens and the last level of unit costs that will be disclosed is close to $k = 2$. Since there is no full disclosure equilibrium for $\phi = [0; 1)$, a level of unit costs of $k = 2$ will never be disclosed to the supplier under uncertainty.

5.6.2.1.4 Special Disclosure Cases

If the special case of certainty were to occur, i.e. $\phi = 1$, the disclosure recommendation to the seller would be full disclosure for all $k = [1; 2]$. If the seller is certain that the supplier will acquire his company, only the price effect will be considered. That is, the profit of the seller in the product market if there is no acquisition is irrelevant. Based on equation (5.60), the seller will disclose all private information on unit costs if

$$\left(\frac{1}{3}\delta - \frac{1}{2}(1-s)k + \frac{1}{6}(1+s)\cdot E[k]\right)^2 > \left(\frac{\delta - (1-2s)\cdot E[k]}{3}\right)^2$$

or $-\frac{1}{2}k + \frac{1}{2}sk > -\frac{1}{2}E[k] + \frac{1}{2}sE[k] \Rightarrow$

$$\frac{1}{2}(s-1)k > \frac{1}{2}(s-1)E[k] \qquad \left| \div \frac{1}{2}(s-1) \right. \quad < 0 \text{ for } s \leq 0.5$$

$$k < E[k]$$

That is, the seller should only fully disclose his private information on unit costs, if actual unit costs were smaller than what the supplier expects. However, the reaction of the supplier upon observing non-disclosure has to be taken into account. The supplier who holds rational expectations would conclude from non-disclosure of the private information under certainty that he underestimated unit costs, i.e. $E[k|N] < k$. He would increase his estimate of unit costs. If the seller still did not disclose the private information, the supplier would again increase his estimate of unit costs. This process would continue until all k, even k = 2, is disclosed. Therefore, a full disclosure equilibrium exists for the case of certainty.[307] Taking into account the expectations of the vertical buyer, the seller should fully disclose all private information on unit costs for all $k = [1; 2]$, if it is certain that the supplier will acquire the seller.

Another special case that might occur is the case of no competitive damages. Based on equation (5.60) and for c = 0, the seller will disclose all private information on unit costs to the supplier if

$$\phi \cdot \left[\left(\frac{1}{3}\delta - \frac{1}{2}(1-s)k + \frac{1}{6}(1+s) \cdot E[k]\right)^2\right] + (1-\phi) \cdot \left[\left(\frac{1}{3}\delta - \frac{1}{2}k + \frac{1}{6}E[k]\right)^2\right]$$

$$> \phi \cdot \left[\left(\frac{\delta - (1-2s) \cdot E[k]}{3}\right)^2\right] + (1-\phi) \cdot \left(\frac{1}{3}\delta - \frac{1}{2}k + \frac{1}{6}E[k]\right)^2 \Rightarrow$$

$$\left(\frac{1}{3}\delta - \frac{1}{2}(1-s)k + \frac{1}{6}(1+s) \cdot E[k]\right) > \left(\frac{\delta - (1-2s) \cdot E[k]}{3}\right)^2$$

$$\rightarrow k < E[k]$$

If there are no competitive damages, the profit of the seller in the product market if the acquisition fails will remain the same both under disclosure and under non-disclosure of the private information on unit costs. Therefore only the effect of the disclosure of private information on the purchase price has to be considered. As under certainty and based on the same reasoning a full disclosure equilibrium results. Taking into account the expectations of the vertical buyer, the seller should fully disclose all information on unit costs for all $k = [1; 2]$, if there are no competitive damages or potential misappropriation of the private information with the supplier as a buyer.

[307] See Milgrom (1981) for voluntary disclosure of verifiable information and Crawford and Sobel (1982) and Gigler (1994) for voluntary disclosure of unverifiable information.

In the next section, the decision about disclosing private information on unit costs to the customer of the seller will be made. Depending on the probability of acquisition and the level of private information k, the seller will either not disclose any information or partially disclose some private information to the customer.

5.6.2.2 Disclosure to the Customer

5.6.2.2.1 Disclosure Decision

Customers as vertical buyers (VBC) derive their synergies from an increase in demand by "d". This increase in demand is generated because the customer obtains all of his products from the seller if he acquires the target. If the customer already obtained all his products from the seller, his synergies would be $d = 0$. But if any part of his products that were obtained from the strategic buyer before the acquisition are now obtained from the seller, then $d > 0$. Since in reality the competing firms will have multiple customers, a likely interval for synergy benefits of $d = [0; 0.5]$ is set. If the customer does not acquire the seller but the private information on unit costs was disclosed, competitive damages may result. As described before, competitive damages through customers may reduce profits because of lower demand. Let the lower demand be equal for both seller and strategic buyer, and let it be denoted with "h" and defined by $h = (0; 0.2]$. Additionally, let demand be $\delta \geq 2.5$ and the probability of the supplier acquiring the seller be $\phi = [0; 1)$. The issue now is for which probability of acquisition the seller should disclose the private information on unit costs to his customer.

The investment banker will recommend to the seller to disclose his private information for any ϕ, for which

$$\begin{aligned} &\phi \cdot \left(\frac{1}{3}(1+3d)\delta - \frac{1}{2}k + \frac{1}{6}E[k]\right)^2 + (1-\phi)\cdot\left(\frac{1}{3}(1-h)\delta - \frac{1}{2}k + \frac{1}{6}E[k]\right)^2 \\ &\quad > \phi\left(\frac{(1+3d)\delta - E[k]}{3}\right)^2 + (1-\phi)\left(\frac{1}{3}\delta - \frac{1}{2}k + \frac{1}{6}E[k]\right)^2 \end{aligned} \tag{5.69}$$

The left hand side of inequality (5.69) shows the expected gain to the seller for the full disclosure case, while the right hand side of the inequality shows the expected gain to the seller for the non-disclosure of private information on unit costs k.[308] In the disclosure case, the private information on unit costs is fully disclosed to the supplier. The competitor (HB), on the other hand, does not know the private information on unit costs (E[k]) but knows the level of synergies. Both horizontal buyer and seller know the level of competitive damages "h" that will arise if the private information on unit costs is disclosed to the customer but the acquisition fails (vertical buyers synergy and damages assumption).

On the right hand side of the inequality (non-disclosure case), the customer does not know the private information on unit cost, which is given by E[k]. This is the only factor about which the customer as a buyer is uncertain. Because the customer does not have any influence on the production decision of the seller in the non-disclosure case, the last term of the inequality gives the base profit of the seller in the product market. Equation (5.69) reduces to:

$$\frac{1}{3}\phi\delta E[k]-\phi d\delta k-\frac{1}{3}\phi\delta k+\phi d\delta E[k]-\frac{2}{9}h\delta^2+\frac{1}{9}h^2\delta^2+\frac{1}{3}h\delta k-\frac{1}{9}h\delta E[k]+\frac{2}{9}\phi h\delta^2$$
$$-\frac{1}{9}\phi h^2\delta^2-\frac{1}{3}\phi h\delta k+\frac{1}{9}\phi h\delta E[k]-\frac{1}{9}\phi E[k]^2+\frac{1}{4}\phi k^2-\frac{1}{6}\phi E[k]k+\frac{1}{36}\phi E[k]^2>0 \Rightarrow$$

$$\begin{aligned}&\frac{1}{4}\phi k^2-\frac{1}{6}\left[2(\phi(3d+1+h)-h)\cdot\delta+\phi E[k]\right]\cdot k-\frac{1}{12}\phi E[k]^2\\&\quad+\frac{1}{9}\delta\cdot\left[(\phi-1)h+3(1+3d)\phi\right]\cdot E[k]+\frac{1}{9}(\phi-1)(2-h)\cdot h\cdot\delta^2>0\end{aligned} \tag{5.70}$$

Based on equation (5.70), the expected gain difference curve T that shows the difference between expected gain to the seller in the disclosure case and in the non-disclosure case is given by

$$\begin{aligned}T=&\frac{1}{4}\phi k^2-\frac{1}{6}\left[2(\phi(3d+1+h)-h)\cdot\delta+\phi E[k]\right]\cdot k-\frac{1}{12}\phi E[k]^2\\&+\frac{1}{9}\delta\cdot\left[(\phi-1)h+3(1+3d)\phi\right]\cdot E[k]+\frac{1}{9}(\phi-1)(2-h)\cdot h\cdot\delta^2\end{aligned} \tag{5.71}$$

If the expected gain difference curve is positive, i.e. T > 0, the expected gain to the seller in the disclosure case is larger than in the non-disclosure case. In addition, if the expected gain difference curve is negative, i.e. T < 0, the expected gain to the seller in the disclosure case is smaller than the profit in the non-disclosure case.

---

[308] Note that in the derivation of equation (5.69) the subscript "i", which indicates that there may be multiple customers, was omitted. This was done to reduce the clutter in the subsequent calculations. The derived expected gain to the seller may easily be applied to multiple customers with different synergy potential, if necessary.

5.6.2.2.2 Theorem 3

Theorem 3: Given that

1) *The seller has private information about unit costs k, which is unknown to the customer and the competitor;*
2) *The customer as a vertical buyer is able to derive synergy "d" from the acquisition of the seller;*
3) *The seller may incur competitive damages "h" if the private information is disclosed to the customer and the acquisition fails;*
4) *The probability of acquisition "ϕ" is a constant;*

   then

(i) There is no full disclosure equilibrium for any probability of acquisition, with $\phi = [0;1)$.

(ii) A non-disclosure equilibrium exists for low to average probabilities of acquisition, i.e. if

$$0 \leq \phi \leq \frac{(-3+4\delta-2h\delta)\cdot h\delta}{3(3d+1-h)\delta+2h\delta^2(2-h)-3.375}$$

(iii) A partial disclosure equilibrium exists for average to high probabilities of acquisition, i.e. if $\frac{(-3+4\delta-2h\delta)\cdot h\delta}{3(3d+1-h)\delta+2h\delta^2(2-h)-3.375} < \phi < 1$

The proof is in the Appendix. It is reasonable that for uncertainty, i.e. for $\phi < 1$, no full disclosure equilibrium can exist. If there are competitive damages, i.e. $h > 0$, the profit component of the expected gain of the seller is always smaller under disclosure than under non-disclosure. Therefore, there is always non-disclosure of private information for low levels of acquisition probability. Hereby, the range of the non-disclosure interval will increase with an increasing level of competitive damages. That is, with higher competitive damages there will be non-disclosure of the private information for a larger acquisition probability interval. For private information to be disclosed, the probability of acquisition has to be sufficiently high so that the price effect can dominate the profit effect. The price component of the expected gain to the seller based on equation (5.69) and under full disclosure becomes

$$\phi\cdot\left(\frac{1}{3}(1+3d)\delta-\frac{1}{2}k+\frac{1}{6}E[k]\right)^2 \tag{5.72}$$

and under non-disclosure

$$\phi\left(\frac{(1+3d)\delta - E[k]}{3}\right)^2 \tag{5.73}$$

Comparing equation (5.72) with (5.73) shows that the price component will be higher under full disclosure than under non-disclosure of the private information if $k < E[k|N]$. Given that $E[k|N] = 1.5$ under non-disclosure for $k = [1; 2]$, low k or favorable private information on unit costs should be disclosed first.[309] A full disclosure equilibrium could thus only exist for a high probability of acquisition and if for $k = 2$ the expected gain to the seller under full disclosure was higher than under non-disclosure. Because of the competitive damages this is never the case, so no full disclosure equilibrium can exist.

Competitive damages may occur if the seller discloses the private information on unit costs and the acquisition fails. Therefore, the effect of disclosure on the product market is always negative. For sufficiently small probabilities of the customer acquiring the seller, non-disclosure equilibria will exist because the negative profit component of the expected gain of the seller will dominate any price effect (see Figure 5-14 for an illustrative example).

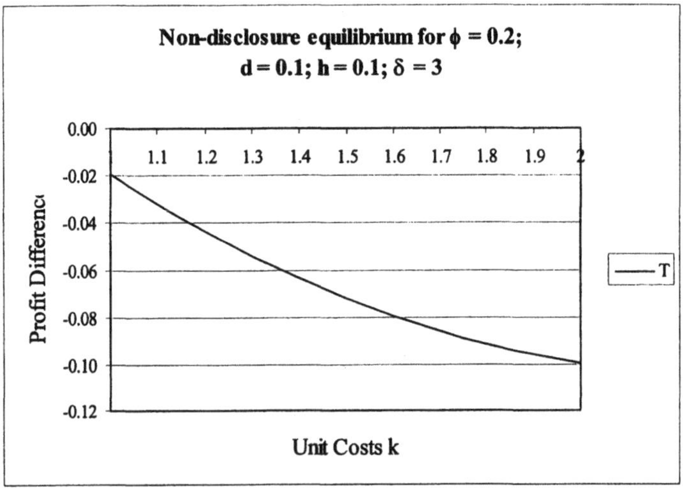

Figure 5-14: An Example for a Non-Disclosure Equilibrium for the Disclosure Decision to the Customer

[309] This effect can also be examined for the illustrative partial disclosure equilibrium example in the next section.

Table 5-6 shows different scenarios for different values of synergies, competitive damages, and demand (columns 1-3). The fourth column shows the upper bound of the non-disclosure interval that results based on the level of the input parameters. The acquisition probability non-disclosure region is given in the last column. The smallest non-disclosure region (row 1) results if synergies are high and competitive damages and demand are low. The non-disclosure region becomes largest for a high level of demand (row 11 and 12). Thereby, both the level of synergies (rows 2, 3, and 6 and rows 9 and 10) and the level of competitive damages (rows 1, 2, and 4) have an effect on the non-disclosure region. With higher synergies, all else constant, the non-disclosure region decreases (the non-disclosure region decreases from $\phi = [0; 0.3094]$ for no synergies to $\phi = [0; 0.1164]$ for high synergies with h = 0.1 and $\delta = 3$). The seller will disclose more information for a high synergy level, holding everything else constant. That is, with high synergies disclosure will occur for a lower level of acquisition probability. Because of the higher synergy benefits, the price component will outweigh the profit component for a larger number of ϕ.

	d	h	δ	ND Equilibrium
1	0.5	0.01	3	$\phi = [0; 0.0138]$
2	0.5	0.1	3	$\phi = [0; 0.1164]$
3	0.3	0.1	3	$\phi = [0; 0.1551]$
4	0.5	0.2	3	$\phi = [0; 0.1966]$
5	0.5	0.2	3	$\phi = [0; 0.2543]$
6	0	0.1	3	$\phi = [0; 0.3094]$
7	0.5	0.2	8	$\phi = [0; 0.4216]$
8	0.5	0.2	20	$\phi = [0; 0.6531]$
9	0.5	0.2	150	$\phi = [0; 0.9349]$
10	0	0.2	150	$\phi = [0; 0.9730]$
11	0	0.2	1,000,000,000	$\phi = [0; 1.0000]$
12	0.5	0.1	1,000,000,000	$\phi = [0; 1.0000]$

Table 5-6: Non-Disclosure Equilibria for Customer Depending on Synergy, Competitive Damages, and Demand

With higher competitive damages, all else constant, the non-disclosure region increases (the non-disclosure region increases from $\phi = [0; 0.0138]$ for no competitive damages to $\phi = [0; 0.1966]$ for high competitive damages with d = 0.5 and $\delta = 3$). The seller will disclose less information for a high level of competitive damages, holding everything else constant. That is, for more levels of acquisition probability non-disclosure will occur. Because of the higher competitive damages, the profit component will dominate the price component for a larger number of ϕ, resulting in less disclosure.

The level of demand has a large effect on the disclosure decision of the seller. With increasing demand, the non-disclosure region increases (rows 5 and 7-9, and rows 2 and 12). For a very high level of demand, only non-disclosure equilibria result for all levels of $\phi = [0;1)$. The reasoning here is that with high demand, the effect of the private information on price becomes negligible, while the effect of competitive damages may be large. Therefore, non-disclosure results for a very high level of demand. For a lower level of demand, the non-disclosure region becomes smaller. For a high probability of acquisition disclosure now becomes more advantageous than non-disclosure, i.e. the price effect dominates the profit effect for high levels of ϕ.

For a sufficiently large probability of the supplier acquiring the seller and not a very high level of demand, partial disclosure results. In the next section, sample partial disclosure equilibria will be shown for specific levels of synergies, competitive damages, demand, and probability of acquisition.

5.6.2.2.3 Illustrative Examples for Partial Disclosure Equilibrium

Two examples can show the properties of a partial disclosure equilibrium as determined under Theorem 3(iii).

First, assume that the level of synergies and demand is low, with $d = 0.1$ and $\delta = 3$. Additionally, the probability of the strategic buyer acquiring the seller and competitive damages are average with $\phi = 0.4$ and $h = 0.1$. From equation (5.71) the second derivative of the expected gain difference function T is determined as

$$\frac{\partial^2 T}{\partial k^2} = \frac{1}{2}\phi$$

It follows that the expected gain difference curve T is convex for all levels of probability of acquisition. Therefore, a partial disclosure equilibrium with a downward sloping expected gain difference curve T must look similar to Figure 5.15.

Next, the level of unit costs k where $T = 0$ will be derived. The expected value of unit costs k given non-disclosure must be between k and 2 and is obtained as

$$E[k|N] = \left[\frac{1}{2}k^2\right]_k^2 \cdot \left(\frac{1}{2-k}\right) = \frac{2-0.5k^2}{2-k} \qquad \text{with } k = [1; 2],$$

since k is identically distributed, i.e. f(k) = 1 for all k.

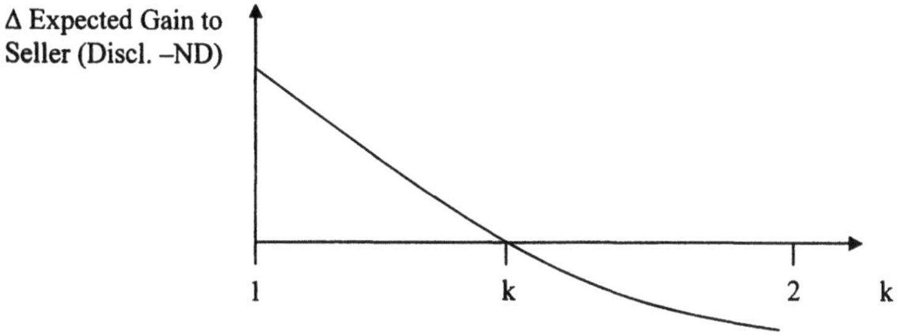

Figure 5-15: Sample Partial Disclosure Equilibrium of Expected Gain Difference Function

Entering this expected value and the values for d, h, δ, and φ in the T function from equation (5.71) results in

$$T = 0.1k^2 - \left(0.46 + \frac{1}{15} \cdot \left(\frac{2-0.5k^2}{2-k}\right)\right)k - \frac{1}{30} \cdot \left(\frac{2-0.5k^2}{2-k}\right)^2 + 0.5 \cdot \left(\frac{2-0.5k^2}{2-k}\right) - 0.114 \quad (5.74)$$

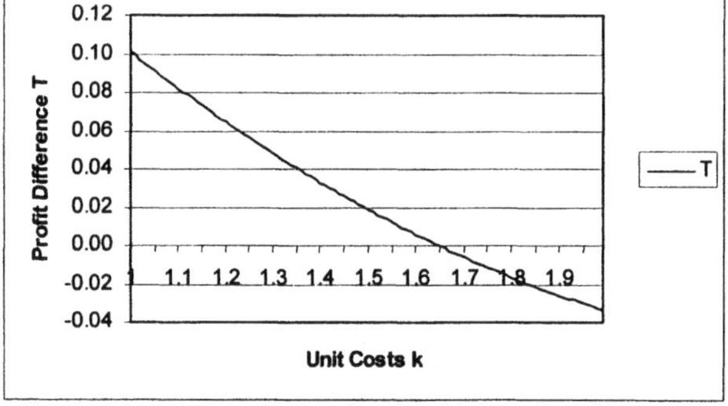

Figure 5-16: Partial Disclosure Equilibrium for Average Acquisition Probability and Competitive Damages, and for Low Synergies and Demand

Solving equation (5.74) for the specific level of unit costs for which there is no expected gain difference between disclosure and non-disclosure, i.e. for T = 0, results in $k = 1.6498$ and $E[k|N] = 1.8249$ (values rounded). The partial disclosure equilibrium for this convex expected gain difference curve is graphed in Figure 5-16.

Second, assume that the level of synergies, competitive damages, and probability of acquisition is high, with $d = 0.5$, $h = 0.2$, $\phi = 0.9$. Additionally, the demand is low with $\delta = 3$. Again, the second derivative is positive, the function is convex, and the expected value of unit costs k given non-disclosure is $E[k|N] = \frac{2-0.5k^2}{2-k}$. Entering this expected value and the values for d, h, δ, and φ in the expected gain difference equation (5.71) results in

$$T = 0.225k^2 - \left(2.23 + 0.15 \cdot \left(\frac{2-0.5k^2}{2-k}\right)\right)k - \frac{3}{40} \cdot \left(\frac{2-0.5k^2}{2-k}\right)^2 + 2.2433 \cdot \left(\frac{2-0.5k^2}{2-k}\right) - 0.036 \qquad (5.75)$$

Solving equation (5.75) for the specific level of unit costs k for which T = 0, results in $k = 1.9884$ and $E[k|N] = 1.9942$ (values rounded). The partial disclosure equilibrium for this convex expected gain difference curve is graphed in Figure 5-17.

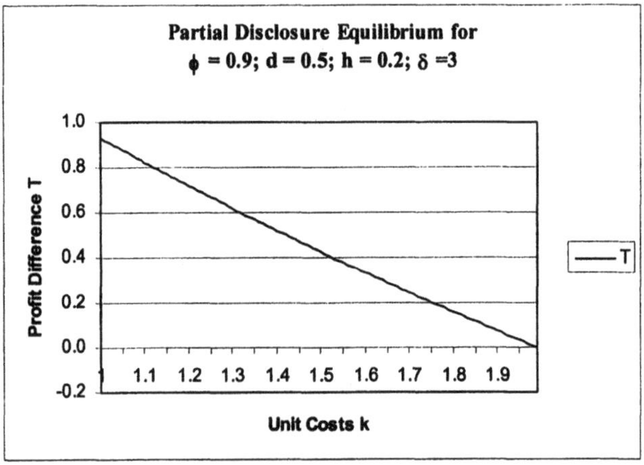

Figure 5-17: Partial Disclosure Equilibrium for High Acquisition Probability, Synergies, and Competitive Damages, and for Low Demand

One general inference that can be drawn for partial disclosure equilibria is that with an increase in the probability of acquisition, all else equal, the full disclosure interval within the partial disclosure equilibrium increases while the non-disclosure interval decreases. That can be explained by the fact that with a larger probability of acquisition the weight of the profit effect if the acquisition fails becomes reduced, while the price effect becomes more and more important. That is, since the effect of competitive damages becomes smaller with larger acquisition probability, the full disclosure region within the partial disclosure equilibrium increases with an increase in the probability of acquisition.

An additional inference is that the expected gain difference curves are downward sloping. That means that the disclosure of private information on unit costs to the customer as to the supplier will first be recommended for a low level of unit costs. That full disclosure region within the partial disclosure equilibrium widens with an increasing probability of acquisition and the last level of unit costs that will be disclosed is close to k = 2. Since there is no full disclosure equilibrium for $\phi = [0; 1)$, a level of unit costs of k = 2 will never be disclosed to the supplier under uncertainty.

5.6.2.2.4 Special Disclosure Cases

If the special case of certainty were to occur, i.e. $\phi = 1$, the disclosure recommendation to the seller would be full disclosure for all $k = [1; 2]$. Reasoning in a manner similar to the disclosure to the supplier as vertical buyer, one can show that the seller will take into account the expectations of his customer; and will be prompted to disclose all private information on unit costs for all $k = [1; 2]$ under certainty. Similarly, if there were no competitive damages, a full disclosure equilibrium would result. Taking into account the expectations of the customer, the seller will be induced to fully disclose all information on unit costs for all $k = [1; 2]$, if there are no competitive damages or potential misappropriation of the private information with the customer as a buyer.

The last special case is the case of certainty about the acquisition failing, i.e. $\phi = 0$. If the seller is certain that the customer will not acquire his company, only the profit effect will be considered. That is, the price effect in the event of the acquisition is irrelevant. For $\phi = 0$, the left hand side of equation (5.69) is always smaller than the right hand side of the equation, since h > 0. That implies that the seller will never disclose his private information on unit costs. That is, for the case of certainty about the acquisition failing, the seller will never disclose any private information on unit costs to the customer as a vertical buyer if competitive damages exist, i.e. if $h > 0$.

5.7 Investment Banker's Recommendation to the Seller

The seller desires to achieve maximum price from the sale of the company. Therefore, the investment banker will recommend a sale to that buyer, from whom the seller can derive the highest expected gain. Depending on the acquisition probability[310] of each buyer, the investment banker will recommend disclosure, partial disclosure, or non-disclosure of the private information on unit costs. To summarize, the expected gain functions under non-disclosure and disclosure of the private information on unit costs are given for the financial buyer, the horizontal strategic buyer, suppliers, and customers.

$$p_{FB} = \left(\frac{1}{3}\delta - \frac{1}{2}k + \frac{1}{6}E[k]\right)^2 - (K_S + \Delta K) \tag{5.14}$$

$$\begin{aligned} g_{HB}(ND) = {} & \frac{\phi_{HB}}{36} \cdot \left[9\left(\delta^2 - 2\delta \cdot E[k] + E[k^2]\right) - 4(\delta - E[k])^2\right] \\ & + \frac{(1-\phi_{HB})}{36}\left[(2\delta - 3k + E[k])^2\right] - (K_S + \phi_{HB} \cdot \Delta K) \end{aligned} \tag{5.40}$$

$$g_{HB}(Discl) = \frac{1}{36}(\phi_{HB} + 4)(\delta - k)^2 - (K_S + \phi_{HB} \cdot \Delta K) \tag{5.41}$$

$$\begin{aligned} g_{VBS,m}(ND) = {} & \phi_{VBS,m} \cdot \left[\left(\frac{\delta - (1 - 2s_m) \cdot E[k]}{3}\right)^2\right] \\ & + (1 - \phi_{VBS,m}) \cdot \left(\frac{1}{3}\delta - \frac{1}{2}k + \frac{1}{6}E[k]\right)^2 - (K_S + \phi_{VBS,m} \cdot \Delta K) \end{aligned} \tag{5.42}$$

$$\begin{aligned} g_{VBS,m}(Discl) = {} & \phi_{VBS,m} \cdot \left[\left(\frac{1}{3}\delta - \frac{1}{2}(1 - s_m)k + \frac{1}{6}(1 + s_m) \cdot E[k]\right)^2\right] \\ & + (1 - \phi_{VBS,m}) \cdot \left[\left(\frac{1}{3}\delta - \frac{1}{2}(1 + c_m)k + \frac{1}{6}(1 - c_m) \cdot E[k]\right)^2\right] - (K_S + \phi_{VBS,m} \cdot \Delta K) \end{aligned} \tag{5.49}$$

[310] Note that in the preceding text the subscripts for the acquisition probabilities of different buyers were omitted to reduce the clutter. In this summary these subscripts are given to show that acquisition probabilities may vary among different buyer types.

$$g_{VBC,i}(ND) = \phi_{VBC,i}\left(\frac{(1+3d_i)\delta - E[k]}{3}\right)^2 + (1-\phi_{VBC,i})\left(\frac{1}{3}\delta - \frac{1}{2}k + \frac{1}{6}E[k]\right)^2 - (K_S + \phi_{VBC,i} \cdot \Delta K) \tag{5.50}$$

$$g_{VBC,i}(Discl) = \phi_{VBC,i} \cdot \left(\frac{1}{3}(1+3d_i)\delta - \frac{1}{2}k + \frac{1}{6}E[k]\right)^2 + (1-\phi_{VBC,i}) \cdot \left(\frac{1}{3}(1-h_i)\delta - \frac{1}{2}k + \frac{1}{6}E[k]\right)^2 - (K_S + \phi_{VBC,i} \cdot \Delta K) \tag{5.52}$$

Generally, the expected gain functions for different buyers show that the expected gain to the seller increases with a higher level of demand. The expected gain to the seller also increases with better private information on unit cost for a given probability of acquisition. In respect to the expected value of unit costs under non-disclosure, there is a trade off between a profit and a price effect. The price effect implies that if strategic buyers overestimate unit costs, i.e. $E[k] < k$, then these buyers bid a higher price for the target. The profit effect only takes the competitor's expected value of unit costs into account. If the competitor underestimated unit costs, i.e. $E[k] > k$, he would produce less, thereby increasing the profit of the selling firm.

Table 5-7 shows disclosure recommendations for different buyers and different input parameters.[311] Input parameters are given in columns 1-9 with the level of demand, the level of unit cost, the buyer-specific probability of acquisition, and synergies and competitive damages for both supplier and customer. Additionally, the header row gives the specified intervals for the different input parameters. For instance, unit costs are defined to range from 1 to 2. Thereby, low private information on unit costs (or $k = 1$) is favorable information, whereas high private information on unit costs (or $k = 2$) is unfavorable. The level of unit costs is varied in column two, which results in different information disclosure and sale recommendations.

The upper bounds of the acquisition probability for disclosure, partial disclosure, and non-disclosure intervals from Theorems 1-3 for the strategic buyers are given in columns 10-15. For demand $\delta = 3$ (row 1) for instance, the lower disclosure interval for the horizontal strategic buyer is $\phi = [0; 0.167)$, and the upper partial disclosure interval is $\phi = [0.346; 0.375]$.

[311] For these illustrations, only one supplier and one customer are considered. The examples could easily be extended to multiple suppliers and multiple customers. This extension was not undertaken here, because it would complicate sample calculations unnecessarily without providing more insight.

1	2	3	4	5	6	7	8	9	10	11	12	13	14	15	16	17	18
			Supplier			Customer			Upper Bound ϕ of the						HB Discl Decision	VBS Discl Decision	VBC Discl Decision
δ	k	ϕ_{HB}	ϕ_{VBS}	s	c	ϕ_{VBC}	d	h	Discl. Interval	PD Interval	ND Interval	PD Interval	ND Interval	ND Interval			
>=2.5	[1;2]	[0;1]	[0;1]	[0;0.5]	]0;0.2]	[0;1]	[0;0.5]	]0;0.2]	HB				VBS	VBC			
3	1	0.3	0.39	0.01	0.2	0.25	0.08	0.15	16.7%	22.1%	34.6%	37.5%	39.2%	31.9%	ND	ND	ND
4	2	0.28	0.2	0.1	0.1	0.3	0.02	0.1	21.9%	24.7%	32.3%	34.2%	25.0%	34.3%	*ND*	ND	ND
150	1	0.9	0.9	0.4	0.2	0.8	0.02	0.1	28.5%	28.5%	28.6%	28.7%	49.8%	94.7%	*Discl*	PD (Discl)	ND
4	1	0.3	0.2	0.5	0.15	0.15	0.1	0.2	21.9%	24.7%	32.3%	34.2%	39.8%	42.7%	ND	*ND*	ND
3	1.4	0.9	0.9	0.4	0.01	0.9	0.01	0.2	16.7%	22.1%	34.6%	37.5%	3.7%	44.3%	Discl	*PD (Discl)*	PD (Discl)
150	1	0.9	0.9	0.4	0.2	0.8	0.3	0.2	28.5%	28.5%	28.6%	28.7%	49.8%	95.0%	Discl	PD (Discl)	*ND*
3	1.6	0.4	0.4	0.2	0.2	0.4	0.1	0.1	16.7%	22.1%	34.6%	37.5%	38.8%	23.2%	Discl	PD (ND)	*PD (Discl)*

Table 5-7: Disclosure Recommendation for Different Buyers Depending on δ, k, ϕ, s, c, d, and h

1	2	3	4	5	6	7	8	9	10	11	12	13	14	15	16	17	18	19
			FB	HB			VBS				VBC				FB	HB	VBS	VBC
δ	k	ΔK	E[k]	ϕ_{HB}	E[k]	[k^2]	ϕ_{VBS}	E[k]	s	c	ϕ_{VBC}	E[k]	d	h	g(FB)	g(HB)	g(VBS)	g(VBC)
>=2.5	[1;2]		[1;2]	[0;1]	[1;2]	[1;4]	[0;1]	[1;2]	[0;0.5]	]0;0.2]	[0;1]	[1;2]	[0;0.5]	]0;0.2]				
3	1	-0.1	1.5	0.3	1.5	2.33	0.39	1.5	0.01	0.2	0.25	1.5	0.08	0.15	*0.6625*	0.5238	0.4836	0.5838
4	2	0.15	1.5	0.28	1.5	2.33	0.2	1.5	0.1	0.1	0.3	1.5	0.02	0.1	0.1903	*0.4519*	0.4164	0.4434
150	1	50	1.5	0.9	1.5	2.33	0.9	1.8202	0.4	0.2	0.8	1.5	0.02	0.1	2425.06	*2976.80*	2462.68	2660.01
4	1	1	1.5	0.3	1.5	2.33	0.2	1.5	0.5	0.15	0.15	1.5	0.1	0.2	0.1736	0.7882	*1.0944*	1.0757
3	1.4	0.2	1.5	0.9	1.5	2.33	0.9	1.9981	0.4	0.01	0.9	1.9697	0.01	0.2	0.1025	0.1684	*0.8439*	0.2283
150	1	150	1.5	0.9	1.5	2.33	0.9	1.8202	0.4	0.2	0.8	1.5	0.3	0.2	2325.06	2886.80	2372.68	*7519.21*
3	1.6	-0.2	1.5	0.4	1.5	2.33	0.4	1.5197	0.2	0.2	0.4	1.8249	0.1	0.1	0.4025	0.3196	0.3971	*0.4367*

Table 5-8: Expected Gain to the Seller Based on Different Buyers' Bids Depending on δ, k, ΔK, E[k], ϕ, s, c, d, and h

Hereby, the upper bound of the disclosure interval for the strategic buyer only depends on demand, while the disclosure interval for vertical buyers depends on demand, synergies, and competitive damages. Depending on the level of these input parameters, different upper bounds of the disclosure interval result. In line with Theorem 1, the investment banker will recommend full disclosure of the private information to the strategic buyer, if the acquisition probability is within the lower disclosure interval (column 10) or if the acquisition probability is higher than the upper bound of the partial disclosure equilibrium (column 13). Based on Theorems 2 and 3, the investment banker will recommend partial disclosure of the private information to the supplier or the customer, if the acquisition probability is higher than the upper bound of the non-disclosure interval (columns 14 and 15, respectively).

Disclosure recommendations for the strategic buyers are given in columns 16-18. For a strategic buyer (HB) acquisition probability of 30% and a level of demand $\delta = 3$ for instance, the investment banker will recommend non-disclosure to the seller (column 16), because the acquisition probability is within the non-disclosure interval $\phi = (0.221; 0.346)$ (row 1, column 12). Additionally, the investment banker will recommend non-disclosure of the private information both to supplier and customer (column 17-18) for their specified acquisition probabilities (row 1, column 4 and 7), because the upper bound of the non-disclosure interval is 39.2% or 31.9%, respectively. For an HB acquisition probability of 40% (last row, column 3), the seller should fully disclose the private information on unit costs to the strategic buyer (column 13 and 16). For the vertical buyers who have the same acquisition probability, partial disclosure equilibria result (columns 14-15 and 17-18).

Partial disclosure equilibria imply that the private information on unit costs will be disclosed for low levels of unit costs and not disclosed for high levels of unit costs for a given acquisition probability. At what unit cost level the disclosure recommendation changes from disclosure to non-disclosure depends on the level of acquisition probability, the level of demand, and the level of synergies and competitive damages. Additionally, the buyer's expected value of unit costs upon observing non-disclosure must be taken into account.

Figure 5-18 shows a partial disclosure equilibrium for the disclosure decision for the supplier. The difference between the expected gain to the seller from the supplier's bid under disclosure and non-disclosure is depicted by the expected gain difference curve T and its magnitude is given on the vertical axis. If the difference curve T is negative, the expected gain to the seller is higher under non-disclosure than under disclosure of the private information on unit costs. The private information on unit costs with k = [1; 2] is given on the horizontal axis. Figure 5-18 shows that private information on unit costs is first disclosed for favorable levels of unit costs. For the given input parameter combination for the supplier with low to average acquisition probability, synergies, competitive damages, and demand (last row in Table 5-7), the investment banker will recommend non-disclosure of the private information for almost all levels of k. Taking into account what the supplier concludes from the non-disclosure of the private information, the supplier's expected unit costs can be determined as $E[k|N] = 1.5197$.[312]

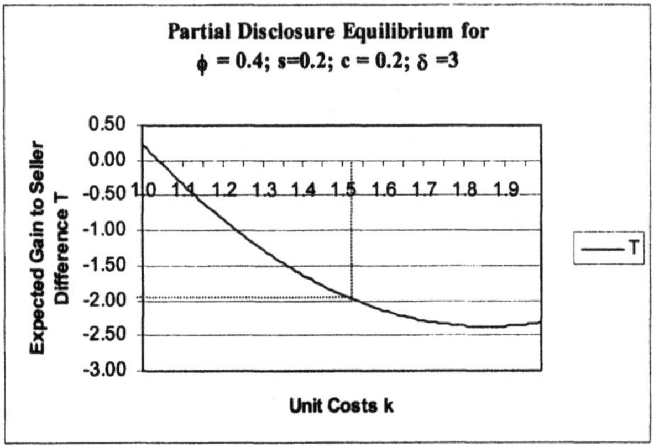

Figure 5-18: Partial Disclosure Equilibrium for the Supplier with Average Acquisition Probability, Low Demand and Synergies, and High Competitive Damages

Table 5-8 shows the expected gain to the seller based on different buyers' bids. Columns 1-2, 5, 8, 10-12 and 14-15 show the input parameters from Table 5-7 in the same combination. In addition to these input parameters, the differential cost of new capital[313] (column 3) and the expected values of unit costs of the buyers (columns 4, 6-7, 9, and 13) have to be taken into account to determine the expected gain to the seller from a buyer's bid (columns 16-19). The supplier data underlying Figure 5-18 is given in the last row of Table 5-8. Column 9 shows the expected value of unit costs upon observing non-disclosure of

[312] Hereby, the supplier's expected unit costs are derived analogous to section 5.6.2.1.3.

[313] The expected gain figures in Table 5-7 are before cost of old capital. Since the cost of old capital (K_S) is the same for all buyers, it does not have to be taken into account for the sale decision. The cost of new capital term however differs between the financial buyer (ΔK) and strategic buyers ($\phi\Delta K$), and thus was accounted for in Table 5-7. Note that different differential cost of new capital (ΔK_i) among buyers could also be considered. Since this modification changes results only insignificantly, it was omitted for ease of interpretation.

$E[k|N]=1.5197$. Since the actual level of unit costs is k = 1.6 (column 2), it can be concluded from Figure 5-18 that the seller should not disclose the private information to the supplier, because the expected gain to the seller is higher under non-disclosure than under disclosure of the private information, i.e. T < 0. This disclosure recommendation to the seller is also formulated in the last row of column 17 in Table 5-7.

The customer on the other hand expects unit costs to be $E[k|N]=1.8249$ (last row of column 13 in Table 5-8) upon observing non-disclosure and for an acquisition probability of 40%, low synergies, and average competitive damages. Figure 5-16 shows that the seller's expected gain from the customer's offer is higher under disclosure than under non-disclosure for low to average levels of unit costs. For a private information level of 1.6 and the given acquisition probability, the investment banker will recommend the seller to disclose the private information on unit costs to the customer (last row of column 18 in Table 5-7).

Once the disclosure recommendation is made (columns 16-18 in Table 5-7), the expected gain to the seller from each buyer's offer is derived. For each combination of acquisition probability, demand, unit costs, cost of new capital, synergies, and competitive damages in Table 5-8, the investment banker will make a sale recommendation for one specific buyer (columns 16-19). The maximum expected gain that can be expected for each input combination is highlighted in Table 5-8, while the respective disclosure strategy for these optimal buyers is highlighted in Table 5-7. Row 1 of Table 5-8 shows a combination of input factors that leads the investment banker to recommend a sale to the financial buyer. If the acquisition probabilities of strategic buyers are low to average, the differential cost of new capital is negative, private information on unit costs is high, and the competitor in the duopoly underestimates unit costs (i.e. the competitor underproduces), the expected gain from a financial buyer's offer becomes high. The expected gain to the seller from the financial buyer's offer becomes highest, if synergies for the strategic buyers are low, competitive damages are high, the differential cost of new capital is negative, and the strategic buyers underestimate unit costs.

The seller's expected gain will become highest for the horizontal strategic buyer, if acquisition probabilities are low, demand is average, private information on unit costs is unfavorable, the strategic buyers are overestimating the private information, synergies for vertical buyers are low and competitive damages about average (row 2). In this case, the investment banker will recommend a sale to the strategic buyer under non-disclosure of the private information. The investment banker will recommend a sale to the strategic buyer under disclosure of the private information, if acquisition probabilities, the demand, and the private information on unit costs are high, but synergies for the customer are low and competitive damages are average (row 3).

The investment banker will recommend a sale to the supplier under non-disclosure of the private information, if acquisition probabilities are low, demand is average, unit costs are favorable and are underestimated, synergies of the supplier are high, while synergies of the customer are low (row 4). The competitive damages derived from the supplier and buyer do not have to be considered in this case, since the disclosure decision to all buyers is to not disclose the private information. On the other hand, the target will be sold to the supplier under disclosure of the private information if the acquisition probability is high, demand and unit costs are average, synergies of the supplier are high while competitive damages are low, and synergies of the customer are low while his competitive damages are high (row 5). Since the investment banker recommends partial disclosure to vertical buyers at this level of acquisition probability and demand, their expected values of the private information upon observing non-disclosure change to 1.9981 for the supplier and 1.9697 for the customer. The recommendation based on an actual level of unit costs of 1.4 is disclosure of the private information. Hereby, the expected gain from the supplier's bid is much higher than the expected gain from any other buyer's bid, because the input parameters for the supplier are favorable (high synergies and low competitive damages), while the input parameters for other buyers are unfavorable.

The target should be sold to the customer under non-disclosure, if all the same parameters as in row 3 prevail[314], except that the synergy and competitive damage parameters of the customer are increased (row 6). Variation of the customer's input parameters shows that the crucial determinant of the expected gain from the customer's offer is the level of synergies. The higher the customer's synergies, the higher the expected gain from his offer. A small increase in the customer's synergy level greatly increases the expected gain to the seller from the customer's offer. Already an average level of synergies (row 6) results in an expected gain from the customer's offer that is more than three times higher the expected gain from the other buyers' offers. Finally, the target will be sold to the customer under full disclosure, if the acquisition probability is sufficiently high, the level of unit costs is sufficiently

[314] Acquisition probability, demand, and private information on unit costs are high, but synergies for the customer are low and competitive damages are average.

low, and the synergies of the customer are sufficiently high while his competitive damages are average (last row).

Generally it can be concluded that the investment banker will recommend a sale to the financial buyer for a negative cost of new capital combined with a low to average acquisition probability of strategic buyers. With an increase in acquisition probability, synergies of strategic buyers must be very low and competitive damages very high so that a sale recommendation for the financial buyer nevertheless results. This result has two implications. Generally, a target should be sold to strategic buyers at a higher price because of synergy benefits. If the acquisition probability and synergies of those strategic buyers are sufficiently small and competitive damages are sufficiently high, a sale to a financial buyer may generate more value. The second implication is that financial buyers will generate the highest expected gain for the seller, if the differential cost of new capital is negative. In a favorable financing environment, financial buyers can take advantage of their industry expertise and reap financial benefits, which strategic buyers may not be able to access. Kaplan (1989) shows on the example of the acquisition of Federated Department Stores by Campeau Corporation that a highly leveraged transaction may greatly increase company value.

The investment banker will recommend a sale to the customer, if synergies are at least average and the differential cost of new capital is positive. Since the customer's synergy benefits are captured by an increase in demand of the seller and a simultaneous decrease in demand of the strategic buyer, the effect of synergy value on the level of expected gain is multiplied. On the one hand, the seller produces more and has a higher profit because his demand increased. On the other hand, the seller's competitor in the duopoly produces less because of the decrease in his demand. Taking this reduced production quantity of his competitor into account, the seller produces more, thereby increasing his profit even further. Therefore, the synergy benefit of the customer is extremely influential in determining the expected gain to the seller. With an average to high level of synergies, the seller is able to multiply his expected gain by selling to the customer rather than to any other buyer.

The target should be sold to the supplier if the differential cost of new capital is positive and the supplier's synergies from the acquisition are highest, while his competitive damages are sufficiently low. The supplier's synergies do not have the influential magnitude of the customer's synergies. This is because the supplier's synergies are captured by a decrease in unit costs, while the competitor's unit costs remain at the same level. Therefore, the profit of the seller only increases based on his own synergy benefits and not based on any negative effect on the competitor. If the synergy benefits of other strategic buyers are sufficiently small and competitive damages are high, the investment banker will recommend a sale to the supplier.

The investment banker will recommend a sale to the horizontal strategic buyer, if his synergies are highest and the differential cost of new capital is positive. Generally, a sale to a particular kind of strategic buyer implies that his synergies are high, while other strategic buyer's synergies are low and their competitive damages are high. Thereby the actual level of the private information on unit costs generally does not change the decision whom to sell to. Instead, the level of private information influences the disclosure decision that the investment banker will recommend for each strategic buyer and the level of expected gain that the seller is able to derive from the sale.

5.8 Chapter Summary and Discussion

5.8.1 Chapter Summary

This section of the dissertation theoretically analyzes information asymmetries in mergers and acquisitions within a modeled economy. Modeling reality, a seller, an investment banker as intermediary, a horizontal buyer or competitor, multiple suppliers as vertical buyers, multiple customers as vertical buyers, and various financial buyers in an auction are presented. The seller and his competitor operate in a Cournot duopoly and the parties to the selling process have differing degrees of information. The seller alone has private information on unit costs. However, the financial buyer possesses private information on the appropriate cost of new capital for the target company, which can be revealed through an auction (for example). All buyers expect to be provided with proprietary information during the evaluation period to decide whether to acquire the target firm.

One contribution of this model is that it specifically shows that the involvement of the investment banker and the financial buyers strengthen the bargaining position of the seller and add value to the sale process. The investment banker is in the unique position of having access to financial buyers. He intermediates (or deals) with the financial buyers in order to facilitate (1) a price discovery function by determining the appropriate cost of new capital and (2) a maximum sale price by generating additional potential buyers from the financial buyer pool. Additionally, the involvement of the investment banker allows the seller to separate the private information into two different components resulting in different disclosure recommendations.

The proprietary information is modeled by two variables with unique and differing characteristics: uncritical information on cost of new capital (ΔK) and critical information about variable unit costs (k). First, the private information of the financial buyer about the uncritical private information and the proper disclosure recommendation to the seller is discussed. Uncritical private information on cost of capital is unique in that it is irrelevant for the production decision of seller and strategic buyer in the Cournot duopoly. Additionally, the information about cost of new capital is only relevant if the acquisition takes place. Therefore, the investment banker recommends to the seller to disclose this private information fully to all buyers.

Critical private information is modeled with the private information of the seller about unit costs. This information category differs from the first one in that it is relevant for the production decision and has the potential to harm the seller competitively if the acquisition fails. That is, if the private information is disclosed to a strategic buyer and the acquisition is completed, a high price for the target results. If the private information is however disclosed to a strategic buyer and the acquisition fails, the strategic buyer may affect the seller's production quantity either directly as a competitor or indirectly as a vertical buyer based on this additional information. Therefore, the disclosure recommendation of the investment banker becomes more complex. The investment banker recommends that the seller disclose the private information, if the expected gain to the seller from the buyer's offer price is higher under disclosure of the private information than under non-disclosure. That is, depending on the probability of the strategic buyer acquiring the target company, the investment banker will recommend full disclosure, partial disclosure, or non-disclosure of the private information on unit costs.

In addition to differentiating between different kinds of private information, an important contribution of the model is that it attributes the knowledge about proprietary information to different players. The private information on unit costs is known by the seller. The private information about cost of capital has two components, 1) the sunk cost of capital of the selling company K_S known by the seller and 2) the differential cost of new capital ΔK for a firm of the same risk as the one offered for sale, which is known by the financial buyers as a whole. That is, an auction amongst financial buyers serves a price discovery function by revealing the differential cost of capital through the valuation. The model thus links the price discovery function with information about cost of capital and asset valuation in an economy.

An important contribution of the model is also that it differentiates between three buyer categories. Non-strategic buyers (financial buyers) are industry outsiders and as such cannot influence the production decision in the Cournot duopoly. Therefore, the investment banker recommends to the seller to fully disclose company information to financial buyers. The disclosure recommendation concerning strategic buyers is more complex. The horizontal strategic buyer who is the competitor of the target in the duopoly has a high potential to harm the target competitively if the private information is disclosed but the acquisition fails. If the acquisition fails, the seller and the horizontal strategic buyer remain competitors. If the disclosed information were favorable, the competitor would then increase his production quantity, thereby decreasing the profit of the seller in the duopoly market. Therefore, both the profit effect and the effect of disclosed information on purchase price have to be taken into account and weighted by the respective probability, to quantify the seller's expected gain. This trade-off between the effect of private information disclosure on price if the acquisition takes place and on profit if the acquisition fails leads to different disclosure strategies that depend on the probability of the competitor acquiring the target. To derive a maximum expected gain from the competitor's offer price, the investment banker recommends that the seller fully disclose his private information for low and high probabilities of the competitor acquiring the firm, and partial disclosure or no disclosure of the private information for average probabilities of the competitor acquiring the target.

The last buyer category consists of vertical buyers that are either suppliers or customers. Both suppliers and customers have synergy benefits arising from the acquisition. Suppliers may be able to take advantage of a reduction in unit costs, while customers may take advantage of an increase in demand. If the acquisition with vertical buyers fails, they cannot influence the production in the duopoly directly. However, vertical buyers may influence the production decision indirectly through an increase in their bargaining power. For instance, the suppliers may be able to increase the seller's unit costs and the customers may decrease the seller's demand if the information is disclosed and the acquisition fails. That means that the disclosure of private information to a vertical buyer may also result in competitive damages for the seller if the acquisition fails. Therefore, the expected gain of the seller from a vertical buyer's bid is the appropriate decision parameter, consisting of a price and a profit component, each weighted by its respective probability.

The disclosure recommendations vary with the probability of the vertical buyer acquiring the target. To maximize the seller's expected gain from the vertical buyers' offer prices, the investment banker recommends the seller to not disclose the private information on unit costs for low probabilities of the vertical buyer acquiring the target. For higher probabilities of acquisition, partial disclosure of unit cost information is recommended. That is, for a given level of acquisition probability with partial disclosure, unit cost information will be disclosed for lower levels of unit cost information (i.e. positive private information on unit costs) and not disclosed for higher levels of unit costs.

Therefore, the sale recommendations the investment banker is able to provide can be generalized as follows:

1. The seller should always disclose his uncritical private information to all buyers, thereby decreasing the degree of hidden information.
2. The seller should not necessarily reveal his proprietary information for as long as possible, as the standard recommendation in investment banking says. Rather, full or partial disclosure of the private information may generate a higher expected gain to the seller for a certain combinations of input parameters, since the buyer adjusts his expectations of the private information upon observing non-disclosure.[315]
3. The seller should sell either to the financial buyer, the horizontal strategic buyer, or a vertical buyer, depending on who provides him with the highest expected gain. The expected gain takes both the price effect for the acquisition and the profit effect in case that the acquisition fails into account.
4. A sale to the financial buyer is only advantageous if the differential cost of new capital (ΔK) is negative or if synergies of strategic buyers are negative or zero.
5. The seller should generally sell to the strategic buyer with the highest level of synergy, given that the synergy of other strategic buyers is lower and their competitive damages are higher.

5.8.2 Discussion

A limitation of the model is the separability assumption. In the advanced economies of this world, such as the European Union or the US, separability is in place. In other countries, e.g.

[315] See Theorems 1-3 for specific disclosure recommendations for the different buyer types.

in Latin America, this separability may however break down. In Argentina, for instance, the confidentiality agreement as an instrument for keeping the private company information that is disclosed during acquisition negotiations confidential is not effective. The author personally experienced the violation of the separability assumption in Argentina, which resulted in numerous potential buyers in the Latin American region being aware of the seller's intent to sell as well as of private details about the company's affairs. If the separability assumption were to break down, the contribution of the investment banker in this model would diminish.

An additional limitation is the maximum bid assumption. If in practice, a competitive auction environment cannot be created, then rational buyers may not reveal their maximum price. If the financial buyer was to offer a lower price, the seller may overestimate the cost of new capital from his offer price, resulting in a lower expected gain to the seller.

A restriction is also that the model assumes the seller and strategic buyer to operate in a Cournot duopoly, and that synergy benefits of the strategic buyer after acquisition are derived based on the monopoly surplus. Practically no industry exhibits duopoly features in reality, and antitrust laws will generally prevent acquisitions striving for monopoly power. An interesting extension would therefore be to include multiple horizontal strategic buyers. This extension would not have a major effect on the results, but rather affect the relative magnitude of the competing firms' profit.

A simplification of the model is also that expected unit costs are assumed equal for all buyers. The model could easily be adapted to different unit cost expectations for each buyer; however then the calculations become much more complex. Another limitation of the model is that the acquisition probability of the buyer is assumed exogenous. It would be very interesting to model the buyer's choice among several investment opportunities, yet this approach would complicate the model greatly. Another interesting extension of this model for further research would be the extension to a multi-period model to include the reputation capital of the investment banker and the industry expertise of the financial buyer.

6 Conclusion

The dissertation examined information asymmetries in mergers and acquisitions, specifically in respect to the role of the investment banker. After an introduction into mergers & acquisition transaction types, the M&A process, and key intermediaries, capital market imperfections in respect to M&A and investment banking are examined. It is derived that the investment banker may exist because (1) he reduces transaction costs and because (2) he mitigates information asymmetries.

Both ex ante information asymmetries (hidden information) and ex post information asymmetries (moral hazard) are analyzed. In respect to hidden information during the implementation stage of mergers and acquisitions, the main issue is that sellers have private information on their company. If this private information is not disclosed the buyer assumes the worst, which translates into a negative effect on purchase price. If the private information is disclosed the buyer may negatively influence the target's competitive position if the acquisition fails and buyer and seller continue to operate in the industry independently. Section 3.2.2.2.2 describes potential solution approaches that mitigate the described problem. All the described solution approaches have shortcomings that limit their use. Similarly, when the investment banker adds value by mitigating the hidden information problem, potential moral hazard issues limit this mitigating contribution. However, the incentives of principal and agent can be sufficiently aligned using incentive-based fee structures and the self-policing reputation effect of the investment banker. This allows the investment banker to contribute to a workable solution to the hidden information problem.

Despite reporting regulations, the hidden information issue is rather large for most transactions. This is especially the case for small and private target companies, but also to a certain degree for large public firms. By categorizing information and buyers into appropriate classes, it can be shown that only the information disclosure of critical private information to strategic buyers is problematic. Critical private information is information that has the potential to influence the seller's competitive position negatively, if disclosed. Hereby, only the information disclosure to strategic buyers is problematic, because only strategic buyers who operate in the same industry can influence the seller's competitive position. In order to maximize his value derived from the sale, the seller now has to decide whether and what kind of information to disclose to a particular buyer.

A theoretical model is developed in Chapter 5 that reflects this hidden information set-up. The players in the model are one seller and financial buyers as industry outsiders with no synergy value. Additionally, strategic buyers who operate in the same industry are considered. There is a horizontal strategic buyer, who is the direct competitor of the seller within the assumed Cournot duopoly. Additionally, there are forward and backward vertical buyers, i.e. suppliers to and customers of the seller. The M&A process is facilitated by the investment banker. The model is set up based on the seller's perspective. That allows interpretation of the results from a financial point of view as well as recommendations to the seller on how to maximize his expected gain from the sale.

The model shows that the investment banker is able to reduce the degree of hidden information between seller and buyer. The private information can be categorized into two components: critical and uncritical. Considering these information components, the investment banker makes two different disclosure decisions. Uncritical information is modeled by the cost of capital parameter. Since that uncritical information does not have the potential to influence the competitive position of the seller negatively, the private information can be disclosed to all buyers. The disclosure of this uncritical information reduces the degree of hidden information between buyer and seller from the outset. An additional benefit arising from the involvement of the investment banker is the access to all buyer categories. The access to three buyer categories (financial buyers, horizontal strategic buyers, and vertical buyers) increases both the selling choices of the target company and the offer price. Depending on the level of input parameters, the seller will sell to a particular buyer (see Table 5-8). If the seller has access to more buyers, his expected gain for a given set of input parameters increases.

The investment banker is also able to make universally valid recommendations to the seller:

1. The seller should always disclose his uncritical private information to all buyers, thereby decreasing the degree of hidden information.
2. The seller should only disclose critical private information if his expected gain based on the buyer's offer is higher under disclosure than under non-disclosure for a given set of input parameters. Hereby, the disclosure recommendation considers that the buyer will adjust his expectations of the private information upon observing non-disclosure.
3. The seller should sell to the buyer, from whom he expects maximum gain under a given set of input parameters, specifically a given level of acquisition probability. Hereby, the expected gain to the seller takes both the offer price of the buyer and the target's profit if

the acquisition fails into account. Therefore, the expected gain to the seller under disclosure also considers potential competitive damages to the seller if the acquisition fails, as well as the probability of the acquisition failing.

4. A sale to the financial buyer is only advantageous if the differential cost of new capital (ΔK) is negative[316] or if synergies of strategic buyers are negative or zero.
5. The seller should generally sell to the strategic buyer with the highest level of synergy, given that the synergy of other strategic buyers is lower and their competitive damages are higher.

In summary, it can be concluded that the investment banker has a mitigating role in respect to the hidden information problem between buyer and seller during the M&A process. Thereby, the investment banker contributes greatly by allowing the seller to maximize his expected gain. In addition to modeling the role of the investment banker, this study contributed to understanding the information flow between buyer and seller during an acquisition. Since many acquisition negotiations break down during the implementation phase, the information flow between buyer and seller is a topic worthy of future research that has the potential to contributing to this academic literature. Considering that this specific problem has not been widely researched, there is ample room for additional research.

[316] A negative cost of new capital may arise within a financing environment that is favorable to financial buyers. This may be the case for an LBO transaction, where financial buyers can take advantage of their industry expertise and reap financial benefits, which strategic buyers may not be able to access.

APPENDIX

Proof of Theorem 1(i)[317]

The Seller will disclose any private information on unit costs, for which the expected gain to the seller from the horizontal buyer's bid is higher under disclosure than under non-disclosure (equation (5.53)),

$$(\phi+4)(\delta-k)^2 > \phi\cdot\left(9\left(\delta^2-2\delta\cdot E[k]+E\left[k^2\right]\right)-4(\delta-E[k])^2\right)+(1-\phi)[2\delta-3k+E[k]]^2.$$

It will be shown in the following that a full disclosure equilibrium exists for very high and very low acquisition probabilities, because of the level of unit costs that the competitor HB expects upon observing non-disclosure.

Let N denote the subset of private information on k, which is not disclosed in equilibrium. In equilibrium the non-disclosure set is defined as

$$N=\left\{k\left|\begin{array}{l}(\phi+4)(\delta-k)^2\le\phi\cdot\left[9\left(\delta^2-2\delta\cdot E[k|N]+E\left[k^2|N\right]\right)-4(\delta-E[k|N])^2\right]\\ \qquad+(1-\phi)\left[(2\delta-3k+E[k|N])^2\right]\end{array}\right.\right\}$$

If $N=\{1\}$, $E[k|N]=1$ and $E\left[k^2|N\right]=1$. That is, the seller will disclose any information on unit costs k, for which

$$(\phi+4)(\delta-k)^2>\phi\cdot\left(9\left(\delta^2-2\delta+1\right)-4(\delta-1)^2\right)+(1-\phi)\cdot(2\delta-3k+1])^2\Rightarrow$$

$$\begin{aligned}&\phi\delta^2-2\phi\delta k+\phi k^2+4\delta^2-8\delta k+4k^2\\&\quad>5\phi\cdot\left(\delta^2-2\delta+1\right)+(1-\phi)\left(4\delta^2-12\delta k+4\delta+9k^2-6k+1\right)\Rightarrow\end{aligned}$$

$$4\phi\delta^2-2\phi\delta k+\phi k^2-8\delta k+4k^2+10\phi\delta-5\phi>(1-\phi)\left(4\delta^2-12\delta k+4\delta+9k^2-6k+1\right)\Rightarrow$$

$$\begin{aligned}4\phi\delta^2-2\phi\delta k+\phi k^2-8\delta k+4k^2+10\phi\delta-5\phi&>4\delta^2-12\delta k+4\delta+9k^2-6k-4\phi\delta^2\\&\quad+12\phi\delta k-4\phi\delta-9\phi k^2+6\phi k-\phi\Rightarrow\end{aligned}$$

$$5\cdot(2\phi-1)k^2+6(1-\phi)k+2\delta(2-7\phi)k+2(7\delta-2)\phi-(4\delta+1)>0 \qquad \text{(A.1)}$$

The quadratic function (A.1) per construction holds with equality for k = 1. The slope is

[317] The proof of Theorem 1 generally follows Wagenhofer (2000), p. 67.

$$10(2\phi-1)k+6(1-\phi)+2\delta(2-7\phi).$$

The slope is positive for k = 1 if

$$10(2\phi-1)+6(1-\phi)+2\delta(2-7\phi)>0$$

$$20\phi-10+6-6\phi+4\delta-14\phi\delta>0$$

$$14(1-\delta)\phi>4(1-\delta)$$

$$\phi<\frac{2}{7}$$

Since the slope is positive if $\phi<\frac{2}{7}$ at k = 1 and the second derivative is negative for $\phi<\frac{2}{7}$, the maximum must be reached at a value $k>1$. Consequently it suffices to examine if equation (A.1) is greater than zero for $k=2$. If this stands, then equation (A.1) is positive for all $k\in[1;2]$.

$$5\cdot(2\phi-1)2^2+6(1-\phi)2+2\delta(2-7\phi)2+2(7\delta-2)\phi-(4\delta+1)>0\Rightarrow$$

$$24\phi-9+4\delta-14\phi\delta>0\Rightarrow$$

$$(24-14\delta)\phi>9-4\delta$$

The demand assumption says that $\delta\geq 2.5$.[318] That is, both numerator and denominator are negative and the inequality sign changes direction.

$$\Rightarrow\phi<\frac{4\delta-9}{2(7\delta-12)} \qquad \text{Q.E.D.}$$

That means that for $\phi<\frac{4\delta-9}{2(7\delta-12)}$, the seller will fully disclose his private information on unit costs to the horizontal strategic buyer for all levels of k.

Recall that in equilibrium the non-disclosure set is defined as

---

[318] Note that $\delta>2$ based on the non-triviality assumption. $\delta\geq 2.5$ ensures that the profit of seller and competitor does not become trivially small. If demand was assumed $2<\delta<2.5$, the categorization of ϕ in Theorem 1 would not hold. For $\delta=2.2$, for instance, non-disclosure equilibria for average levels of ϕ and otherwise partial disclosure equilibria would result. Therefore, to be able to develop a general disclosure recommendation and to ensure that profit does not become trivially small, $\delta\geq 2.5$ is assumed.

$$N = \left\{ k \left| \begin{array}{l} (\phi + 4)(\delta - k)^2 \le \phi \cdot \left[9\left(\delta^2 - 2\delta \cdot E[k|N] + E[k^2|N]\right) - 4\left(\delta - E[k|N]\right)^2\right] \\ \qquad + (1-\phi)\left[(2\delta - 3k + E[k|N])^2\right] \end{array} \right. \right\}$$

If $N = \{2\}$, $E[k|N] = 2$ and $E[k^2|N] = 4$. That is, the seller will disclose any information on unit costs k, for which

$$(\phi + 4)(\delta - k)^2 > \phi \cdot \left[9\left(\delta^2 - 2 \cdot 2\delta + 4\right) - 4(\delta - 2)^2\right] + (1-\phi)\left[(2\delta - 3k + 2])^2\right] \Rightarrow$$

$$\begin{aligned} \phi\delta^2 - 2\phi\delta k + \phi k^2 + 4\delta^2 - 8\delta k + 4k^2 > {} & 5\phi \cdot \left(\delta^2 - 4\delta + 4\right) \\ & + (1-\phi)\left(4\delta^2 - 12\delta k + 8\delta + 9k^2 - 12k + 4\right) \Rightarrow \end{aligned}$$

$$\begin{aligned} \phi\delta^2 - 2\phi\delta k + \phi k^2 + 4\delta^2 - 8\delta k + 4k^2 > {} & 5\phi\delta^2 - 20\phi\delta + 20\phi + 4\delta^2 - 12\delta k + 8\delta + 9k^2 \\ & - 12k + 4 - 4\phi\delta^2 + 12\phi\delta k - 8\phi\delta - 9\phi k^2 \\ & + 12\phi k - 4\phi \Rightarrow \end{aligned}$$

$$5 \cdot (2\phi - 1)k^2 + 12(1-\phi)k + 2\delta(2 - 7\phi)k + 4(7\delta - 4)\phi - 4(2\delta + 1) > 0 \tag{A.2}$$

The quadratic function (A.2) holds per construction with equality for k = 2. The slope is

$$10(2\phi - 1)k + 12(1-\phi) + 2\delta(2 - 7\phi).$$

The slope is negative for k = 2 if:

$$10(2\phi - 1)2 + 12(1-\phi) + 2\delta(2 - 7\phi) < 0$$

$$40\phi - 20 + 12 - 12\phi + 4\delta - 14\phi\delta < 0$$

$$14(2 - \delta)\phi < 4(2 - \delta)$$

The demand assumption says that $\delta \ge 2.5$. That is, if divided by $2 - \delta$, the divisor becomes negative and the inequality sign changes direction.

$$\Rightarrow \phi > \frac{2}{7}$$

Since the slope is negative if $\phi > \frac{2}{7}$ at k = 2, the maximum must be reached at a value $k < 2$. Consequently it suffices to examine if equation (A.2) is greater than zero for $k = 1$. If this stands, then equation (A.2) is positive for all $k \in [1; 2]$.

$$5\cdot(2\phi-1)1+12(1-\phi)1+2\delta(2-7\phi)1+4(7\delta-4)\phi-4(2\delta+1)>0\Rightarrow$$

$$10\phi-5+12-12\phi+4\delta-14\delta\phi+28\delta-16\phi-8\delta-4>0\Rightarrow$$

$$-18\phi+3-4\delta+14\phi\delta>0\Rightarrow$$

$$2(7\delta-9)\phi>4\delta-3$$

The demand assumption says that $\delta\geq 2.5$. That is, if divided by $7\delta-9$, the divisor is positive and the inequality sign remains the same.

$$\Rightarrow\phi>\frac{4\delta-3}{2(7\delta-9)}. \qquad \text{Q.E.D.}$$

That means that for $\phi>\frac{4\delta-3}{2(7\delta-9)}$, the investment banker will recommend to the seller to fully disclose his private information on unit costs to the horizontal strategic buyer for all levels of k.

Proof of Theorem 1(ii)

Let T depict the expected gain difference curve between disclosure and non-disclosure based on equation (5.53),

$$T=(4+\phi)(\delta-k)^2-\phi\left(9\left(\delta^2-2\delta E[k|N]+E[k^2|N]\right)-4(\delta-E[k|N])^2\right)-(1-\phi)(2\delta-3k+E[k|N])^2$$

$$\begin{aligned}T=&(4+\phi)(\delta^2-2\delta k+k^2)-5\phi\delta^2+10\phi\delta E[k|N]-9\phi E[k^2|N]+4\phi E[k|N]^2\\&-(1-\phi)\left(4\delta^2-12\delta k+4\delta E[k|N]+9k^2-6kE[k|N]+E[k|N]^2\right)\Rightarrow\end{aligned}$$

$$\begin{aligned}T=&4\delta^2+\phi\delta^2-8\delta k-2\phi\delta k+4k^2+\phi k^2-5\phi\delta^2+10\phi\delta E[k|N]-9\phi E[k^2|N]\\&+4\phi E[k|N]^2-4\delta^2+12\delta k-4\delta E[k|N]-9k^2+6kE[k|N]-E[k|N]^2+4\phi\delta^2\\&-12\phi\delta k+4\phi\delta E[k|N]+9\phi k^2-6\phi kE[k|N]+\phi E[k|N]^2\Rightarrow\end{aligned}$$

$$\begin{aligned}T=&5(2\phi-1)k^2+2\delta(2-7\phi)k+6E[k|N](1-\phi)k+2\delta(7\phi-2)E[k|N]\\&+(5\phi-1)E[k|N]^2-9\phi E[k^2|N]\end{aligned} \qquad \text{(A.3)}$$

The derivatives of T in respect to k are

$$\frac{\partial T}{\partial k} = 10(2\phi - 1)k + 2\delta(2 - 7\phi) + 6E[k|N](1 - \phi)$$

$$\frac{\partial^2 T}{\partial k^2} = 10(2\phi - 1)$$

Claim: $\frac{\partial^2 T}{\partial k^2} < 0$ for all $\phi \leq \frac{4\delta - 3}{2(7\delta - 9)}$ (from Theorem 1(i))

$$10\left(2 \cdot \frac{4\delta - 3}{2(7\delta - 9)} - 1\right) < 0$$

$$\frac{4\delta - 3}{(7\delta - 9)} < 0$$

$$4\delta - 3 < 7\delta - 9$$

$$\delta > 2$$

It can be concluded from the second derivative being a constant in "k" and less than zero for all $\phi \leq \frac{4\delta - 3}{2(7\delta - 9)}$ and $\delta > 2$ that (A.3) is a strictly concave function. A partial disclosure equilibrium for different values of k cannot exist if all values of T are strictly greater than or less than zero for all $k \in [1; 2]$. Therefore, the disclosure interval in equilibrium must be $D = [k_1; k_2]$ with $k_1 < k_2$ and $k \in (1; 2)$ and the non-disclosure interval in equilibrium is $N = [1; k_1] \cup [k_2; 2]$. Q.E.D.

Proof of Theorem 1(iii)

There can only be a non-disclosure equilibrium if the seller has no incentive to disclose any k with N = k, taking into account what the strategic buyer concludes from non-disclosure. For $k \in [1; 2]$ expected values of k given non-disclosure can be derived as

$$E[k|N] = \left[\frac{1}{2}k^2\right]_1^2 = 2 - \frac{1}{2} = \frac{3}{2},$$

$$E[k^2|N] = \left[\frac{1}{3}k^3\right]_1^2 = \frac{8}{3} - \frac{1}{3} = \frac{7}{3}.$$

Equation (A.3) now reads:

$$T = 5(2\phi - 1)k^2 + 2\delta(2 - 7\phi)k + 6 \cdot \frac{3}{2}(1 - \phi)k + 2\delta(7\phi - 2) \cdot \frac{3}{2} + (5\phi - 1) \cdot \left(\frac{3}{2}\right)^2 - 9\phi \cdot \frac{7}{3} \Rightarrow$$

$$T = 5(2\phi - 1)k^2 + 2\delta(2 - 7\phi)k + 9(1 - \phi)k + 3\delta(7\phi - 2) - \frac{3}{4}(13\phi + 3) \quad \text{(A.4)}$$

For a non-disclosure equilibrium to exist, the expected gain to the seller from the horizontal strategic buyer's bid must be higher under non-disclosure than for disclosure, i.e. (A.4) < 0 for all $k \in [1;\, 2]$. The maximum k* can be determined as

$$\frac{\partial T}{\partial k} = 10(2\phi - 1)k + 2\delta(2 - 7\phi) + 9(1 - \phi) \overset{!}{=} 0$$

$$k^* = \frac{2\delta(7\phi - 2) + 9(\phi - 1)}{10(2\phi - 1)} \qquad \text{for } \phi \neq 0.5 \qquad \text{(A.5)}$$

Figure A-1 illustrates that the maximum of T can lie on either boundary of the interval k = [1; 2] or in the interior of this interval.

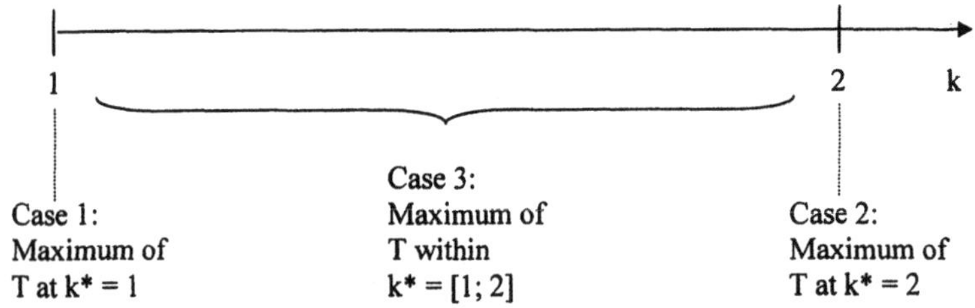

Figure A-1: Maximum of T for k ∈ [1; 2]

Case 1: If the maximum of T lies at the lower boundary k = 1, which implies favorable private information on unit costs, then $k^* \leq 1$.

$$\frac{2\delta(7\phi - 2) + 9(\phi - 1)}{10(2\phi - 1)} \leq 1 \qquad \bigg| \cdot 10(2\phi - 1)$$

Claim: The divisor $(2\phi - 1)$ is negative

$$\Rightarrow \phi = \frac{4\delta - 3}{2(7\delta - 9)} < 0.5 \qquad \Big|\cdot 2(7\delta - 9)$$ [319]

$$\Rightarrow 4\delta - 3 < 7\delta - 9$$

$$\Rightarrow \delta > 2$$

→ For $\delta > 2$, the divisor is negative, i.e. the sign of the inequality changes direction.

$$\Rightarrow 2\delta(7\phi - 2) + 9(\phi - 1) \geq 10(2\phi - 1)$$

$$14\delta\phi - 4\delta + 9\phi - 9 \geq 20\phi - 10 \Rightarrow$$

$$1 - 4\delta \geq (11 - 14\delta)\phi \qquad \Big|\div (11 - 14\delta)$$

Since $(11 - 14\delta) < 0$ for all $\delta \geq 2.5$, the sign of the inequality changes direction.

$$\Rightarrow \phi \geq \frac{1 - 4\delta}{11 - 14\delta}$$

If for such ϕ and for k = 1 the value of T > 0, then no non-disclosure equilibrium can exist.

T at k = 1:

$$T = 5(2\phi - 1)1^2 + 2\delta(2 - 7\phi)1 + 9(1 - \phi)1 + 3\delta(7\phi - 2) - \frac{3}{4}(13\phi + 3) \Rightarrow$$

$$T = 10\phi - 5 + 4\delta - 14\delta\phi + 9 - 9\phi + 21\phi\delta - 6\delta - \frac{39}{4}\phi - \frac{9}{4} \Rightarrow$$

$$T = -\frac{35}{4}\phi + 7\delta\phi + \frac{7}{4} - 2\delta$$

For $\phi \geq \frac{1 - 4\delta}{11 - 14\delta}$, T > 0 for k = 1 if

$$-\frac{35}{4} \cdot \frac{1 - 4\delta}{11 - 14\delta} + 7\delta \cdot \frac{1 - 4\delta}{11 - 14\delta} + \frac{7}{4} - 2\delta > 0 \Rightarrow$$

$$\frac{7\delta(1 - 4\delta)}{11 - 14\delta} - \frac{35(1 - 4\delta)}{4(11 - 14\delta)} > 2\delta - \frac{7}{4} \Rightarrow$$

---

[319] Note that the lower bound of the upper full disclosure interval for ϕ was derived in Theorem 1(i). Additionally, since $\delta \geq 2.5$, the multiplier is positive and the sign of the inequality remains the same.

$$\frac{28\delta(1-4\delta)-35(1-4\delta)}{4(11-14\delta)} > \frac{8\delta-7}{4} \qquad |\cdot 4(11-14\delta)$$ [320]

$$28\delta(1-4\delta)-35(1-4\delta) < (8\delta-7)\cdot(11-14\delta) \Rightarrow$$

$$28\delta-112\delta^2-35+140\delta < 88\delta-112\delta^2-77+98\delta \Rightarrow$$

$$42 < 18\delta \Rightarrow$$

$$\delta > \frac{7}{3}$$

For $\phi \geq \frac{1-4\delta}{11-14\delta} \wedge k=1 \wedge \delta > \frac{7}{3}$, $T > 0$. That is, no non-disclosure equilibrium exists at the lower boundary $k = 1$.

Case 2: If the maximum of T lies at the upper boundary $k = 2$, which implies unfavorable private information on unit costs, then $k^* \geq 2$.

$$\frac{2\delta(7\phi-2)+9(\phi-1)}{10(2\phi-1)} \geq 2 \qquad |\cdot 10(2\phi-1)$$

Claim: The divisor $(2\phi-1)$ is negative

$$\Rightarrow \phi = \frac{4\delta-3}{2(7\delta-9)} < 0.5 \qquad |\cdot 2(7\delta-9)$$ [321]

$$\Rightarrow 4\delta-3 < 7\delta-9$$

$$\Rightarrow \delta > 2$$

→ For $\delta > 2$, the divisor is negative, i.e. the sign of the inequality changes direction.

$$\Rightarrow 2\delta(7\phi-2)+9(\phi-1) \leq 20(2\phi-1)$$

$$14\delta\phi-4\delta+9\phi-9 \geq 40\phi-20 \Rightarrow$$

$$11-4\delta \geq (31-14\delta)\phi \Rightarrow \qquad |\div(31-14\delta)$$

[320] Since $\delta > 2$, the multiplier becomes negative, resulting in a direction change of the sign of the inequality.
[321] Note that the lower bound of the full disclosure interval was derived in Theorem 1(i). Moreover, since, $\delta \geq 2.5$ the multiplier is positive and the sign of the inequality remains the same.

For $\delta \geq 2.5$ (demand assumption), the divisor $31-14\delta<0$ is negative and the sign of the inequality changes direction.

$$\Rightarrow \phi \leq \frac{11-4\delta}{31-14\delta}$$

If for such ϕ and for $k=2$ the value of $T>0$, then no non-disclosure equilibrium can exist. T (equation (A.4)) at $k=2$ is

$$T=5(2\phi-1)2^2+2\delta(2-7\phi)2+9(1-\phi)2+3\delta(7\phi-2)-\frac{3}{4}(13\phi+3)\Rightarrow$$

$$T=40\phi-20+8\delta-28\delta\phi+18-18\phi+21\phi\delta-6\delta-\frac{39}{4}\phi-\frac{9}{4}\Rightarrow$$

$$T=\frac{49}{4}\phi-7\delta\phi-\frac{17}{4}+2\delta$$

For $\phi \leq \frac{11-4\delta}{31-14\delta}$, $T>0$ for $k=2$ if

$$T=\frac{49}{4}\cdot\frac{11-4\delta}{31-14\delta}-7\delta\cdot\frac{11-4\delta}{31-14\delta}-\frac{17}{4}+2\delta>0\Rightarrow$$

$$\frac{49(11-4\delta)}{4(31-14\delta)}-\frac{7\delta(11-4\delta)}{31-14\delta}>\frac{17-8\delta}{4} \qquad |\cdot 4(31-14\delta)$$ [322]

$$49(11-4\delta)-28\delta(11-4\delta)<(17-8\delta)\cdot(31-14\delta)\Rightarrow$$

$$12<18\delta\Rightarrow$$

$$\delta>\frac{2}{3}$$

For $\phi \leq \frac{11-4\delta}{31-14\delta} \wedge k=2 \wedge \delta>\frac{2}{3}$, $T>0$. That is, no non-disclosure equilibrium exists at the upper boundary $k=2$.

---

[322] For $\delta \geq 2.5$, the multiplier becomes negative, resulting in a direction change of the inequality sign.

Case 3: If the maximum of T lies in the interior of k = [1; 2], T (equation (A.4)) has to be evaluated at k^* (equation (A.5)).

$$T = 5(2\phi-1)\cdot\left[\frac{2\delta(7\phi-2)+9(\phi-1)}{10(2\phi-1)}\right]^2 + 2\delta(2-7\phi)\cdot\left[\frac{2\delta(7\phi-2)+9(\phi-1)}{10(2\phi-1)}\right]$$
$$+9(1-\phi)\cdot\left[\frac{2\delta(7\phi-2)+9(\phi-1)}{10(2\phi-1)}\right] + 3\delta(7\phi-2) - \frac{3}{4}(13\phi+3) \Rightarrow$$

$$T = \frac{(14\phi\delta-4\delta+9\phi-9)^2}{20(2\phi-1)} + \frac{(4\delta-14\phi\delta)(14\phi\delta-4\delta+9\phi-9)}{10(2\phi-1)}$$
$$+\frac{(9-9\phi)(14\phi\delta-4\delta+9\phi-9)}{10(2\phi-1)} + \frac{\left(21\phi\delta-6\delta-\frac{39}{4}\phi-\frac{9}{4}\right)\cdot 20(2\phi-1)}{20(2\phi-1)} \Rightarrow$$

$$T = \frac{196\phi^2\delta^2-112\phi\delta^2+252\phi^2\delta-324\phi\delta+16\delta^2+72\delta+81\phi^2-162\phi+81}{20(2\phi-1)}$$
$$+\frac{224\phi\delta^2-32\delta^2+324\phi\delta-72\delta-392\phi^2\delta^2-252\phi^2\delta}{20(2\phi-1)}$$
$$+\frac{162\phi\delta-36\delta+162\phi-81-126\phi^2\delta-81\phi^2}{10(2\phi-1)}$$
$$+\frac{840\phi^2\delta^2-660\phi\delta+120\delta-390\phi^2+105\phi+45}{20(2\phi-1)} \Rightarrow$$

$$T = \frac{196\phi^2\delta^2-112\phi\delta^2+252\phi^2\delta-324\phi\delta+16\delta^2+72\delta+81\phi^2-162\phi+81+224\phi\delta^2}{20(2\phi-1)}$$
$$+\frac{-32\delta^2+324\phi\delta-72\delta-392\phi^2\delta^2-252\phi^2\delta+324\phi\delta-72\delta+324\phi-162}{20(2\phi-1)}$$
$$+\frac{-252\phi^2\delta-162\phi^2+840\phi^2\delta^2-660\phi\delta+120\delta-390\phi^2+105\phi+45}{20(2\phi-1)} \Rightarrow$$

$$T=\frac{(-196\delta^2+588\delta-471)\phi^2+(112\delta^2-336\delta+267)\phi-16\delta^2+48\delta-36}{20(2\phi-1)}$$

For a non-disclosure equilibrium $T < 0$ has to hold.

$$\frac{(-196\delta^2+588\delta-471)\phi^2+(112\delta^2-336\delta+267)\phi-16\delta^2+48\delta-36}{20(2\phi-1)} < 0$$

Solving the quadratic function for $\phi_{1,2}$ that set the function equal to zero,

$$\left(-196\delta^2+588\delta-471\right)\phi^2+\left(112\delta^2-336\delta+267\right)\phi-16\delta^2+48\delta-36=0$$

$$\phi_{1,2}=\frac{-112\delta^2+336\delta-267\pm\sqrt{\begin{array}{l}\left(112\delta^2-336\delta+267\right)^2\\-4\left(-196\delta^2+588\delta-471\right)\cdot\left(-16\delta^2+48\delta-36\right)\end{array}}}{2\left(-196\delta^2+588\delta-471\right)}$$

The square root can be written as

$$\sqrt{\begin{array}{l}12544\delta^4-37632\delta^3+29904\delta^2-37632\delta^3+112896\delta^2-89712\delta+29904\delta^2-89712\delta\\+71289-4\cdot\begin{pmatrix}3136\delta^4-9408\delta^3+7056\delta^2-9408\delta^3+28224\delta^2-21168\delta+7536\delta^2\\-22608\delta+16956\end{pmatrix}\end{array}}\Rightarrow$$

and simplified to

$$=\sqrt{1440\delta^2-4320\delta+3465}\Rightarrow$$

$$=3\sqrt{5\left(32\delta^2-96\delta+77\right)}$$

$\phi_{1,2}$ now becomes

$$\phi_{1,2}=\frac{-112\delta^2+336\delta-267\pm3\sqrt{5\left(32\delta^2-96\delta+77\right)}}{2\left(-196\delta^2+588\delta-471\right)}$$

That is, $T<0$ for

$$\frac{-112\delta^2+336\delta-267+3\sqrt{5\left(32\delta^2-96\delta+77\right)}}{2\left(-196\delta^2+588\delta-471\right)}<\phi<\frac{-112\delta^2+336\delta-267-3\sqrt{5\left(32\delta^2-96\delta+77\right)}}{2\left(-196\delta^2+588\delta-471\right)}$$

Q.E.D.

Proof of Theorem 2(i)

The seller will disclose any private information on unit costs, for which

$$T=\left[9\begin{pmatrix}\phi(1-s)^2\\+(1-\phi)(2+c)c\end{pmatrix}\right]\cdot k^2+6\begin{bmatrix}\phi(s-1)\cdot(2\delta+(1+s)\cdot E[k])\\+(1-\phi)(cE[k]-2\delta)\cdot c\end{bmatrix}k \\ +\left[3\phi(6s-5s^2-1)+c(1-\phi)(c-2)\right]\cdot E[k]^2+4\left[3(1-s)\phi\delta-(1-\phi)\delta c\right]\cdot E[k] \tag{5.61}$$

That is, in equilibrium the non-disclosure set is defined as

$$N=\left\{k\left|\begin{matrix}\left[9\begin{pmatrix}\phi(1-s)^2\\+(1-\phi)(2+c)c\end{pmatrix}\right]\cdot k^2+6\begin{bmatrix}\phi(s-1)\cdot(2\delta+(1+s)\cdot E[k])\\+(1-\phi)(cE[k]-2\delta)\cdot c\end{bmatrix}k \\ +\left[3\phi(6s-5s^2-1)+c(1-\phi)(c-2)\right]\cdot E[k]^2+4\left[3(1-s)\phi\delta-(1-\phi)\delta c\right]\cdot E[k]\end{matrix}\leq 0\right.\right\}$$

If $N=\{1\}$, then $E[k|N]=1$. That is, the seller will disclose any information on unit costs k, for which

$$\left[9\begin{pmatrix}\phi(1-s)^2\\+(1-\phi)(2+c)c\end{pmatrix}\right]\cdot k^2+6\begin{bmatrix}\phi(s-1)\cdot(2\delta+(1+s)\cdot E[k])\\+(1-\phi)(cE[k]-2\delta)\cdot c\end{bmatrix}k \\ +\left[3\phi(6s-5s^2-1)+c(1-\phi)(c-2)\right]\cdot E[k]^2+4\left[3(1-s)\phi\delta-(1-\phi)\delta c\right]\cdot E[k]>0 \tag{A.6}$$

For $E[k|N]=1$, is there any ϕ for which $T>0$ for all k?

Claim: For the lower bound of k, i.e. $k = 1$, $T < 0$ for all levels of ϕ.

See Figure A-2 for the exemplary curvature of T for $E[k|N]=1$, $\phi = 0.7$, $s = 0.4$; $c = 0.1$; $\delta = 3$.

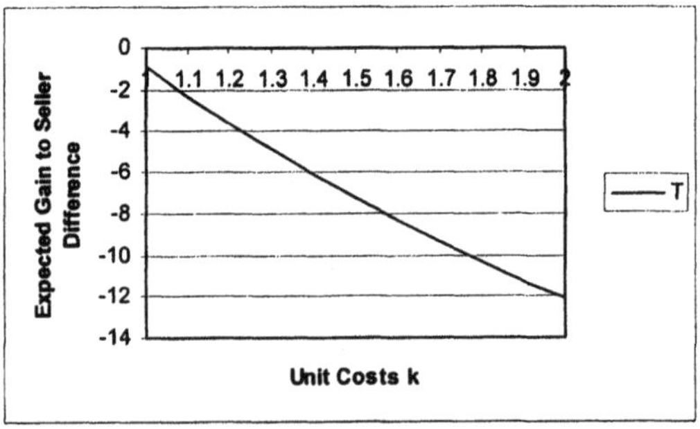

Figure A-2: No Full Disclosure Equilibrium for E[k/N] = 1
(ϕ = 0.7; s = 0.4; c = 0.1; δ =3)

Proof:

At k = 1 and $E[k|N]=1$, the expected gain to the seller difference curve T (equation (A.6)) is

$$T=\left[9\left(\phi(1-s)^2+(1-\phi)(2+c)c\right)\right]+6\left[\phi(s-1)\cdot(2\delta+(1+s))+(1-\phi)(c-2\delta)\cdot c\right]$$
$$+\left[3\phi\left(6s-5s^2-1\right)+c(1-\phi)(c-2)\right]+4\left[3(1-s)\phi\delta-(1-\phi)\delta c\right]>0 \qquad \Rightarrow$$

$$T=16c(1-\phi)(1+c-\delta) \tag{A.7}$$

Recall that $\delta \geq 2.5$ (demand assumption). To see if T in equation (A.7) < 0 for all values of δ, the lower boundary of the demand interval has to be entered into T. For $\delta = 2.5$,

$$T=16c(1-\phi)(-1.5+c)<0$$

For all $c \in (0; 0.2]$ and $\phi = [0; 1)$, $T < 0$.[323] Q.E.D.

The larger the demand, the more negative T becomes. That is, no full disclosure equilibrium exists at the lower bound of k.

As a second step, the upper bound of k has to be examined. If $N = \{2\}$ then $E[k|N]=2$. That is, the seller will disclose any information on unit costs k, for which

$$\left[9\begin{pmatrix}\phi(1-s)^2\\+(1-\phi)(2+c)c\end{pmatrix}\right]\cdot k^2+6\begin{bmatrix}\phi(s-1)\cdot(2\delta+(1+s)\cdot 2)\\+(1-\phi)(2c-2\delta)\cdot c\end{bmatrix}k$$
$$+\left[3\phi\left(6s-5s^2-1\right)+c(1-\phi)(c-2)\right]\cdot 4+4\left[3(1-s)\phi\delta-(1-\phi)\delta c\right]\cdot 2>0 \tag{A.8}$$

For $E[k|N]=2$, is there any ϕ for which $T > 0$ for all $k \in [1; 2]$?

Claim: For the upper bound of k, i.e. k = 2, T < 0 for all levels of ϕ.
See Figure A-3 for the exemplary curvature of T for $E[k|N]=2$, $\phi = 0.9$, $s = 0.4$; $c = 0.1$; $\delta = 3$.

Proof:
At k = 2, the expected gain to the seller difference curve T from (A.8) is

[323] The special case of certainty ($\phi = 1$) will be considered in section 5.6.2.1.4.

$$T=\left[9\begin{pmatrix}\phi(1-s)^2\\+(1-\phi)(2+c)c\end{pmatrix}\right]\cdot 4+6\begin{bmatrix}\phi(s-1)\cdot(2\delta+(1+s)\cdot 2)\\+(1-\phi)(2c-2\delta)\cdot c\end{bmatrix}\cdot 2$$
$$+\left[3\phi\left(6s-5s^2-1\right)+c(1-\phi)(c-2)\right]\cdot 4+4\left[3(1-s)\phi\delta-(1-\phi)\delta c\right]\cdot 2>0 \quad\Rightarrow$$

$$T=32c(1-\phi)\cdot(2c+2-\delta) \qquad \text{(A.9)}$$

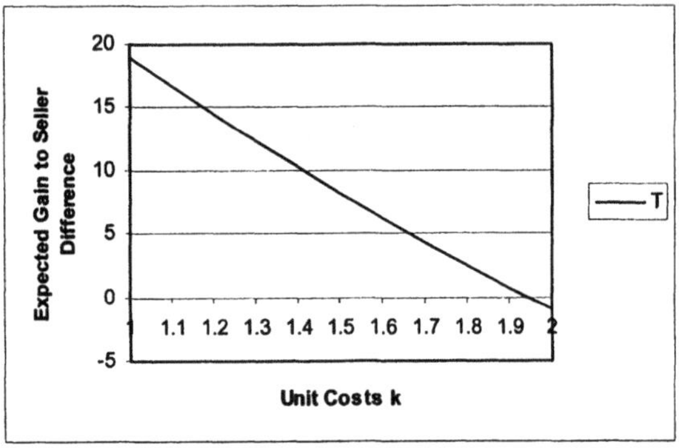

Figure A-3: No Full Disclosure Equilibrium for E[k/N]= 2
(ϕ = 0.9; s = 0.4; c = 0.1; δ =3)

Recall that $\delta \geq 2.5$ (demand assumption). To see if T in equation (A.9) < 0 for all values of δ, the lower boundary of the demand interval has to be entered into T. For $\delta = 2.5$,

$$T=32c(1-\phi)\cdot(2c-0.5)<0$$

For all $c \in (0;\, 0.2]$, $T<0$. Q.E.D.

The larger the demand, the more negative T becomes. That is, no full disclosure equilibrium exists at the upper bound of k.

To show that for all levels of ϕ no full disclosure equilibrium exists, the curvature of the expected gain to the seller difference curve T (equation (5.61)) has to be considered. The first derivative reads

$$\frac{\partial T}{\partial k}=2\left[9\begin{pmatrix}\phi(1-s)^2\\+(1-\phi)(2+c)c\end{pmatrix}\right]\cdot k+6\begin{bmatrix}\phi(s-1)\cdot(2\delta+(1+s)\cdot E[k])\\+(1-\phi)(cE[k]-2\delta)\cdot c\end{bmatrix}$$

and the second derivative

$$\frac{\partial^2 T}{\partial k^2} = 2\underbrace{\left[9\left(\phi(1-s)^2 + (1-\phi)(2+c)c\right)\right]}_{\geq 0}$$

The second derivative is positive for all $s = [0; 0.5]$, $c = (0; 0.2]$, $\delta \geq 2.5$, and $\phi = [0; 1]$. That means that the expected gain difference curve T is convex for all $\phi = [0; 1]$. Because at the lower and upper bound of unit costs the expected gain to the seller difference curve T is below zero for all levels of ϕ, no full disclosure equilibrium can exist for any probability of acquisition.

Proof of Theorem 2(ii)

Recall that the expected gain difference curve T from equation (5.61) reads:

$$T = \left[9\begin{pmatrix}\phi(1-s)^2 \\ +(1-\phi)(2+c)c\end{pmatrix}\right]\cdot k^2 + 6\begin{bmatrix}\phi(s-1)\cdot(2\delta+(1+s)\cdot E[k]) \\ +(1-\phi)(cE[k]-2\delta)\cdot c\end{bmatrix}k$$
$$+\left[3\phi(6s-5s^2-1)+c(1-\phi)(c-2)\right]\cdot E[k]^2 + 4\left[3(1-s)\phi\delta-(1-\phi)\delta c\right]\cdot E[k]$$

and the second derivative

$$\frac{\partial^2 T}{\partial k^2} = 2\left[9\left(\phi(1-s)^2 + (1-\phi)(2+c)c\right)\right]$$

For a non-disclosure equilibrium, the function T has to be smaller than or equal to zero for all $k = [1; 2]$. Recall that

$$N = \left\{ k \left| \begin{matrix} \left[9\begin{pmatrix}\phi(1-s)^2 \\ +(1-\phi)(2+c)c\end{pmatrix}\right]\cdot k^2 + 6\begin{bmatrix}\phi(s-1)\cdot(2\delta+(1+s)\cdot E[k]) \\ +(1-\phi)(cE[k]-2\delta)\cdot c\end{bmatrix}k \\ +\left[3\phi(6s-5s^2-1)+c(1-\phi)(c-2)\right]\cdot E[k]^2 + 4\left[3(1-s)\phi\delta-(1-\phi)\delta c\right]\cdot E[k] \end{matrix} \leq 0 \right. \right\}$$

To determine the upper bound of the non-disclosure interval, it suffices to find the probability of acquisition for which k = 1 and T = 0, since the function is convex and downward sloping for low (i.e. favorable) levels of private information on unit costs. The expected value of k given non-disclosure with $k = [1; 2]$ is $E[k|N] = 1.5$. The function T for k = 1, T = 0, and $E[k|N] = 1.5$ then reads:

$$T = \left(9\left(\phi(1-s)^2 + (1-\phi)(2+c)c\right)\right)\cdot 1^2 + 6\left[\phi(s-1)\cdot(2\delta + (1+s)\cdot 1.5) + (1-\phi)(1.5c - 2\delta)\cdot c\right]\cdot 1$$
$$+ \left[3\phi(6s - 5s^2 - 1) + c(1-\phi)(c-2)\right]\cdot 2.25 + 4\left[3(1-s)\phi\delta - (1-\phi)\delta c\right]\cdot 1.5 = 0 \quad \Rightarrow$$

$$T: -6.75\phi + 22.5\phi s - 15.75\phi s^2 + 20.25c^2 + 13.5c - 20.25\phi c^2 - 13.5\phi c - 6\phi s\delta + 6\phi\delta$$
$$-18\delta c + 18\phi\delta c = 0 \quad \Rightarrow$$

$$\phi_\circ(\phi \mid T = 0) = \frac{9(9c + 6 - 8\delta)c}{9\left(3(1 + (3c+2)c) + (7s - 10)s\right) + 24(s - 1 - 3c)\delta} \tag{A.10}$$

To ensure that for all levels of $0 < \phi \leq \phi_\circ$ from equation (A.10) a non-disclosure equilibrium for the convex function exists, it has to be shown that for k = 2 and $E[k|N] = 1.5$ there is no level of acquisition probability for which T = 0. The expected gain difference curve based on equation (5.61) then reads,

$$T = \left[9\begin{pmatrix}\phi(1-s)^2 \\ +(1-\phi)(2+c)c\end{pmatrix}\right]\cdot 2^2 + 6\begin{bmatrix}\phi(s-1)\cdot(2\delta + (1+s)\cdot 1.5) \\ +(1-\phi)(1.5c - 2\delta)\cdot c\end{bmatrix}\cdot 2$$
$$+ \left[3\phi(6s - 5s^2 - 1) + c(1-\phi)(c-2)\right]\cdot 1.5^2 + 4\left[3(1-s)\phi\delta - (1-\phi)\delta c\right]\cdot 1.5 = 0 \Rightarrow$$

$$\phi = \frac{5\left[6\delta - 2.25(5c+6)\right]\cdot c}{2.25\left[5 - 14s + 9s^2 - 5(5c+6)c\right] + 6(s + 5c - 1)\delta} \tag{A.11}$$

For all $s = [0; 0.5]$, $c = (0; 0.2]$, and $\delta \geq 2.5$, equation (A.11) is not within the defined range of ϕ, with $\phi = [0; 1]$. Therefore, for no probability of acquisition is T = 0 for the upper bound of k, i.e. for k = 2. It can be concluded that for all levels of probabilities of acquisition

$$0 \leq \phi \leq \frac{9(9c + 6 - 8\delta)c}{9\left(3(1 + (3c+2)c) + (7s - 10)s\right) + 24(s - 1 - 3c)\delta}$$

a non-disclosure equilibrium exists. Q.E.D

Proof of Theorem 2(iii)

With the convex and downward sloping expected gain to the seller difference curve T, a partial disclosure equilibrium can only sustain if T = 0 for exactly one level of k, with $1 < k < 2$. The expected value of unit costs k given non-disclosure is:

$$E[k|N] = \left[\frac{1}{2}k^2\right]_k^2 \cdot \left(\frac{1}{2-k}\right) = \frac{2-0.5k^2}{2-k}$$

Then, the expected gain difference curve T becomes

$$T = \left[9\begin{pmatrix}\phi(1-s)^2 \\ +(1-\phi)(2+c)c\end{pmatrix}\right]\cdot k^2 + 6\left[\begin{matrix}\phi(s-1)\left(2\delta + (1+s)\cdot\left(\frac{2-0.5k^2}{2-k}\right)\right) \\ +(1-\phi)\left(c\cdot\left(\frac{2-0.5k^2}{2-k}\right) - 2\delta\right)\cdot c\end{matrix}\right]\cdot k$$
$$+\left[3\phi\left(6s-5s^2-1\right)+c(1-\phi)(c-2)\right]\cdot\left(\frac{2-0.5k^2}{2-k}\right)^2$$
$$+4\left[3(1-s)\phi\delta-(1-\phi)\delta c\right]\cdot\left(\frac{2-0.5k^2}{2-k}\right)=0$$

Setting T = 0 and solving for k results in one specific k with $1 < k < 2$ for all values of $\phi = [0; 1)$; $s = [0; 0.5]$; $c = (0; 0.2]$; and $\delta \geq 2.5$. Q.E.D.

Proof of Theorem 3(i)

From equation (5.71), the Seller will disclose private information on unit costs, as long as

$$\begin{aligned} T: &\frac{1}{4}\phi k^2 - \frac{1}{6}\left[2(\phi(3d+1+h)-h)\cdot\delta + \phi E[k]\right]\cdot k - \frac{1}{12}\phi E[k]^2 \\ &+\frac{1}{9}\delta\cdot\left[(\phi-1)h + 3(1+3d)\phi\right]\cdot E[k] + \frac{1}{9}(\phi-1)(2-h)\cdot h\cdot\delta^2 > 0 \end{aligned} \quad \text{(A.12)}$$

That is, in equilibrium the non-disclosure set is defined as

$$N = \left\{k \left| \begin{matrix}\frac{1}{4}\phi k^2 - \frac{1}{6}\left[2(\phi(3d+1+h)-h)\cdot\delta + \phi E[k]\right]\cdot k - \frac{1}{12}\phi E[k]^2 \\ +\frac{1}{9}\delta\cdot\left[(\phi-1)h + 3(1+3d)\phi\right]\cdot E[k] + \frac{1}{9}(\phi-1)(2-h)\cdot h\cdot\delta^2\end{matrix} \right. \leq 0\right\}$$

If $N = \{1\}$, then $E[k|N] = 1$. That is, the seller will disclose any information on unit costs k, for which

$$T: \frac{1}{4}\phi k^2 - \frac{1}{6}[2(\phi(3d+1+h)-h)\cdot\delta+\phi]\cdot k - \frac{1}{12}\phi + \frac{1}{9}\delta\cdot[(\phi-1)h+3(1+3d)\phi] + \frac{1}{9}(\phi-1)(2-h)\cdot h\cdot\delta^2 > 0 \tag{A.13}$$

For $E[k|N] = 1$, is there any ϕ for which $T > 0$ for all k?

Claim: For the lower bound of k, i.e. $k = 1$, $T < 0$ for all levels of ϕ.

See Figure A-4 for the sample curvature of T for $E[k|N] = 1$, $\phi = 0.7$, $d = 0.4$; $h = 0.1$; $\delta = 3$.

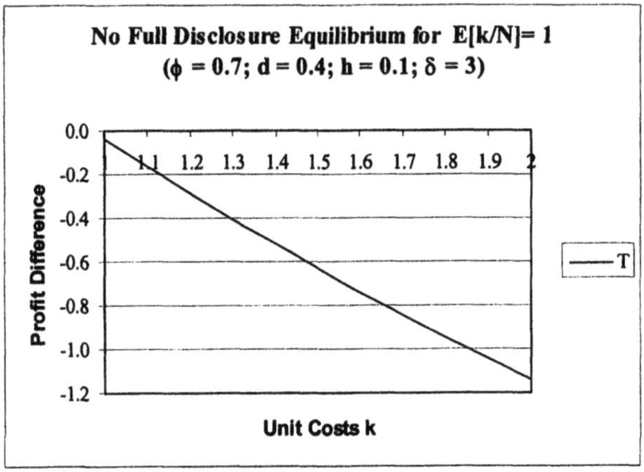

Figure A-4: No Full Disclosure Equilibrium for E[k/N] = 1
(ϕ = 0.7, d = 0.4, h = 0.1, δ = 3)

Proof:

At $k = 1$ and $E[k|N] = 1$, the expected gain to the seller difference curve T (equation (A.13)) is

$$T = \frac{1}{4}\phi - \frac{1}{6}[2(\phi(3d+1+h)-h)\cdot\delta+\phi] - \frac{1}{12}\phi + \frac{1}{9}\delta\cdot[(\phi-1)h+3(1+3d)\phi] + \frac{1}{9}(\phi-1)(2-h)\cdot h\cdot\delta^2 \Rightarrow$$

$$T = -\frac{2}{9}\phi h\delta + \frac{2}{9}h\delta + \frac{2}{9}\phi h\delta^2 - \frac{2}{9}h\delta^2 - \frac{1}{9}\phi h^2\delta^2 + \frac{1}{9}h^2\delta^2 \Rightarrow$$

$$T = \frac{1}{9}(1-\phi)\cdot(2-2\delta+h\delta)\cdot h\delta \qquad \text{(A.14)}$$

Recall that $\delta \geq 2.5$. To see if equation (A.14) < 0 for all values of δ, the lower boundary of the demand interval has to be entered into T. For $\delta = 2.5$,

$$T = \frac{1}{9}(1-\phi)(-3+h\cdot 2.5)\cdot 2.5h < 0$$

For all $h \in (0; 0.2]$ and $\phi = [0; 1)$, $T < 0$.[324] Q.E.D.

The larger the demand, the more negative T becomes. That is, no full disclosure equilibrium exists at the lower bound of k.

As a second step, the upper bound of k has to be examined. If $N = \{2\}$ then $E[k|N] = 2$. That is, the seller will disclose any information on unit costs k, for which

$$\begin{aligned} T: &\frac{1}{4}\phi k^2 - \frac{1}{6}[2(\phi(3d+1+h)-h)\cdot\delta + 2\phi]\cdot k - \frac{1}{12}\phi\cdot 4 \\ &+\frac{1}{9}\delta\cdot[(\phi-1)h + 3(1+3d)\phi]\cdot 2 + \frac{1}{9}(\phi-1)(2-h)\cdot h\cdot\delta^2 > 0 \end{aligned} \qquad \text{(A.15)}$$

For $E[k|N] = 2$, is there any ϕ for which $T > 0$ for all $k \in [1; 2]$?

Claim: For the upper bound of k, i.e. $k = 2$, $T < 0$ for all levels of ϕ.
See Figure A-5 for the illustrative curvature of T for $E[k|N] = 2$, $\phi = 0.9$, $d = 0.4$; $h = 0.1$; $\delta = 3$.

Proof:
At $k = 2$, the expected gain difference curve T from (A.15) is

[324] The special case of certainty ($\phi = 1$) will be considered in section 5.6.2.2.4.

$$T=\frac{1}{4}\phi\cdot 4-\frac{1}{6}\left[2\left(\phi(3d+1+h)-h\right)\cdot\delta+2\phi\right]\cdot 2-\frac{1}{12}\phi\cdot 4$$
$$+\frac{1}{9}\delta\cdot\left[(\phi-1)h+3(1+3d)\phi\right]\cdot 2+\frac{1}{9}(\phi-1)(2-h)\cdot h\cdot\delta^2\Rightarrow$$

$$T=\frac{2}{3}\phi-2\phi d\delta-\frac{2}{3}\phi\delta-\frac{2}{3}\phi h\delta+\frac{2}{3}h\delta-\frac{2}{3}\phi+\frac{2}{9}\phi\delta h-\frac{2}{9}h\delta+\frac{2}{3}\phi\delta+2\phi d\delta$$
$$+\frac{2}{9}\phi h\delta^2-\frac{1}{9}\phi h^2\delta^2-\frac{2}{9}h\delta^2+\frac{1}{9}h^2\delta^2\Rightarrow$$

$$T=\frac{1}{9}(1-\phi)(4-2\delta+h\delta)\cdot h\delta \qquad (A.16)$$

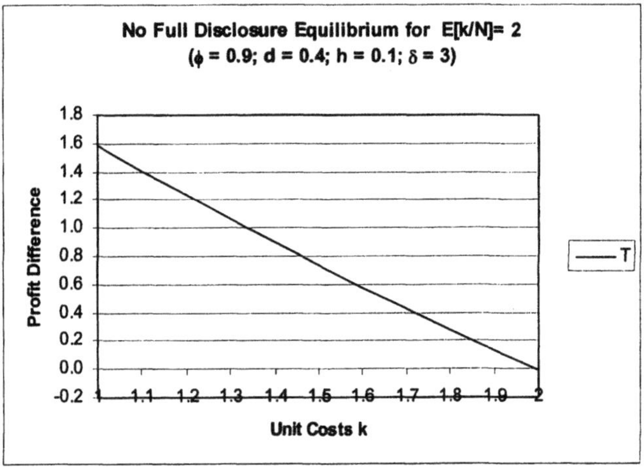

Figure A-5: No Full Disclosure Equilibrium for E[k/N] = 2
(ϕ = 0.9; d = 0.4; h = 0.1; δ = 3)

Recall that $\delta \geq 2.5$ (demand assumption). To see if equation (A.16) < 0 for all values of δ, the lower boundary of the demand interval has to be entered into T. For $\delta = 2.5$,

$$T=\frac{1}{9}(1-\phi)(4-5+h\cdot 2.5)\cdot h\cdot 2.5 \quad <0$$

For all $h \in (0; 0.2]$, $T < 0$. Q.E.D.

The larger the demand, the more negative T becomes. That is, no full disclosure equilibrium exists at the upper bound of k.

To show that for all levels of ϕ no full disclosure equilibrium exists, the curvature of the expected gain to the seller difference curve T (equation (A.12)) has to be considered. The first derivative of equation (A.12) reads

$$\frac{\partial T}{\partial k}=\frac{1}{2}\phi k-\frac{1}{6}\left[2(\phi(3d+1+h)-h)\cdot\delta+\phi E[k]\right]$$

and the second derivative

$$\frac{\partial^2 T}{\partial k^2}=\frac{1}{2}\phi$$

Since the second derivative is positive, the expected gain to the seller difference curve T is convex for all $\phi=(0;1]$. Because T is negative for all levels of ϕ both at the lower and at the upper bound of unit costs, no full disclosure equilibrium can exist for any probability of acquisition.

Proof of Theorem 3(ii)

Recall that the expected gain difference curve T from equation (A.12) reads:

$$\begin{aligned}T:&\frac{1}{4}\phi k^2-\frac{1}{6}\left[2(\phi(3d+1+h)-h)\cdot\delta+\phi E[k]\right]\cdot k-\frac{1}{12}\phi E[k]^2\\&+\frac{1}{9}\delta\cdot\left[(\phi-1)h+3(1+3d)\phi\right]\cdot E[k]+\frac{1}{9}(\phi-1)(2-h)\cdot h\cdot\delta^2>0\end{aligned}$$

and the second derivative is positive for all values of acquisition probability. For a non-disclosure equilibrium, the function T has to be smaller than or equal to zero for all $k\in[1;2]$. Recall that

$$N=\left\{k\left|\begin{aligned}&\frac{1}{4}\phi k^2-\frac{1}{6}\left[2(\phi(3d+1+h)-h)\cdot\delta+\phi E[k]\right]\cdot k-\frac{1}{12}\phi E[k]^2\\&+\frac{1}{9}\delta\cdot\left[(\phi-1)h+3(1+3d)\phi\right]\cdot E[k]+\frac{1}{9}(\phi-1)(2-h)\cdot h\cdot\delta^2\end{aligned}\right.\leq 0\right\}$$

To determine the upper bound of the non-disclosure interval, it suffices to find the probability of acquisition for which k = 1 and T = 0, since the function is convex and downward sloping.

The expected value of k given non-disclosure with $k=[1;2]$ is $E[k|N]=1.5$. The function T for k = 1, T = 0, and $E[k|N]=1.5$ then reads:

$$T:\frac{1}{4}\phi-\frac{1}{6}[2(\phi(3d+1+h)-h)\cdot\delta+1.5\phi]-\frac{1}{12}\phi\cdot 1.5^2$$
$$+\frac{1}{9}\delta\cdot[(\phi-1)h+3(1+3d)\phi]\cdot 1.5+\frac{1}{9}(\phi-1)(2-h)\cdot h\cdot\delta^2=0$$

$$T:\frac{1}{2}\phi d\delta+\frac{1}{6}\phi\delta-\frac{1}{6}\phi h\delta+\frac{1}{6}h\delta-\frac{3}{16}\phi+\frac{2}{9}\phi h\delta^2-\frac{1}{9}\phi h^2\delta^2-\frac{2}{9}h\delta^2+\frac{1}{9}h^2\delta^2=0 \Rightarrow$$

$$\phi_{\bullet}(\phi\mid T=0)=\frac{(-3+4\delta-2h\delta)\cdot h\delta}{3(3d+1-h)\delta+2h\delta^2(2-h)-3.375} \qquad \text{(A.17)}$$

To ensure that for all levels of $0\le\phi\le\phi_{\bullet}$ of equation (A.17) a non-disclosure equilibrium for the convex function exists, it has to be shown that there is no level of acquisition probability for k = 2 and $E[k|N]$ = 1.5 for which T = 0. The expected gain difference curve based on equation (A.12) then reads,

$$T:\frac{1}{4}\phi\cdot 4-\frac{1}{6}[2(\phi(3d+1+h)-h)\cdot\delta+1.5\phi]\cdot 2-\frac{1}{12}\phi\cdot 1.5^2+\frac{1}{9}\delta\cdot[(\phi-1)h+3(1+3d)\phi]\cdot 1.5$$
$$+\frac{1}{9}(\phi-1)(2-h)\cdot h\cdot\delta^2=0 \Rightarrow$$

$$T=\frac{5}{16}\phi-\frac{1}{2}\phi d\delta-\frac{1}{6}\phi\delta-\frac{1}{2}\phi h\delta+\frac{1}{2}h\delta+\frac{2}{9}\phi h\delta^2-\frac{1}{9}\phi h^2\delta^2-\frac{2}{9}h\delta^2+\frac{1}{9}h^2\delta^2\Rightarrow$$

$$\phi=\frac{(-9+4\delta-2h\delta)\cdot\delta h}{5.625+2(2-h)\cdot h\delta^2-3(3d+1+3h)\delta} \qquad \text{(A.18)}$$

For all $d=[0;0.5]$, $h=(0;0.2]$, and $\delta\ge 2.5$, equation (A.18) is not within the defined range of ϕ, with $\phi=[0;1]$. Therefore, for no probability of acquisition is T = 0 for the upper bound of k, i.e. for k = 2. It can be concluded that for all levels of probabilities of acquisition with

$$0\le\phi\le\frac{(-3+4\delta-2h\delta)\cdot h\delta}{3(3d+1-h)\delta+2h\delta^2(2-h)-3.375}$$

a non-disclosure equilibrium exists. Q.E.D

Proof of Theorem 3(iii)

With the convex and downward sloping expected gain to the seller difference curve T, a partial disclosure equilibrium can only sustain if $T = 0$ for exactly one level of k, with $1 < k < 2$. The expected value of unit costs k given non-disclosure is

$$E[k|N] = \left[\frac{1}{2}k^2\right]_k^2 \cdot \left(\frac{1}{2-k}\right) = \frac{2-0.5k^2}{2-k}$$

Then, the expected gain difference curve T becomes

$$T = \frac{1}{4}\phi k^2 - \frac{1}{6}\left[2(\phi(3d+1+h)-h)\cdot\delta + \phi\left(\frac{2-0.5k^2}{2-k}\right)\right]\cdot k - \frac{1}{12}\phi\left(\frac{2-0.5k^2}{2-k}\right)^2$$
$$+\frac{1}{9}\delta\cdot[(\phi-1)h + 3(1+3d)\phi]\cdot\left(\frac{2-0.5k^2}{2-k}\right) + \frac{1}{9}(\phi-1)(2-h)\cdot h\cdot\delta^2 = 0$$

Setting $T = 0$ and solving it for k results in one specific k with $1 < k < 2$ for all values of $\phi = [0;1)$; $d = [0;0.5]$; $h = (0;0.2]$; and $\delta \geq 2.5$. Q.E.D.

REFERENCES

Achleitner, Ann-Kristin (2000), *Handbuch Investment Banking.*

Akerlof, George (1970), The Market for Lemons: Quality Uncertainty and the Market Mechanism, *Quarterly Journal of Economics*, Vol. 84, (3), 488-500.

Anand, Bharat and Khanna, Tarun (2000), The structure of licensing contracts, *Journal of Industrial Economics*, 48, (1), 103-135.

Arrow, Kenneth (1985), The Economics of Agency, in John Pratt and Richard Zeckhauser (eds.), *Principals and Agents: The Structure of Business*, 37-51.

Arrow, Kenneth (1969), The Organization of Economic Activity: Issues Pertinent to the Choice of Market versus Non-Market Allocation, in *The Analysis and Evaluation of Public Expenditures: The PBB-System*, Joint Economic Committee, 91st Congress, 1st session, Vol. 1.

Azarmi, Ted, Eisele, Florian, and Häcker, Christine (2003), Valuation and Market Timing in Private M&A Transactions, *Journal of Business and Economics Research,* 1, (8), 1-7.

Azarmi, Ted and Häcker, Christine (2004), Mergers & Acquisitions, *Das Wirtschaftsstudium,* 33, (7), 887.

Azarmi, Ted and Häcker, Christine (2003), Leveraged Buy Out, *Das Wirtschaftsstudium,* 32, (11), 1367.

Balakrishnan, Srinivasan and Koza, Mitchell (1993), Information Asymmetry, Adverse Selection, and Joint Ventures: Theory and Evidence, *Journal of Economic Behavior and Organization,* 20, (1), 99-117.

Ballwieser, Wolfgang (1997), Die Lageberichte der DAX-Gesellschaften im Lichte der Grundsätze ordnungsmäßiger Lageberichterstattung, in Thomas Fischer and Reinhold Hömberg (eds.), *Jahresabschluss und Jahresabschlussprüfung: Probleme, Perspektiven, internationale Einflüsse, Festschrift für Jörg Baetge*, 153-187.

Beatty, Randolph and Ritter, Jay (1986), Investment Banking, Reputation, and the Underpricing of Initial Public Offerings, *Journal of Financial Economics,* 15, (1-2), 213-232.

Beitel, Derick (2004), *Investmentbanken in M&A Transaktionen – Mandatsvergabe und Erfolgsbeitrag aus Sicht deutscher Käuferunternehmen.*

Beitel, Derick, Boerner, Cristoph, and Schiereck, Dirk (2005), Warum beauftragen deutsche Käuferunternehmen Investmentbanken bei der Durchführung ihrer M&A Transaktionen? *Zeitschrift für betriebswirtschaftliche Forschung,* (6), 283-309.

Benston, George and Smith, Clifford (1976), A Transactions Cost Approach to the Theory of Financial Intermediation, *Journal of Finance*, 31, (2), 215-223.

Berman, Dennis (2004), Dealmakers Got It Right In '03, Study Finds, *Wall Street Journal*, November 9, C1, accessible at http://online.wsj.com/article/0,,SB109994946766667951, 00.html.

Biglaiser, Gary (1993), Middlemen as Experts, *Rand Journal of Economics*, 24, (2), 212-223.

Biglaiser, Gary and Friedman, James (1999), Adverse Selection with Competitive Inspection, *Journal of Economics & Management Strategy*, Vol. 8, (1), 1-32.

Biglaiser, Gary and Friedman, James (1994), Middlemen as Guarantors of Quality, *International Journal of Industrial Organization*, 12, (4), 509-531.

Booth, James and Smith, Richard (1986), Capital Raising, Underwriting and the Certification Hypothesis, *Journal of Financial Economics,* 15, 261-281.

Bowers, Hellen and Miller, Robert (1990), Choice of Investment Banker and Shareholders' Wealth of Firms Involved in Acquisitions, *Financial Management,* 19, 34-44.

Brealey, Richard and Myers, Stewart (2003), *Principles of Corporate Finance*, 7th International Edition.

Bundesrat Drucksache (1999), *Regierungsbegründung zu §264 a HGB*, Nr. 458, dated 13.08.1999.

Campbell, Tim (1979), Optimal Investment Financing Decisions and the Value of Confidentiality, *The Journal of Financial and Quantitative Analysis,* 14, (5), 913-924.

Capen, Edward, Clapp, Raymond, and Campbell, William (1971), Competitive Bidding in High-Risk Situations, *Journal of Petroleum Technology*, (23), 641-653.

Carter, Richard and Manaster, Steven (1990), Initial Public Offering and Underwriter Reputation, *Journal of Finance,* 45, (4), 1045-1067.

Coase, Ronald (1937), The Nature of the Firm, *Economica*, 4, 386-405.

Coenenberg, Adolf Gerhard (2003), *Jahresabschluss und Jahresabschlussanalyse*, 19th Edition.

Copeland, Tom, Koller, Tim, Murrin, Jack (2000), *Valuation: Measuring and Managing the Value of Companies*, 3rd Edition.

Craig, Brian and Smith, Andy (2003), The Art of Earnouts, *Strategic Finance,* 84, (12), 44-47.

Crawford, Vincent and Sobel, Joel (1982), Strategic Information Transmission, *Econometrica,* 50, 1431-1451.

Datar, Srikant, Frankel, Richard, and Wolfson, Mark (2001), Earnouts: The Effects of Adverse Selection and Agency Costs on Acquisition Techniques, *Journal of Law, Economics & Organization*, 17, (1), 201-238.

DePamphilis, Donald (2001), *Mergers, Acquisitions, and Other Restructuring Activities: An Integrated Approach to Process, Tools, Cases, and Solutions.*

Desai, Mihir, Foley, Fritz, and Hines, James (2004), The Costs of Shared Ownership: Evidence from International Joint Ventures, *Journal of Financial Economics*, 73, (2), 323-374.

Der Betrieb (2004), Pflicht zur Offenlegung des Jahresabschlusses einer GmbH & Co. KG: Einsichtsrecht eines Dritten (Konkurrenten) ohne Nachweis eines schutzwürdigen Interesses, 57, (45), 2413-2415.

Der BetriebsBerater, (2004), GmbH & Co. KG: Publizitätspflicht für Jahresabschlüsse besteht ausnahmslos, 59, (45), 2456-2461.

Dibelius, Alexander (2002), Mergers & Acquisitions: Schnittstelle zwischen Unternehmen und Kapitalmärkten, in Gerhard Picot (ed.), *Handbuch Mergers & Acquisitions: Planung, Durchführung und Integration*, 2nd Edition, 39-68.

Dietl, Helmut (1993), *Institutionen und Zeit.*

Dontoh, Alex (1989), Voluntary Disclosure, *Journal of Accounting, Auditing and Finance*, 4, (4), 480-511.

Dufey, Günter, and Hommel, Ulrich (2000), Mergers & Acquisitions, in Georg Obst, Otto Hintner, and Jürgen von Hagen (eds.), *Geld-, Bank- und Börsenwesen, Handbuch des Finanzsystems*, 40th Edition, 963-986.

Eckbo, Espen, Giammarino, Ronald, and Heinkel, Robert (1990), Asymmetric Information and the Medium of Exchange in Takeovers: Theory and Tests, *The Review of Financial Studies*, 3, (4), 651-675.

Eisele, Florian, Häcker, Christine, and Oesterle, Ralf (2004), German Venture Capitalists' Investment Criteria over Financing Stages, International Business & Economics Research Journal, 3, (3), 87-103.

Elschen, Rainer (1991), Gegenstand und Anwendungsmöglichkeiten der Agency-Theorie, Zeitschrift für betriebswirtschaftliche Forschung, 43, 1002-1012.

Ernst, Dietmar, and Häcker, Joachim (2002), *Realoptionen im Investment Banking: Mergers & Acquisitions, Initial Public Offering, Venture Capital.*

Fama, Eugene (1985), What's Different about Banks? *Journal of Monetary Economics*, 15, (1), 29-39.

Fama, Eugene (1980), Agency Problems and the Theory of the Firm, *Journal of Political Economy*, 88, (2), 288-307.

Fama, Eugene and Jensen, Michael (1983), Agency Problems and Residual Claims, *Journal of Law and Economics*, 26, (6), 327-349.

Farrell, Joseph and Gibbons, Robert (1989), Cheap Talk with Two Audiences, *American Economic Review,* 79, (5), 1214-1223.

Fishman, Michael (1989), Preemptive Bidding and the Role of the Medium of Exchange in Acquisitions, *Journal of Finance,* 44, (1), 41-58.

Franke, Günther and Hax, Herbert (2004), *Finanzwirtschaft des Unternehmens und Kapitalmarkt*, 5th Edition.

Freixas, Xavier and Rochet, Jean-Charles (1997), *Microeconomics of Banking.*

Gaughan, Patrick (2002), *Mergers, Acquisitions, and Corporate Restructurings*, 3rd Edition.

Gigler, Frank (1994), Self-Enforcing Voluntary Disclosure, *Journal of Accounting Research,* 32, 261-279.

Giliberto, Michael and Varaiya, Nikhil (1989), The Winner's Curse and Bidder Competition in Acquisitions: Evidence from Failed Bank Auctions, *Journal of Finance,* 44, (1), 59-75.

Grossman, Sanford (1981), The Information Role of Warranties and Private Disclosure about Product Quality, *Journal of Law and Economics*, 24, (4), 461-483.

Grossman, Sanford and Hart, Oliver (1986), The Costs and Benefits of Ownership: A Theory of Vertical and Lateral Integration, *Journal of Political Economy*, 94, (4), 691-719.

Grossman, Sanford, and Stiglitz, Joseph (1980), On the Impossibility of Informationally Efficient Markets, *American Economic Review,* 70, (3), 393-408.

Häcker, Joachim (2005), The Process of Mergers & Acquisitions – Financial Issues, Legal Aspects, the Consummation of the Process, in Ulrich Brecht (ed.), *Trends im Rechnungswesen,* 219-235.

Haller, Axel (2000), Wesentliche Ziele und Merkmale US-amerikanischer Rechnungslegung, in Wolfgang Ballwieser (ed.), *US-Amerikanische Rechnungslegung*, 4th Edition, 1-27.

Hansen, Robert (1987), A Theory for the Choice of Exchange Medium in Mergers and Acquisitions, *Journal of Business,* 60, (1), 75-95.

Hart, Oliver and Moore, John (1990), Property Rights and the Nature of the Firm, *Journal of Political Economy*, 98, (6), 1119-1158.

Hartmann-Wendels, Thomas (1992), Agency-Theorie und Publizitätspflicht nichtbörsennotierter Gesellschaften, *Betriebswirtschaftliche Forschung und Praxis*, 44, (5), 412-425.

Hartmann-Wendels, Thomas, Pfingsten, Andreas, and Weber, Martin (2004), *Bankbetriebslehre*, 3rd Edition.

Hennart, Jean-Francois (1988), A Transaction Cost Theory of Equity Joint Ventures, *Strategic Management Journal*, 9, (4), 361-374.

Hennart, Jean-Francois and Reddy, Sabine (2000), Digestibility and Asymmetric Information in the Choice between Acquisitions and Joint Ventures: Where's the Beef? *Strategic Management Journal*, 21, (2), 191-193.

Hennart, Jean-Francois and Reddy, Sabine (1997), The Choice between Mergers & Acquisitions and Joint Ventures: The Case of Japanese Investors in the United States, *Strategic Management Journal*, 18, (1), 1-12

Hirshleifer, Jack (1971), The Private and Social Value of Information and the Reward to Incentive Activity, *American Economic Review*, 61, (4), 561-574.

Hodgkinson, Lynn (1996), Corporate Restructuring and Leveraged Buyouts, in Edward Gardener and Philip Molyneux (eds.), *Investment Banking: Theory and Practice*, 327-338.

Hölters, Wolfgang (2002), Der Unternehmens- und Beteiligungskauf: Bedeutung, Grundfragen und Abwicklung, in Wolfgang Hölters (ed.), *Handbuch des Unternehmens- und Beteiligungskaufs*, 5th Edition, 3-74.

Holmström, Bengt (1979), Moral Hazard and Observability, *Bell Journal of Economics*, Vol. 10, (1), 74-91.

Hooke, Jeffrey (1997), *M&A: A Practical Guide to Doing the Deal.*

Hopf, Michael (1983), *Informationen für Märkte und Märkte für Informationen.*

Hunter, William and Walker, Mary (1990), An Empirical Examination of Investment Banking Merger Fee Contracts, *Southern Economic Journal*, 56, 1117-1130.

Jansen, Esther (1999), Publizitätsverweigerung deutscher GmbH und ihre Sanktionen im Lichte des KapCoRiLiG, *Deutsches Steuerrecht*, 36, 1490-1497.

Jansen, Stephan (2001), *Mergers & Acquisitions: Unternehmensakquisitionen und -kooperationen*, 4th Edition.

Jansen, Stephan and Müller-Stewens, Günter (2001), Pre- and Post Merger-Integration bei grenzüberschreitenden Zusammenschlüssen, in Gerhard Picot and Dirk Schiereck, *Internationales Fusionsmanagement – Erfolgsfaktoren grenzüberschreitender Zusammenschlüsse*, 3-34.

Jensen, Michael (1986), Agency Costs of Free Cash Flow, Corporate Finance, and Takeovers, *American Economic Review*, 76, 323-329.

Jensen, Michael and Meckling, William (1976), Theory of the Firm: Managerial Behavior, Agency Costs and Ownership Structure, *Journal of Financial Economics,* 3, 305-360.

Jensen, Michael and Ruback, Richard (1983), The Market for Corporate Control, *Journal of Financial Economics*, Apr83, Vol. 11, (1-4), 5-50.

Kajüter, Peter and Winkler, Carsten (2003), Die Risikoberichterstattung der DAX100-Unternehmen im Zeitvergleich, *Zeitschrift für kapitalmarktorientierte Rechnungslegung,* 5, 217-228.

Kaplan, Steven (1989), Campeau's Acquisition of Federated – Value Destroyed or Value Added, *Journal of Financial Economics,* 25, 191-212.

Kierulff, Herbert (1981), Finding the Best Acquisition Candidates, *Harvard Business Review*, 59, (1), 66-68.

Kohers, Ninon, and Ang, James (2000), Earnouts in Mergers: Agreeing to Disagree and Agreeing to Stay, *The Journal of Business,* 73, (3), 445-476.

Korn, Evelyn (2004), Voluntary Disclosure of Partially Verifiable Information, *Schmalenbach Business Review,* 56, 139-163.

Kosnik, Rita, and Shapiro, Debra (1997), Agency Conflicts Between Investment Banks and Corporate Clients in Merger and Acquisition Transactions: Causes and Remedies, *Academy of Management Executive,* 11, (1), pp. 7-20.

KPMG (2003), *Rechnungslegung nach US-Amerikanischen Grundsätzen*, 3rd Edition.

Leland, Hayne and Pyle, David (1977), Informational Asymmetries, Financial Structure, and Financial Intermediation, *Journal of Finance*, 32, (2), 371-387.

Lizzeri, Alessandro (1999), Information Revelation and Certification Intermediaries, *RAND Journal of Economics*, 30, (2), 214-232.

M&A International (2006), *Strategische Käufer bestimmen die Marktdynamik – Mergers and Acquisitions mit deutscher Beteiligung im Jahr 2005*, Pressemitteilung, available at http://www.m-a-international.de/PDF-Files/Pressemitteilung%20Volljahr%202005.pdf.

Maksimovic, Vojislav and Phillips, Gordon (2001), The Market for Corporate Assets: Who Engages in Mergers and Asset Sales and Are There Efficiency Gains? *Journal of Finance,* 56, (6), 2019-2065.

Marshall, John F. and Ellis, M.E. (1994), *Investment Banking and Brokerage.*

Mastracchio Jr., Nicholas and Zunitch, Victoria (2002), Differences Between Mergers and Acquisitions, *Journal of Accountancy*, 194, (5), p. 38-41.

Matthews, Russel (1986), The Economics of Institutions and the Sources of Growth, *Economic Journal*, 96, (384), 903-10.

McLaughlin, Robyn (1996), Adverse Contract Incentives and Investment Banker Reputation: Target Firm Tender Offer Fees, *Journal of Financial Research*, 19, (1), 135-156.

McLaughlin, Robyn (1992), Does the Form of Compensation Matter? Investment Banker Fee Contracts in Tender Offers, *Journal of Financial Economics*, 32, (2), 223-260.

McLaughlin, Robyn (1990), Investment-Banking Contracts in Tender Offers: An Empirical Analysis, *Journal of Financial Economics*, 28, (1/2), 209-232.

Mergers & Acquisitions: The Dealmaker's Journal, (2000), Hiring Dealmaker's in the 21st Century, 35, (6), 16-17.

Milde, Hellmuth (1988), Die Theorie der Adversen Selektion, *Wirtschaftswissenschaftliches Studium*, 17, 1-16.

Milgrom, Paul (1981), Good News and Bad News: Representation Theorems and Applications, *Bell Journal of Economics*, 12, (2), 380-391.

Milgrom, Paul and Roberts, John (1992), *Economics, Organization and Management.*

Moeller, Sara, Schlingemann, Frederik, and Stulz, Rene (2005), Wealth Destruction on a Massive Scale? A Study of Acquiring-Firm Returns in the Recent Merger Wave, *Journal of Finance*, 60, (2), 757-782.

Müller-Stewens, Günter, Spickers, Jürgen, and Deiss, Christian (1999), *Mergers & Acquisitions – Markttendenzen und Beraterprofile.*

Nash, John (1953), Two-Person Cooperative Games, *Econometrica*, 21, (1), 128-140.

Neus, Werner (2005), *Einführung in die Betriebswirtschaftslehre*, 4th Edition.

Neus, Werner (1999), Unternehmungen in unvollkommenen Märkten, *Das Wirtschaftsstudium*, 28, (7), 955-961.

Neus, Werner (1995), *Zur Theorie der Finanzierung kleinerer Unternehmungen.*

Neus, Werner, (1989), Die Aussagekraft von Agency Costs. Eine Untersuchung anhand von Finanzierungsbeziehungen im Kapitalmarktzusammenhang, *Zeitschrift für betriebswirtschaftliche Forschung*, 41, (6), 472-490.

Neus, Werner and Walz, Uwe (2005), Exit Timing of Venture Capitalists in the Course of an Initial Public Offering, *Journal of Financial Intermediation*, 14, (2), 253-277.

Niemann, Claus (1995), *Informationsasymmetrien beim Unternehmensverkauf: Gesellschaftsrechtliche und auktionstheoretische Analyse unter besonderer Berücksichtigung des Management Buy-Outs.*

Noth, Michael (1994), *Regulierung bei asymmetrischer Informationsverteilung.*

Oxley, Joanne (1997), Appropriability Hazards and Governance in Strategic Alliances: A Transaction Cost Approach, *Journal of Law, Economics and Organization,* 13, (2), 387-409.

Penno, Mark (1997), Information Quality and Voluntary Disclosure, *Accounting Review,* 72, (2), 275-284.

Picot, Arnold, Reichwald, Ralf, and Wigand, Rolf (2003), *Die grenzenlose Unternehmung: Information, Organisation und Management,* 5th Edition.

Picot, Gerhard (1998), Vertragsrecht, in Gerhard Picot (ed.), *Unternehmensverkauf und Restrukturierung,* 2nd Edition, 10-117.

Ragotzky, Serge (2003), *Unternehmensverkauf und asymmetrische Information.*

Rau, P. Raghavendra (2000), Investment bank market share, contingent fee payments, and the performance of acquiring firms, *Journal of Financial Economics,* 56, (2), pp. 293-324.

Reed, Stanley and Reed Lajoux, Alexandra (2000): *The Art of M&A – A Merger and Acquisition Buyout Guide.* 3rd Edition.

Reuer, Jeffrey and Koza, Mitchell (2000), On Lemons and Indigestibility: Resource Assembly through Joint Ventures, *Strategic Management Journal,* 21, (2), 195-197.

Reuer, Jeffrey, Shenkar, Oded, and Ragozzino, Roberto (2004), Mitigating Risk in International Mergers and Acquisitions: The Role of Contingent Payouts, *Journal of International Business Studies,* 35, (1), 19-32.

Richter, Rudolf and Furubotn, Eirik (1999), *Neue Institutionenökonomik: Eine Einführung und kritische Würdigung,* 2nd Edition.

Ross, Stephen (1989), Institutional Markets, Financial Marketing, and Financial Innovation, *Journal of Finance,* 44, (3), 541-556.

Ross, Stephen (1973), The Economic Theory of Agency: The Principal's Problem, *American Economic Review,* 63, (2), 134-139.

Rothschild, Michael and Stiglitz, Joseph (1976), Equilibrium in competitive insurance markets, *Quarterly Journal of Economics,* 90, (4), 629-649.

Rubinstein, Ariel (1982), Perfect Equilibrium in a Bargaining Model, *Econometrica,* 50, (1), 97-109.

Rubinstein, Ariel and Wolinsky, Asher (1987), Middlemen, *Quarterly Journal of Economics,* 102, (3), 581-593.

Salant, Stephen, Switzer, Sheldon, and Reynolds, Robert (1983), Losses from Horizontal Merger: The Effects of an Exogenous Change in Industry Structure on Cournot-Nash Equilibrium, *The Quarterly Journal of Economics*, 98, (2), 185-199.

Saunders, Anthony and Srinivasan, Anand, (2001), *Investment Banking Relationships and Merger Fees,* University of Georgia Department of Banking and Finance Working Paper, available at http://ssrn.com/abstract=288725.

Scherer, Frederic (2002), The Merger Puzzle, in Wolfgang Franz, Hans Jürgen Ramser, and Manfred Stadler (eds.), *Fusionen*, 1-22.

Schindhelm, Malte and Stein, Klaus (2000), Offenlegung, in Norbert Winkeljohann and Malte Schindhelm (eds.), *Das KapCoRiLiG: Ein Praxisleitfaden zum Kapitalgesellschaften- und Co-Richtlinie-Gesetz,* 191-245.

Schmidt, Reinhard H. (1993), Finanzierung und unsichere Erwartungen, in Waldemar Wittmann (ed.), *Handwörterbuch der Betriebswirtschaft*, 5th Edition, 1038-1050.

Schmidt, Reinhard H. (1979), *Die Rolle von Informationen und Institutionen auf Finanzmärkten.*

Schmidt, Reinhard H. and Terberger, Eva (1997), *Grundzüge der Investitions- und Finanzierungstheorie*, 4th Edition.

Schumann, Jochen, Meyer, Ulrich, and Ströbele, Wolfgang (1999), *Grundzüge der mikroökonomischen Theorie*, 7th Edition.

Servaes, Henri and Zenner, Marc (1996), The Role of Investment Banks in Acquisitions, *The Review of Financial Studies,* 9, (3), 787-815.

Shen, Jung-Chin and Reuer, Jeffrey (2005), Adverse Selection in Acquisitions of Small Manufacturing Firms: A Comparison of Private and Public Targets, *Small Business Economics,* 24, 393-407.

Shleifer, Andrei and Vishny, Robert (1997), A Survey of Corporate Governance, *Journal of Finance*, 52 (2), 737-783.

Shleifer, Andrei and Vishny, Robert (1989), Management Entrenchment: The Case of Manager-Specific Investments, *Journal of Financial Economics*, 25, 123-140.

Spence, A. Michael (1973), Job Market Signaling, *Quarterly Journal of Economics*, 87, (3), 355-374.

Spremann, Klaus (1990), Asymmetrische Information, *Zeitschrift für Betriebswirtschaft*, 60, (5/6), 561-586.

Stiglitz, Joseph (1975), The Theory of „Screening", Education, and the Distribution of Income, *American Economic Review,* 65, (3), 283-300.

Stiglitz, Joseph, and Weiss, Andrew (1981), Credit Rationing in Markets with Imperfect Information, *American Economic Review,* 71, (3), 393-410.

Strasser, Brigitte (2000), *Informationsasymmetrien bei Unternehmensakquisitionen.*

Stuart, Toby, Ha, Hoang, and Hybels, Ralph (1999), Interorganizational Endorsements and the Performance of Entrepreneurial Ventures, *Administrative Science Quarterly*, 44, (2), 315-349.

Sutton, John (1986), Non-Cooperative Bargaining Theory: An Introduction, *Review of Economic Studies,* 53, (5), 709-724.

Titman, Sheridan and Trueman, Brett (1986), Information Quality and the Valuation of New Issues, *Journal of Accounting and Economics,* 8, 159-172.

Varaiya, Nikhil (1988), The 'Winner's Curse' Hypothesis and Corporate Takeovers, *Managerial and Decision Economics,* 9, (3), 209-219.

Varian, Hal (1999), *Grundzüge der Mikroökonomik*, 4th Edition.

Vault (2006), *Top 50 Consulting Firms – 2006,* available at http://www.vault.com/nr/Consulting_rankings/consulting_rankings.jsp?consulting2006=2&ch_id=252, retrieved on March 1, 2006.

Verrechia, Robert (1990), Information Quality and Discretionary Disclosure, *Journal of Accounting and Economics,* 12, 365-380.

Verrechia, Robert (1983), Discretionary Disclosure, *Journal of Accounting and Economics,* 5, 179-194.

Vincenti, Aurelio (2002), Wirkungen asymmetrischer Informationsverteilung auf die Unternehmensbewertung, *Betriebswirtschaftliche Forschung und Praxis*, 55-68.

Wagenhofer, Alfred (2000), Disclosure of proprietary information in the course of an acquisition, *Accounting and Business Research*, 31, (1), 57-69.

Wagenhofer, Alfred (1990), Voluntary disclosure with a strategic opponent, *Journal of Accounting and Economics*, 12, (4), 341-363.

Weston, Fred, Siu, Juan, and Johnson, Brian (2001), *Takeovers, Restructuring, and Corporate Governance*, 3rd Edition.

Williamson, Oliver (1985), *The Economic Institutions of Capitalism - Firms, Markets, Relational Contracting.*

Williamson, Oliver (1964), *The Economics of Discretionary Behavior: Managerial Objectives in a Theory of the Firm.*

Wilson, Charles (1977), A Model of Insurance Markets with Incomplete Information, *Journal of Economic Theory*, 16, 167-207.

Winkeljohann, Norbert and Schindhelm, Malte (2000), Grundlagen des Kapitalgesellschaften- und Co-Richtlinie-Gesetzes, in Norbert Winkeljohann and Malte Schindhelm (eds.), *Das KapCoRiLiG: Ein Praxisleitfaden zum Kapitalgesellschaften- und Co-Richtlinie-Gesetz*, 1-15.

Wirtschaftsprüferkammer (1998), Untersuchung zu den Jahresabschlüssen 1997, *Zeitschrift für Wirtschaftsrecht*, A 50, Nr. 130.

Wittmann, Waldemar (1959), *Unternehmung und unvollkommene Information. Unternehmerische Voraussicht – Ungewissheit und Planung.*

Wohlschieß, Volker (1996), *Unternehmensfinanzierung bei asymmetrischer Informationsverteilung.*